Rebirth III

By:
Jonathan

Rebirth III
Book Six of the Series *The Nine*
May 22, 2018, *First Edition*

Copyright © 2018

Cover Photo Credit: Olivier Fahrni

All rights reserved. This book or any portion thereof may not be reproduced or used in any manner whatsoever without the express written permission of the publisher except for the use of brief quotations in a book review or scholarly journal.

ISBN-13: 978-1-942967-34-7

KreativeMinds Publishing
www.kreativeminds.net

Ordering Information:

Special discounts are available on quantity purchases by corporations, associations, educators, and others. For details, contact the publisher at the above listed address or the email address below.

U.S. trade bookstores and wholesalers: Please use the email address below.
email: publishing@kreativeminds.net

To My Creator, through whom all things are possible.

Always,
Jonathan

Introduction

...

This is the third book of my journals, the words of the experiences shown to me by God. Book VI – Rebirth III covers a period of time from March 25, 2014, through September 10, 2014. This was a time measured by faith, experienced through an exodus from Nashville, Tennessee, into the continued journey through the desert preceding the Promised Land. In all of my life, I have never felt as blessed and held as I have since the beginning of these days. The end of this book closes with the witnessing of a wedding ceremony in the heavens. At the time my soul experienced this grand wedding, the meaning was not yet apparent. But as these books have begun to take their final form, the meaning could not be clearer. There is a concept spoken about by Jesus of a Wedding Banquet and of Christ's Bride. The groomsmen have a role to play, as does the bridegroom. And though I now understand that only through this divine ceremony of the soul to Christ's Bride can the unity of man and spirit become one, I can now look back and see how God was telling this story all along. While these books began with God saying, "Come here, son – we've got a story to tell," perhaps the greatest part of the story was not knowing how it would one day be told... for that part of this journey is what has made this ride so divine.

Always,
Jonathan

Wonders (Part 3)

As it was revealed to me by the Lord during the winter of 2013 in Book IV- Rebirth I, I learned I was "one of two," though the meaning was absent of any substance and glue. It would not be until the winter of 2014 that my Father would begin to allow it all to fall into view. And though the portion of the journey covered in this book are the moments leading up to His grand revealing, it is important for the reader to look beyond the words written and see the beacon of light guiding my soul home. For this is the story leading up to that grand moment of revelation: the understanding that for the last three years, my Father has been preparing me through every step of this journey, so that one day I could share a specific message with the world...a message and all of its glory detailed in the continuation of Wonders in Book VII – Glory. But the highlights to the revealing must be foreshadowed here, for the messages in this book are easy to miss without the understanding of what is to come.

The second book of my journals ended in a leap of faith in understanding the free-fall of Love into His Almighty Hands. And though the ending of His script did not end in the way I had hoped, His ending was better than I could have ever imagined. For this was the time that I would come to understand the bounds of His Love and the manner of His instructions. The symbolism in all of the steps I was asked to make only became apparent in hindsight. I was blinded to the purpose of attending His class and only saw the lesson after it came to pass.

This was my Abraham and Isaac moment, even if the world would never see it as such. It was the one and only time I thought I would shatter into a million pieces by following His will, only to feel the magnitude of His Love as He caught me at the bottom of the fall. The truth is His hands were always there. He was not just prepared to catch me, but rather already holding me with all of His Love. It would take that leap of faith for me to realize I no longer had to hold on, for I was always being held. That was my fault, my naiveté to His grand design.

It would only be appropriate from that point forward that I would follow His every will as He asked me to move to Fort Lauderdale for reasons then unknown. I moved blindly, but in complete faith. It was clear that He was preparing the way for me, and that I was only following His lead. The place I would stay, the people I would meet, the interactions I would have...these were all parts of His grand plan.

The journal entries in this book cover the almost-indescribable experiences of a child learning to communicate through the language of the Divine. These were the months of true devotion. Every second, every breath was devoted to His call. There would be no other distractions. This was the beginning of a ministry unfolding, though, again, I was not yet

Wonders (Part 3)

prepared to see it as such during those days. The lessons and communication from God ramped up to unfathomable levels as He continued preparing me to hear the grand message that would one day be revealed.

This book ends with the witnessing of a marriage in the heavens and a conversation with my bride-to-be. It would only be as these books would take their final form during the last days of 2014 and the beginning of 2015, that the revelation of His message – and in effect, the meaning of this particular experience of the wedding in the heavens – would be unveiled. For just as a bride walks down the aisle with a veil covering her face as she slowly approaches her man, the wedding ceremony I experienced in the heavens of the Bride of Christ should be viewed in the same light as She slowly approaches Her man.

Confidently, with each step drawing closer, the moment of complete commitment draws near – each stride as She approaches Her man begins to reveal that the seemingly opaque veil from afar is more transparent than it appeared, with so much more beauty and Love to be revealed. The eyes speak wonders to All That Is, and are a doorway to a cosmic bound. As She approaches Her man holding Her Father's arms, the man begins to see Her eyes – a face hidden from afar when She began Her approach down the aisle. Though She could see his eyes alight in wonder and awe from afar, Her eyes were carefully veiled and shielded from his, until the moment of the grand reveal.

Rebirth III

It is at this point Her Father prepares to give His daughter to a man worthy of Her Love. He lets go of her hands as their approach down the aisle draws to a close. He turns to Her and pulls the veil above Her head igniting the room in brilliance Divine. The man is speechless. There are no words to describe the moment he first sees Her eyes. Her Father kisses Her on the cheek and turns to take His seat, to witness the ceremony of His daughter's Love to a man who will never be worthy enough, though he has proven all of the worth that he can.

God's face hidden from man is how every story has been told. And with every awestruck moment of seeing His infinite Love, I was always blinded to His face, though now I can see that it was only behind a veil. The daughter of our Father, the Bride of Christ, these are One and the same. For as the Bride's face is slowly revealed upon Her presentation to the man Her Father deems worthy enough to stand by Her side at the alter, so is the face of God Our Father revealed – for they are One.

So it can be seen in the very action of a wedding ceremony on Earth, that the symbolism, the traditions, and the efforts for all of it to remain Holy in His eyes, are like unto a child "playing house" or "playing teacher" as the child learns to take baby steps into becoming an adult. This does not take away from the meaning of marriage or lessen the amount of Love that is to be experienced and revealed. Instead, it amplifies those very practices. For in the earthly experience, we are to live our lives as if we are in Heaven performing the work of our Lord. Each action should be taken with the Love and care

Wonders (Part 3)

on Earth as it is in Heaven, coated in the splendor of His Divine.

The witness to the wedding celebration in the heavens would reveal yet another marker on His divine timeline and would challenge me to explore the origin of my earthly marriage, and its eventual end. The portion of my journey that involved my marriage occurred prior to the Genesis of my rebirth. This portion of time – the first thirty years of my life – should be seen as the time God stood over the waters of the deep, when it was void and without form. These were the days that God allowed it to take shape in such a manner – in such a specific way – that one day I would be able to see in hindsight the meaning all along.

I met my ex-wife in December of my senior year of college, though we would not go out on our first date until March 9, 2002. On May 25, 2003, we would become husband and wife and journey into the sunset. Everything was seemingly perfect, a forever-until-the-end. She was my soulmate, my Love. She was everything that I had to give, and everything that I never was. She was the flash of color to an otherwise serene painting of my life. For seven years, we spent our lives together. I never once contemplated there could ever be an end.

It was only upon the day that she surprised me with a conversation expressing her desire to separate, was the impending ending revealed. Even in that conversation, it turned from separation and holding on, to a finite ending as soon as we could work out the terms. I was a father to a two-year-old,

Rebirth III

and had just become a broken man. It was only a little over a month after we celebrated our fifth wedding anniversary together on May 25, 2008, that we would separate. It would be just days over seven years from the moment I first saw her to when we would legally bring it to an end. I was twenty-seven years old and I would not see how any of those dates would matter. But in hindsight, the meaning is so grand.

So as the words in this book are being read, understand that a story is unfolding more grand than the experiences stand on their own. For each experience is just another small piece of His revealing, done so in a manner that was always under His guidance and His control. It was never meant for me to understand the immediate meaning during each point in time, for that would have tempted ego to seize control. It would have been like giving a child "playing doctor" a scalpel and telling him he was now knowledgeable enough to perform surgery on any man. This was always the story being told, though I would have to learn to hear and understand His words through His divine language before I could realize His story of Ever-After was in motion before I was even born. So as these words are written, see them for the foreshadowing being told, the hindsight drawing near, the point of reason approaching the point of surrender to spiritual understanding through all that will eventually be revealed.

The Written (cont'd)

"The Written" is the continued portion of the journey from the moment when God called upon me to take a leap of faith so as I could learn that He was holding me all along. At the time of the leap, it defied logic and placed the most fragile part of my being into a position of vulnerability. It was a point in time during the free-fall when I feared an unfavorable outcome would result in my soul being shattered into a million pieces as it was once before. But this time I feared it would be un-repairable.

The point of being caught by the hand of God when a free-fall into the thickness of dark seemed all that remained is where this book begins. The experiences continue from that point forward through my pilgrimage to Fort Lauderdale until His ultimate reveal. The move to Fort Lauderdale was a panacea from the destruction of the Earth, and ultimately a version of the Promised Land intended for my eyes to see. But though I would only begin to see bits and pieces of His grand unveiling during the time in which they occurred, by the end of this book, the story had more than just legs, it was beginning to move before me. The words had been in motion, though at the time it was difficult to see.

Rebirth III

There is a time in a child's life that he is sitting in the backseat of a car. Inside of the car everything is moving at the same rate as the child, so everything inside appears to be stationary. Now imagine a car has pulled up alongside of the child's vehicle, and now each vehicle is traveling at the same rate of speed as the other. When the child looks out the window, the car appears to be stationary as well. Glancing at the wheels of the tires offers the same illusion. The motion of the spinning of the wheel is moving faster than the mind can digest, thus causing a motion blur that appears static in real time. This is how God's message was delivered to me over the course of this journey.

For a child to understand all that is to be learned, the surroundings must first appear stationary. Each part of the message holds substance and glue. It is not until the child begins to see objects passing that motion is understood. And, only then, is it understood for the visualization alone. In the beginning, the child does not recognize the concept of distance, much less understand the roadmap that leads him to his intended destination. It takes much more time of experiencing the ride and learning the concepts of motion and time before the child can understand how the roads crossing and diverging on his map were always leading to a divine destination.

It is only after all of these concepts are learned that the story is revealed. This is the manner in which God used to communicate to me. I was a child. I am a child. We are all children. But, we are all children learning to become men unto the face of the Lord. So as this portion of "The Written" be-

The Written (cont'd)

gins, understand that the words through the first two books had already been in motion long before I understood there was motion surrounding the messages being taught to me. These were the days that it all would begin to come clear. By the end of this book, the Lord chose to deliver a message through the witnessing of a wedding in the heavens, a celebration still to be told. But it was during this book's portion of the journey, that the concept of motion and roadmaps began to fall into view.

...

March 25, 2014

After waking up this morning, I shut my eyes to meditate. I became aware that there were angels in my room. As I meditated within (the same context of what I did yesterday in discovering the letters TAJ), I had the experience of being the observer and being observed at the same time. I could see around my apartment, and down upon my bed. But, I still felt that I was lying on my side in the bed. This is the most pure mind-soul duality I have experienced to date. As I lay there, I knew there were two people who were standing off in the distance of my room. I could not see any definition in them. They were more like silhouettes – black or dark gray in color, but definitely in the shape of humans. It was not that I was scared, or even that I was excited. I just wanted to continue my state of meditation. The female walked around the room

Rebirth III

trying to make enough noise to get my attention. Their conversation became louder. The male would make sure his voice was loud enough to awaken most people. But I just lay there. Eventually they walked toward my bed – the male leading the way. I heard the female say, "Awww. He's trying to pretend like he's sleeping – like he doesn't hear us." The male laughed and said, "Maybe we should wake him up." They both came closer to my bed, the male in front. He reached out his hand and touched my neck. Instantly I was jolted into earthly reality with my eyes wide open.

March 27, 2014

There were several experiences in the heavens this morning, but only one that I was allowed to bring back in detail. This one experience placed my soul in a room with Chris's soul. Chris is the guy who has just started dating Lindsey. I did not ask to be in the room with him, nor did I ever expect to find myself in such a precarious situation in a spiritual sense. But, it was clear why I was there.

As I stood in the room, Chris stood along the opposite wall. There were windows with sunlight streaming in behind him. The setting was similar to that of a school classroom with desks separating us from each other. He paced around nervously. He eventually began to ask me why I would try to mess up his opportunity with Lindsey. He did not leave much room for me to answer before he moved on to other questions. He

The Written (cont'd)

started asking whether any of the words in the book were true – whether I really had seen angels. But eventually he circled back to anger.

He was very angry at my words in the book. He was almost pleading to me for answers to his discomfort. Up until this point I was just observing him and his words. But when he started pleading for answers, I knew it was time to respond. But for every question he asked, I replied with a question. My own answers surprised me. There was never a direct answer to his questions, but rather a question that redirected his thoughts to help him find resolve. It was a very spiritual conversation – one that in context, followed the manner in how Jesus responded to his disciples or how Buddha answered questions.

I became aware as I observed my soul in conversation with Chris that the lesson was one that I needed to see. Since words have now been written that disclose some pretty heavy spiritual concepts, it is now necessary for me to understand how to be able to answer questions that will come my way. The most important piece that I took away from the experience was that I should only answer with questions and parables. I should never try to prove my words in description, but rather ask questions that help others find truth in the words I have written. Any attempt in supporting the words will only inject a lens of distortion to the truth in His words thus potentially introducing doubt.

While I do believe that I directly addressed Chris's soul in the heavens, I think that it was more important for the lesson gleaned than in the resolve that I attempted to give Chris. In

Rebirth III

truth, I wish him the best with Lindsey. God purposed her into my life for a specific reason, and I have complete resolve in how it has played out. In fact, I probably learned more by observing her being shown the key within the clay and the box – and choosing to not open the box – than I would have ever learned had everything worked out in a blissful fairytale ending. And in that, I find complete peace.

March 29, 2014

The experience this morning began on an island with a group of people. The island was rocky, but also contained green pastures. The settlements were mostly along the mountain coastline, though there were beaches dividing the mountains from the ocean. Some of the people on the island were called to war. I was called to save them. I was taken to a religious building on a cliff some distance away. The building was white and resembled a chapel. I took several people with me to the top of the cliff to enter the building.

Once we were inside of the building we began pulling drapes down. The drapes were purple and hung perpendicular to the walls – almost like banners hanging down in a grand hall of a medieval castle. They reached twenty feet or so above us into the heights of the room. The windows were between the drapes and were tall and slender with no glass. Sunlight was pouring in. Wind blew through the windows and blew one of the drapes upwards so that it was parallel to the floor. This

The Written (cont'd)

moment caught my attention – and in the wind I heard God's voice.

After the drapes were pulled down, they were all given to me. We left the chapel where I then led a group two hundred miles away to survive some sort of culling. Our destination was an inlet – a sandy lagoon with calm, blue water. In the middle of the lagoon was a large square box floating upon the waters. It looked to have been made of bamboo. There was a girl with a baby in the floating box. A man pulled it from the water and tossed it to the shore where the box was broken open. The woman and baby were okay, but after the box was smashed open, I helped rescue and save her.

After this happened, two angels pulled me aside and took me to another setting. If the first setting in the heavens resembled a medieval time period, the new time period was more modern. It was now dark outside and raining. We were in an urban environment with electricity and modern conveniences. I was taken to a restaurant where we chatted over coffee (or some similar type of beverage). We sat in a booth. The seats were red, the table was a pearl-like laminate. I sat at the end of the booth in a chair. On my left was an elder angel. On my right was a skeptical younger angel. He communicated without words – only by writing on a piece of paper and pushing it to me. I think this was partly to see how well I could read his words. Reading in the heavens is extremely difficult and takes much will and concentration. But above all, it takes experience and knowledge. It is no different than being a baby trying to

Rebirth III

understand the words in an encyclopedia – all in a language that is unfamiliar.

The younger angel wrote a sentence on the paper mentioning "Thomas" and then in parentheses it said something about "a an AP and then". I knew the "Thomas" that he was talking about was the biblical Thomas who wrote the Book of Thomas – a book which was left out of the modern Biblical canon. When I read the words on the narrow piece of paper, I looked at him and said, "I feel comfortable telling you about my experiences." He looked uneasy about my answer. I said, "You mentioned AP which I have to assume means astral projection." The angel nodded, acknowledging I was correct. I was not arrogant, but I was confident in my words. I knew I was taken to the restaurant for an important reason, though the meeting seemed somewhat secretive from everyone around. So I just responded, "I thought so. We are on the same page. Trust me."

The younger angel looked at the elder who smiled and said, "See. I told you. I have a really good feeling about this one." The elder was proud of my spiritual growth and progress. The younger angel said something again about Thomas, though this time it was communicated without words or writing. I acknowledged I knew a good bit about him. The angels seemed happy about our conversation. We left the restaurant and parted ways. It was important to know that the meeting was under a veil of privacy and secrecy, and that I may be the only person who "survived" a meeting with those two angels.

The Written (cont'd)

As I left the restaurant, I was imparted to me that I was the only person who ever was able to leave the restaurant under my own will before. Apparently no one else had "made it that far"...whatever that may mean in terms of my earthly and spiritual journey. I was left with many questions, though I felt a great peace that I was doing all that was possible to rapidly advance in growth... possibly even faster than the angels expected. At least, it would seem that way based on the recent conversations with the angels in the heavens. Ironically, this is a time where I have felt more lost after being shown my seat as a King – without any full understanding of whether I am one, or how I am to take action in God's will. I continue to pray for guidance, but only find answers of this type. So, apparently I am on the right course...

March 30, 2014

The main experience in the heavens took place in a valley among mountains. The surroundings were rocky and the cliffs were exceedingly high along the borders of the land in which I was to experience this lesson. There were two angels with me and other people mulling about the land. They appeared to be farming, though there were no plants to be seen. The angels continued to talk to me about my "ability being special." I was not sure what "ability" they were talking about, so I continued to try to understand what it was they were addressing. But, as much as I tried to seek answers about this "ability," I only

Rebirth III

found that their answers went in circles. They clearly could not tell me what my "ability" was, but only offer me guidance in helping me find it.

The angels gave me a lot of tests which involved something actionable to a given situation. I completed every test quickly and efficiently. The tests all involved the demonstration of my faith in God. The situations involved camping out in the wilderness in a barren land with a wall dividing us from the world. After the tests, the angels continued to speak highly of my "ability." They asked me about the visions that I have and then proceeded to have me act out certain ones. I never quite understood why I was doing anything, but I managed to perform everything better than expected.

Eventually, the final test involved me performing two tasks at once. I was tasked with removing every snake from the ground and still maintaining all of my tasks on the upper plane. This is difficult to describe as it would have been an impossible experience on Earth. Essentially, the ground represented one physical plane/dimension. Everything above the ground represented a spiritual plane/dimension. But, to understand the test, I had to see the two as one. As soon as they told me I was to rid the ground of snakes and crawling creatures, I felt a feeling of dread. I hate snakes. I decided it best to create a device that would suck up the snakes without me having to physically touch them. I thought that I could push the device while I performed all of the other tasks in the upper plane. I quickly crafted a vacuum-like device and moved speedily across the barren land sucking up the snakes.

The Written (cont'd)

It still made me queasy to have to deal with the snakes, but at least I did not have to touch them.

As I reached the end of the land, the angels stopped me and looked at me puzzled. They asked why I created a machine. I told them that I did not want to touch the snakes, and that handling the snakes with a device would free up the burden of the thought of the snakes from my mind so I could devote my mind to the other tasks I had been given. The angels had never seen this type of answer before. I could tell my response was new to them. One took the device and began pushing it around. I showed the angel how it just sucked up the snakes. The angel pushed it around and was entertained at the device. They all looked at each other in a way that I can only assume meant, "Well, that's not what we expected, but it clearly works and achieves the goal." I knew that whatever caused me to create the device was related to my "ability," but I still could not understand what this "ability" was.

March 31, 2014

While the experiences in the heavens were numerous again, I could only bring back one brief part of the experience. Standing among angels, I was continually asked how I did things differently than everyone else. I was somewhat confused by the question since I have always assumed that the angels already knew everything before I did. So, logically, I have to assume that either they were trying to understand something

Rebirth III

they had never seen before (unlikely), or they were trying to help me understand my own ability – even as unaware as I may be about my use of it. The latter is the more likely scenario because I have to believe the angels are teaching me and not the other way around. But as much as I think it is the latter, the scenario presented itself where I was the teacher and not the student.

All of the angels around me continued to ask me over and over about how I executed all of the tasks laid out before me with such fluidity and grace. They seemed to genuinely desire an answer, to which I did not have a solid response. One word that was continually repeated to me by the angels was a word that began with the letter R. I had never heard the word before, and as many times as I repeated it to try to help me retain it for when my soul returned to Earth, I was unsuccessful. But, whatever the strength the word held, I knew that the answer to their questions about my ability resided in that word.

There were activities such as deejaying for a crowd of angels all of the way through to tutoring children where the word applied. The tasks I was given to demonstrate my ability spanned any and all possibilities I would never have lumped into one concept. Within those tasks, the meaning of the word could be found – and therefore the answer to how I did everything so differently would find resolve. It has been my understanding that my actions of doing things differently are part of the gift – I see tasks differently than most. But still – I cannot even begin to put into words the archetypal and con-

The Written (cont'd)

ceptual lessons I am being taught. Though I try, I know that it is important for me to understand this word that begins with R – and whatever method/how I am able to do whatever it may be that has found favor in the eyes of the angels.

Talk about a tough task. It is like saying, "Good job buddy. Keep doing what you are doing, and then tell us whatever your secret is that makes you complete these tasks so well." All the while, there is no baseline to see how your performance is better than someone else's. To me, everything just *is* because that is where I have progressed. I do not know what to even compare my actions to so that I can begin to understand what is different. Maybe that is the starting line. Maybe I should seek out baselines to compare my own actions against. But to do so, I suppose I need to understand *what* I am comparing as the baseline scenario. I know I am talking in circles, but this is the conundrum I find myself in as I seek to understand this ability. I suppose if I knew the baseline, I would already be able to see the variance and thus the "ability." It is a paradox that actually has an answer – a point of entry into something seemingly undefined.

April 1, 2014

I had numerous experiences in the heavens throughout the night/early morning hours, but every one left me with a divide in bringing back the information. I was able to bring back some of it, but the details – which were the most im-

Rebirth III

portant part – were unable to be brought back to Earth. I often wonder if this is because of the nature of spiritual knowledge and where it must remain, or whether it has to do with my own inability to maintain harmony/balance enough to bring the information back. Whatever the case may be, the experiences were tacked onto the previous several days' experiences in the heavens that focused on some specific ability I have been gifted by God (which I still have not figured out what it is or how to use it). In fact, most of the last several days' experiences involved me only seeing glimmers of what I could do. I used the gift intuitively, but without understanding I was using it. Definitely, it should be seen as a grand conundrum for my personal growth.

The first experience in the heavens began with me sitting next to an angel on a plane. Vehicles are typically used to illustrate traveling or personal progress, and this time was no different. I was being given wisdom from the angel about this particular gifted ability that I still am unsure what it is. It is difficult to even comprehend the conversations because it is as if we talk in circles. The angel cannot reveal what the gift is within me, for I must find it on my own. But, the angel can be a guide, which typically means the conversations seem like gibberish and circles in meaning. Because the guidance is so misconstrued from earthly context, it is difficult to retain and bring the information back to Earth. But they are trying to help me nonetheless… and I am trying as hard as I can to understand.

The Written (cont'd)

After the experience in the plane ended, I found myself sitting next to an angel in a car – another vehicle to illustrate personal progress. The car was parked in a parking lot. In front of us was a rectangular-shaped restaurant that had a line of other vehicles circling it in the drive-thru line. Diagonally right from the car was a smaller building – like a security booth. It was maybe 30 yards or so from where we were sitting.

As we sat there, I was recounting a story to the angel. He listened intently. But, the focus was on my conversation. I believe I was discussing the conversation from the plane, but again, it seemed disjointed in an earthly-sense – yet fluid in a spiritual sense. Eventually, I observed someone come out of the restaurant carrying a bag. The person walked over to the building that was diagonally right from us and handed the bag of food to the person in the booth. It was important that I understood that the person who received the food was the "director," and that she received her food before everyone else waiting in line.

We laughed and chatted about it – the absurdity of the prioritization in the heavens. We walked over to the director's building and began conversing. For all intents and purposes, I believe "the director" is "the girl" I talk about frequently in the heavens, but she appeared slightly different this time. During our conversation, she talked about the "great moments" in my life so far and talked about me not having any clear direction before. The purpose of both the conversation and the journey so far has been to understand what *I thought* God was say-

Rebirth III

ing to me and then doing it. Depending on my actions, the rest of the journey would unfold the way it needs to for me to learn. Everything – all outcomes – are directly related to helping my own spiritual growth. In a global sense, the purpose of the journey is to learn to discern God's voice and will.

We continued to talk about me not knowing the outcomes of situations before taking my leaps of faith. I desired guidance. I wanted to make the right decision – the decision that God intends. I want to be a pure, unobstructed vessel for God, but it would seem that I still have a lot to learn. The answers I was given left me feeling there was still a tremendous gap from where I am today in my spiritual growth to what I will one day become.

In the end, I was told that when I take a leap of faith based on what I thought was God's will, then the answers/outcomes are just. Obviously, the leaps must be vetted and prayed about. The leaps are based on what I believe God's answer is – not what I want the answer to be or even think the answer could be. This is the divide in the ego and the soul. A pure soul will abide by God's will – not his own desires or formed conclusions. I was likely left with more questions than answers in the conversation, but before I left I was imparted one last important piece of wisdom.

With any call to action invoked by the hand of God, our body is called to serve as a vessel for Him to speak and act through. While I understood the concept of this, I have been praying a lot recently about help in discerning *what* the call to action is specifically for each scenario. I can now tell when I

The Written (cont'd)

have been called, but discerning the action is where I am struggling. I often feel that there are numerous possibilities, but I want to make sure I choose the way that God intends me to choose. For me, I do not want to stumble or choose incorrectly.

So, as I chatted with the angels, they imparted me this answer: For any call-to-action, there are four possible directions/methods of action. The first is the best way (the way that God ideally desires you choose). The second is the wrong way (the way that goes against God's will). The other two ways will help get you to the right answer eventually, but they are not wrong. They are placed there to help you learn. So, to better understand the angel's answer, it could be summed up as follows: There are four cardinal directions for any question/answer/call-to-action. One action moves with the direction of the wind. One goes against the wind. The other two still push forward, but deviate from the course as the sail seeks to find the most optimal direction to catch the wind.

Until this moment, I would not have assumed there was anything other than two directions, but alas, there are four. And truthfully, this just makes me realize how much more of a challenge it is to hear God's intention. If there is a clear right and wrong, I can run with that much more easily. But apparently, there is a window of grace as long as action is done in the way that we best can understand God's direction. Perhaps this knowledge was imparted to help me feel more comfortable in taking action, for the odds just went to 75% in not making the wrong decision. But as much as the odds have increased, I

Rebirth III

suppose I now am faced with the greater task of seeing the window of grace and trying to find the eye of the needle between the expanse of possibility.

April 3, 2014

Before bed, I prayed to God to help me to have a better hold on my harmony in the heavenly experiences I typically have. It has been several days since my last experience in which I could maintain harmony. I know I have introduced a lot of variables recently into my earthly life, so I have to assume these variables are causing me to drift from my normal balance. Just to make note of those variables – I have taken a week or two off from working out, taken a week or two off of my diet (more specifically, I have allowed myself to eat more greasy foods and sweets), and changed up my sleep schedule. Each of those individually affect biological balance, so I assume all three are having a greater, more complicated effect. I need to get back into my routine to maintain optimal body/soul balance – or, at least back to the balance I can more spiritually recognize.

But with that said, I experienced three separate heavenly experiences that were all incredibly hyper-sensory. The first one began with me standing near a child and an older girl. The boy child was maybe around eight years old or so. The girl appeared to be in her twenties. Each should be understood to be angels – guardians and guideposts for me along my jour-

The Written (cont'd)

ney. It was readily apparent that we all knew each other very well. I recognized everyone's familiarity, but I did not know their names, nor could I identify why I knew them.

As we talked, the boy called us to follow him. We all mounted ourselves on top of a rocket. It was a long, slender rocket with an end cap that had a curved taper spanning about fifteen or twenty feet and forming into a point. We all hung onto the end cap. It looked like something from a fiction comic book – something that could never happen on Earth. As we were all holding onto the rocket, it launched into the stratosphere. Only space surrounded us with a great sense of speed and rumbling encompassing our souls. I knew that the experience was metaphorical to my soul leaving my body and traveling to the heavens. Sometimes I get to experience the "takeoff" through similar visualizations. Sometimes it is a train or plane. Other times it is a tornado or thunderstorm. This time it was a rocket – a first for me.

As we were traveling to the heavens, I looked at the boy and noticed that his appearance changed slightly. It was in that moment I realized the boy's appearance was a cloak to who he really was – whether it was my mind causing his identity to be misrepresented or whether it was controlled from the heavenly side, I do not know. The boy could tell that I saw his appearance change briefly. He looked at me, smiled and said, "I know! I'm not who you think I am. I've been dying to tell you all of this time…" Suddenly, I was booted out of the experience and back into my body. I recognized that I was not supposed to hear the boy's answer. I also knew he was about

Rebirth III

to reveal both his identity and the girl's identity to me. I would Love to have known who they were, but apparently it was not my time to know yet.

As I digested everything that happened, I focused back on returning to the heavens. Suddenly, I found myself standing outside of a cedar plank house in the middle of a thick forest. The trees towered above the house. Outside, night had fallen. I walked up to the house and stepped inside. The house was oblong and was divided in half along the length of the building. I walked to my right with the dividing wall to my left. I could see a door at the end of the building. It looked to be another entrance into the house. As I reached the end of the building, I noticed on my left was a hidden door that would allow me to pass through the divider wall. I noticed it was spring mounted and was a sliding door.

I pulled the door open. It took a lot of strength and effort to keep the door open long enough for me to jump through, but I managed. As I jumped through, the door shut behind me. I heard someone tell me that if the room was not to my liking, to let them know. It reminded me of a hotel concierge speaking to a visitor, though I could not identify where the voice came from. The room was initially dark, but as my eyes adjusted, I could see I was standing in a bedroom. It was cedar planked on the inside and was very rustic. I noticed a bed off to my left. If it is understood in relative directions that I entered the door in the North and walked East before crossing the divider, the bed was also facing East. As I approached the bed, I could not manage to observe if anyone was in it. Along

The Written (cont'd)

the foot of the bed, in the bottom right hand corner (Southeast corner), I saw a square of glowing light that was illuminating the comforter. It looked like how sun would pass through a window and light up a specific part of a room. I looked around to see if I could find a window where light would be passing through, but, alas, the room seemed to have no windows. Suddenly, I heard a female's voice boom out, "Jonathan"...and then I lost harmony in the moment and returned to my body.

When discussing this experience with Bryan, he felt it was important to break the experience down into thirds. Actually, this concept of thirds was something he had begun to do earlier in the day and was applying it to everything that he was doing to better understand God's message. When we broke it down the thirds indicated 1) stepping into a house, 2) finding the door, and 3) finally seeing the light on the corner of a bed with no source of light. Bryan thought the message was explaining how God continues to communicate with me. Perhaps it was even offering guidance to an alignment of my body, but mostly it was capped by hearing my spiritual name from the voice of an angel. Spiritual names are another story all together, but the fact that my spiritual name is the same as my earthly name has extremely strong implications.

The final experience involved me walking toward some type of club in the night. The building was lighted with a neon-like sign, but appeared to be very dirty and poorly constructed. When I walked up to it, there was a Gatekeeper. In earthly terms, it would appear more like a bouncer to a

Rebirth III

club, but I knew this was a Gatekeeper to a spiritual experience in a specific setting for me to learn and grow from. The other people in the line in front of me were carefully scrutinized before they were allowed in the building. Many were turned away by the gatekeeper. When I approached him, I was nervous I would be turned away. But, as I approached him he just smiled at me and waved me right on in. He did not even think twice. I realized I must be a familiar soul for him to just allow me to pass on through.

When I walked in, there was a row of booths along the left hand side. They were dimly lighted – mostly hidden in the shadows. As I walked past the row of booths, I noticed two familiar male angels sitting at a table talking to two female angels across from them. For some reason, one of the female angels I knew as "Lauren." One of the male angels and a female angel each had red hair. The two others had brown hair. The brown-haired male reminded me of Joey. The red-haired male reminded me of Jonathan C. I did not acknowledge I saw them, but spiritually, we acknowledged each other's presence.

I walked to the back of the club and saw the spirit of an angel that reminds me of a girl on Earth named Natalie. I do not believe they are the same entity, but it at least helps me remember when I see her time and time again. We interact quite a bit in the heavens – typically involving me teaching and her learning. In fact, most of the souls in the building seemed to be the souls of others I help teach. When I reached "Natalie" she was on her knees leaning against a wall. She was distraught and upset – having just collapsed to the floor.

The Written (cont'd)

When I reached her, I gave her a big hug and we caught up. She was wearing a really "look at me" revealing piece of clothing. I would struggle to call it a dress, but it was similar and made of large rectangles of fabric with equally large rectangles of nothing where the skin was revealed. This particular dress was meant to show off her breasts – which I have to say looked very nice, but abnormally large. From a spiritual standpoint, I knew that her soul was battling with image issues and trying to make people like her for her body. In fact, the reason she was collapsed on the floor was because she could not understand why no one was paying her attention – for she had no idea that she was in the heavens.

I comforted her and began to help her stand when another girl walked up to me. This was another familiar soul, though I cannot recall specifically where we had met before. When she reached me, she wanted me to help her get home. After helping "Natalie," I left the club with the other soul. She was wearing tall boots and a short dress. She was sleepy and struggling to understand where she was. She was very incoherent – similar to someone being drunk. But, her incoherence stemmed from a soul not understanding why they were in the heavens. In her bodily form, I am sure she probably had no idea we interacted in the heavens, which is why she was "drunk."

As I walked her toward her house, the sun was coming up. I know it may seem odd to relate the experience in the heavens to a drunk person, but when you really think about it, how else would a person be in a locale that does not adhere to earthly

Rebirth III

rules...one that requires "awakening" the spirit. It would appear metaphorically as how a groggy soul would try to see the surroundings with no understanding of what was happening to them. It is at this point along my spiritual journey that I have been tasked with helping awaken the souls of those around me – those that are within a certain radius of my earthly soul...those I have interacted with in the past and have left a seed in their minds. This is how one can help awaken others spirits.

April 4, 2014

The first experience began with me standing in a house/office. A business (represented by a company I consult with on Earth) was close to closing a deal that they wanted me to see. Everyone of the people involved in the deal closing joked with me about being in a meeting that I was not invited to. This type of kidding around with me was done in a form of jealousy, rather than of scolding. For some reason, I apparently am included in this group's meetings because of something special – something that they cannot see. So instead of seeking understanding, they joke with me about how I am always present in their meetings without being invited. This occurred over the course of several meetings.

Finally, I found myself using a bathroom in an office when a group came into the adjoining conference room to meet. This was yet another meeting I was not invited to, but one I

The Written (cont'd)

did not want to be coincidentally in the room when the meeting began. As they began to gather, I exited the bathroom and walked through the conference room – excusing myself from the group. Everyone exchanged pleasantries with me. One guy made it a point to tell me how happy he was with me. I assumed he was referring to my contributions to the team.

Outside in a lounge, a couple of others who should have been in the meeting were just hanging out and relaxing. They sarcastically asked how I was in that meeting too and made more jokes about it. On that note, I walked out of the lounge. When I reached the door to leave, a girl tried to get my attention. I turned around to see a group of gorgeous women standing beside me. They laughed and giggled at the circumstance of standing by me. It seemed celebrity-esque to them for whatever reason. Each of them began talking to me. I heard one voice say, "Boy, won't the other girls be jealous tonight? Look how beautiful we all are."

The excitement of being around me was an odd feeling for me. I could not understand the situation, but I embraced it and just "went with it" without acting special at all. They wanted me to go wherever they were going, so I just tagged along. When we reached the next destination, I was held outside of the main room by a group of girls. They tried to be discreet in keeping me outside of it. I could tell they had a purpose, but I did not let on I could see through their ploy.

We chatted for a bit when suddenly a bride walked up. She was beautiful. Her gown was gorgeous – long and flowing white. The top had a deep V in the front and a deeper V in

Rebirth III

the back. The bride knew me. She immediately gave me a big hug. At that point, the other girls dispersed, leaving just me and the bride. It was clear they were wanting her and me to meet. After we talked, we all headed inside to the party. Everyone was dancing. I was pulled onto the dance floor where all of the girls wanted to dance with me. Everyone was extra physical to me – something that is atypical in the heavens, but seemed okay in this context. It was more of a flirty spiritual celebration of sorts. It would seem that the celebration was for the bride….or for me….or for both of us. It is hard to say, but it was important I was there. Most of the others at the party were reserved, but it became clear as we were dancing that the girls intended to get everyone to "live a little" and have fun in the celebration. Eventually, all of the partygoers were dancing and enjoying the moment.

    I eventually lost harmony with the moment, but managed to return almost instantly to the heavens. This time I was standing outside of two buildings. I could now see how the first location with the offices was connected to the other location where the party was being held. The party was on a covered patio on the building to my right side. It was clear that I could go back, but this time I did not see anyone in the buildings. They each appeared empty. As I stood there observing the buildings, I began pondering questions about life and existence. I still am not sure why the questions entered my head. But, nonetheless, those were the thoughts running rampant through my mind. As I contemplated on the theme, one specific thought entered my mind: "Why does one feed the

The Written (cont'd)

intellect so long?" Immediately I heard a whip sound and returned to my body. I made sure to write the question down word-for-word since whatever I had arrived at caused me to be kicked back to my body. Perhaps I was kicked back to write down the thought – to explore the meaning of it. It is an interesting question…

After I journaled the previous experience, I closed my eyes. Immediately a great light filled my periphery. I found myself standing in the middle of jumbled symbols. There were nine. The symbols represented all that I have learned so far. A hand started sliding the symbols around. I could not see who the hand was attached to as there was only darkness outside of the symbols. The angel left me in the middle of the symbols and then began to form an octagon, or maybe a nine-shaped figure around me illustrating how I could find clarity within. The shape is similar to others I have seen in occult drawings… but somehow more precise in design. I am not sure how a shape can be more "geometrically precise" than another drawing made geometrically, but that was the case with this shape. Suddenly, my mind's eye was shown a wiki-like article about me and had an image of a collection of nine books. These books represented the books I will eventually write and leave behind for everyone. They were each different colors – all bright. The baby-blue, red, and ochre yellow stood out the most. They looked like colors from the 1970s. Each book was bound in leather and was held within a red rectangular case. With that, I returned to my body.

Rebirth III

April 6, 2014

While I cannot recall the experience with much clarity, I know there was an important circumstance in which I was interacting with Chris (the guy Lindsey is dating). It was all positive – some sort of a learning experience for me, but most of the emphasis in the experience pertained to our conversation (of which I cannot recall with any clarity). So I will write this down in hopes that some clarity will be added at a later point in time.

April 8, 2014

The heavenly experience this morning placed me in the same room as from days before with Chris's soul (the guy who is now dating Lindsey). I assume this is a continuation of what I could not recall with much clarity from a couple of days ago. I cannot tell you if I was truly interacting with Chris or if it was an angel in disguise to test my growth, but it felt more like a test than an actual encounter with Chris's soul. I suppose for someone reading this who may have never experienced an angelic encounter in the heavens, it will be more difficult to understand why I thought it was a test versus an actual soul, but I will try to disambiguate my statement.

To date, when I have encountered tests, there is a strong sense of oversight from someone I cannot see. It is akin to the feeling of "being watched" but the feeling would not be identi-

The Written (cont'd)

cal in spiritual terms. The spirit is much more difficult to put into words. In fact, I have trouble putting many of the feelings during the experiences in words, which is why I believe that the concept is so difficult for people to understand. How can a person explain something that is incomprehensible in earthly words, yet is able to be experienced by each and every person?

Anyway, much of the time I spent in the heavens with Chris was of a very friendly nature. We spoke to each other as if we had been friends for ages. Everywhere we would go and everything we would do in the heavens was similar to how two friends on Earth would interact. Eventually, there came a point where I said, "Chris – I suppose we should talk about the elephant in the room." He looked at me somewhat saddened that we had to talk about it. I told him that I was extremely happy for him and Lindsey. I explained that while he may not understand much of what I was about to say, that I hoped he would think about it. I went on to explain that what I had experienced and written about with Lindsey was about a spiritual Love that transcends time and space. I explained that his anger toward me in an earthly sense was misguided because he did not understand – nor did she – what the meaning of my words in the book actually meant. I explained that I was at peace with him and with Lindsey because I could now see what greater message God was allowing me to see and also to share with him. Chris looked frustrated at my explanation, but I continued to offer him reassurance that if Lindsey is the person he wants to be with, then he should continue forward – and that God would watch over them. I also said that if I

Rebirth III

could ever be of help to him along his journey, that he should always know that I will be here to help in whatever way I can help. With that, the experience ended and I returned to my body.

As I digested all that had occurred, I realized that God must be showing me that I have earthly emotions still wrapped up in the situation with Lindsey and Chris. I found truth in frustration with Chris, because I could not understand why he was so angry with me when we saw each other at Jason's wedding reception. As much as I was dealing with spiritually, the last thing I expected was the anger he exuded. And while he never went out of his way to do anything to me to exhibit the anger, it was the subtleties that disheartened me. I could not process in my mind why a person would have so much anger directed toward another, whether he acted on it or not. I guess it would be appropriate to relate it to a demon, for the emotion he was experiencing was the living embodiment of a negative entity within his mortal body. And, I suppose if it could be said that he was battling a demon inside, then it would also make sense how Jesus was said to be able to rid a person of demons – because it is within the abundance of Love that negative energy runs away. So, perhaps it could be seen that what I was offering to Chris in a laborious conversation in the heavens was equivalent to how the spirit has a conversation with the soul of another and cleanses it of negative feelings. This is just my guess from my experience, though. It would also make sense that I was interacting with a representation of Chris so I could learn how to grow in this regard, for I

The Written (cont'd)

do not think that I would have been tested in a real-world scenario if I had the potential of failing. Either way, these are just my thoughts for now, but there is a greater application to the scenario than just a random encounter in the heavens – that part is for sure.

April 9, 2014

This morning was filled with numerous experiences in the heavens. Sometimes it seems like I can write a lot about the experiences. Other times the details "are what they are," and I cannot discern any more at the point of the experience. Much of what happened in each of the experiences this morning falls into this category of bullet-point details.

The first experience began with me standing amongst a group of angels. They were all circled around me asking me questions. It seemed like a Q&A session with my angelic advisors – though I had never thought of them as "advisors" before now. I cannot recall any of the questions asked except for one question specifically. I have to believe that question contained so much gravity within it that it resonated deep within my core.

As the group of angels was taking turns asking me questions and hearing my answers, a jolly upper-middle aged man leaned over to ask me a question. He looked like Albert Einstein, but his hair was salt-and-peppered instead of the traditional white hair as Einstein is typically portrayed. The

Rebirth III

question he asked was simple and was clearly the important take-away from the experience. He asked, "Are you trying the family thing first?" When he asked this, I scrunched up my face as if to show disgust that he would ask such a question. The feeling of my face scrunching in a spiritual sense was a sensation I had not felt before the other night (in which the experience kicked me back to my body causing me not to be able to recount the experience at all). This time it kicked me back to my body as well.

After I journaled the previous experience, I found my way back to the heavens. In this particular experience, I was arrested and taken into custody. I was led to a booking room where there were a couple other souls sitting in seats awaiting the next part of the process after being arrested. Eventually, I was released since there was nothing to charge me with. The detective who arrested me wanted to lock me up for "spiritual reasons" but could not make his desires manifest into anything that could tangibly stick in the judge's eyes. More or less, it was a demonstration of someone resistant to allowing me to grow spiritually while attempting to invoke his will of suppressing me. But, alas, it was to no avail.

After leaving, I experienced about a week's worth of life in the heavens. Typical routines to start and end the day occurred. After about a week from when I was first arrested, I was approached by officers again. I was not doing anything abnormal. They sought me out. This was on a Friday. The officers escorted me to the station where I was booked again. As I sat in the waiting room, I realized it was taking forever.

The Written (cont'd)

There was no one watching the doorway that I had entered, so I just decided to get up and leave. I had no intention of running away from the charges. I just wanted to be more productive with my time and face my charges whenever they finally got processed. When I stood up to leave, the other people who had been booked all looked at me amazed that I would do such a thing. I just looked at them and said I would see them later – that I did not have time to wait. I walked out.

I was expecting my mother to arrive on Saturday, and I really did not want her to see me locked up for no apparent reason – even if I did not know what the officers would attempt to pin on me. It was clear this was still a spiritual battle. When I left, I planned to return after my mother left for the weekend.

After leaving, I saw my mother and spent the weekend with her. While I am still sorting out my spiritual brethren by names and titles, the mother I am speaking of is my "spiritual mother." She is not my earthly mother…at least not that I can yet tell. They could be one and the same, but I think they are two distinctly different spiritual embodiments.

The weekend came and went, and I returned to the police station on Sunday. I sat in the waiting room alone. No one was around. Eventually I noticed a receptionist had arrived behind a glass window, and I went up to speak with her. I explained I was arrested and decided to leave on Friday, but now I was back and wanted to wrap up whatever it was that the detective had started on Friday. I knew whatever the reasoning, it was just a spiritual flailing of suppression from the

Rebirth III

detective's side, so I really was not concerned about the outcome. I had faith that all would be okay.

The receptionist looked at me as if I had lost my mind when I told her I just up and left on Friday. But after a while, she just laughed about it and realized I was not in the wrong. She tried to contact the detective, but could not. I knew that when I was booked, there was a rule that I had "three days to speak with the detective from the time I was booked." Since this was the end of the three days, I was anxious to make sure we met. But when the receptionist was unable to reach the detective, she just laughed and said it did not seem like anyone really cared about my case, and that I was free to go. And with that, I left. I returned to my body and journaled the experience.

I returned one last time to the heavens this morning. This time I saw Mary, an old friend from my middle school and high school days. She had been on my mind a lot recently. Back in December/January, she reached out to me explaining how she was excited that she and her fiancé were moving to Nashville. She wanted me to help them find a place up here, or at least point them in the direction of a good realtor. I put them both in touch with a good friend here in Nashville-- Leah. She was planning to help them find a home. I never heard back, though.

Some time had passed, so I decided to reach out to Mary to see if they ever made it up to Nashville. But, when I went to reach out to her on Facebook (the way we initially had chatted), I discovered that she had deleted her Facebook account.

The Written (cont'd)

That is the only way we communicated, so I had to assume something happened for her to delete it. I had wondered if she and her fiancé had broken up – which may have caused her to remove her profile.

So, when I saw her soul in the heavens I was surprised. This is the first time I have seen her soul during my heavenly experiences. I walked over and talked with her. I asked how she was doing – careful not to pry about anything too sensitive. She told me about how she and her fiancé were struggling with their relationship. I assumed their relationship at a delicate point, but that part was not evidently clear. It was just clear that she was experiencing some major challenges in her relationship. With that response, I lost harmony with the moment and returned to my body.

April 10, 2014
Early Morning

Last night I went to bed somewhat frustrated about my stalemating of spiritual encounters. I know that I have not been "abandoned" or anything like that. It is just that over the last week or two, it has seemed that my experiences have not been as fluid as they have been in the past. I know that may sound like I am complaining about not getting enough "face time" in the heavens, when others may not receive any at all – but the truth is that it is more about spiritual growth.

Rebirth III

It could be that I am just getting a spiritual breather for a bit. Perhaps I need to catch my breath before the next breakneck acceleration into the next phase of my life. After all, I had asked God for a chance to catch my spiritual breath after I reached the 28th of March. I guess this is just me saying, "Put me back in, Coach," to The Big Guy Upstairs. So, for anyone who may read this, please do not think that I am pouting or anything along those lines. I am just extremely excited to keep moving forward. But I suppose sometimes space is what makes the more intimate times that much more special.

So, as I went to bed, I prayed for heightened guidance. And as God would have it, He offered several experiences in the heavens that had heightened sensitivity. They were so brilliant in experience that I did not think I had to journal them immediately upon returning to my body. Sometimes there are experiences that will last an eternity. I thought that each of the experiences I had this morning would be the same due to the amount of awareness and sensation I felt during my travels. But, this would be where my ego interfered with my spirit. For, when I finally got out of bed this morning, nearly every experience had vanished from my mind. There was only the lingering understanding of the scenario and one important question I was asked. In retrospect, I assume that what lingered in my mind the most must have been the most important part of the experience. But, I am extremely disappointed that I abandoned my normal policy of journaling immediately upon returning to my body in lieu of being lazy. That is really what it is when it comes down to it… laziness.

The Written (cont'd)

So with that said, the memories that did linger in my mind involved three experiences. Each of the three experiences involved me being escorted through the heavens while having intimate conversations with one particular angel. I know I was shared direction, guidance, and answers to some extremely important questions I have had about the heavens, but unfortunately I did not write them down. Heavenly experiences are not like normal memories. They are archetypal ripples in a spiritual aether that the soul understands how to interpret. But, when the body is fully awake and in motion, it is extremely difficult to recall the ripples. The one important question I was asked in the heavens that caused me to return to my body came from a group of angels that walked up to us as we were walking around the heavens. One younger angel who was very familiar, came up and said hello to me as the group seemed excited to see us. But after he said hello, he then said, "The only question I have is why is your coat so large?"

This question immediately sent my soul hurtling back to Earth. Over the course of my journeys, the symbolism in the coat I am wearing has become increasingly apparent and important. While it is not important to delve into it too much in this part of my journal, the coat should be thought of as tantamount to the biblical "coat of many colors" that Joseph "wore." If I could just add one thing to the thought of the coat, it is that Joseph's coat was symbolic of what He received from God in the heavens. It is the same coat I wear. But this time, it was important for me to hear about the coat being too large. I had never heard that about the coat. In fact, I thought it al-

Rebirth III

ways fit me extremely well. While I could not explain what it looks like, I just know that it is a garment that seems to fit me in a very tailored fashion when I wear it in the heavens. I never put it on by choice. It is symbolic in nature and appears on me when it is important for my understanding of growth. I did not even think about the "coat" that continued to recur in my experiences to be like Joseph's coat until a conversation with Bryan where he offered that guidance. After understanding that aspect, it has helped me understand a lot more about the symbolism in each and every part of the experiences in the heavens.

Anyway, when I returned to my body, the question I was asked resonated deep within my soul. All I could think about is why would the coat be too large? Is it because my spirit has "shrunk" from where it was when I was given the coat? This would not seem to be the case because I have grown so much spiritually, but anything is an option. Keep in mind that the more spiritual and "elder" angels are in heaven, the larger they appear. Is it supposed to mean that I am not as close to God in the recent weeks as I have been over the last few months? Possibly – but not for lack of trying. Could it be just to remind me of the coat itself, and that God had given it to me for a reason? Quite possibly. Is it possible that it is meant to represent the amount of growth that remains before me to "grow into the coat" that I have been given? This seems most likely, but again all of these questions and potential answers have rattled through my mind to think about.

The Written (cont'd)

April 10, 2014

Afternoon

To date, this may be one of the most prolific experiences I have ever had. Today during meditation around lunch, I prayed to God asking him to help me understand why I felt that I was in a spiritual funk over the last week. It was not that I did not think He was speaking to me. It was just that the experiences felt distant to me. It could possibly be due to something I was doing, or maybe something else. In a stream-of-consciousness fashion, I wondered aloud to God if it was the lack of Love in my life. I wondered if the absence of the feelings I felt during the last several months about Lindsey had created an insurmountable spiritual chasm that even I did not recognize. Really, I was just looking for answers. I honestly am not upset or even feeling down about Lindsey. It is evident that God had prepared that test for me and caught me when it did not play out. So, as I rambled on about that and other thoughts about physical workouts and diets possibly introducing variables into my walk with God, my phone rang.

It was my insurance company seeking to finish my insurance questionnaire for a personal articles policy I took out over an item God led me to purchase for Lindsey – though she never received it. It was at this point along the journey that I now had to remove any reference to Lindsey on my file (insurance wise and spiritually). It was a little frustrating, but it would be

Rebirth III

the period at the end of a sentence to the closure of the ride my soul took with Lindsey.

After I hung up, I realized that on top of having just prayed about the concept of "Love" and the experience with Lindsey, I was wearing the same shirt and suit I had worn the night I saw Lindsey with Chris. Oh, the irony. It is a combination of clothes I maybe have worn one or two other times, and I only wore it today because all of my other shirts were dirty… and I had rotated through my other suits. Everything is connected, and it was clear in this moment that my clothes, the phone call, and the prayer were all interconnected.

Even so, I did not think too much more about it, and I began praying about my next spiritual steps. I did not know where I was being called to live, but I knew that God was calling for a change in my location. Was Florida still a consideration? These were the types of questions I was speaking aloud to God. Eventually, I wrapped up my prayer and decided to pray internally in the same way I had done the time that God showed me the Kingdom and my seat. This is what Bryan calls "the wormhole inside." It is different than praying internally, though I do not know how I can differentiate it through words. Anyway, as I chased the wormhole around inside, I suddenly arrived in the heavens…or maybe I should call it the border of Heaven and Hell.

I was standing on a rocky ledge next to a brunette girl. There was no apparent path that helped us arrive on this ledge. Beneath us about one hundred feet below, was a dark, formless matter. It was reddish in color – sort of like lava – but

The Written (cont'd)

mostly it was dark. It should be understood as "formless matter." It rolled around like a great ocean below. Intuitively, my soul understood the motion of the rolling matter and the location we were in. I could see both sides simultaneously while standing on the edge of the cliff. The best manner I could explain the scenario, is to be standing inside an active volcano near the point where magma erupts from the core of the Earth. Though the motion was not explained to me, I knew at some point prior, the knowledge to the motion of the formless matter had been imparted to me so that I could understand it in this moment.

As we stood on the cliff's edge, I saw that the girl could not make a decision about something I was not privy to. The point I was to observe was that she could not make a decision. As I watched her pleading for help because she was not able to make a decision, I saw a hand (larger than our souls) reach down from above, reach into her body, and pull out a smoky-formed spirit within. I knew instantly it was a demon residing inside of her. As the hand pulled it out, I saw that both the girl and the demon were yelling and crying out unsure of what was happening. To me, it was as if her soul had been split into two mirrored souls – one evil, one with the potential for good. The hand that took the smoky demon out of her cast it down into the formless matter. The smoky soul was screaming as it descended. I knew it was not killed, but rather sent to reside on the other side of the dark matter.

At the moment the demon was cast to the underside, the voice of God rang out in response to the girl's cries. He said,

Rebirth III

"Don't worry about below. There is only light up here. I am light." With that, God revealed himself as a blinding white light, glowing like a star. He stood between her and me. From the light, a hand protruded holding a great golden staff. To my eyes, I saw a great blinding light holding a staff. The girl kept saying how she was terrified of being cast below. She seemed suddenly familiar. Though she was brunette, I began to realize the girl was Lindsey (Lindsey has blonde hair). I had never seen her in the form she was in. As all of this was occurring, I heard the voice of the smoky demon crying out from below.

It began calling out Lindsey's name in a terrifying voice. It was in agony and suffering below the formless matter. When God cast the evil out of her, she was terrified of hearing the screams because they were in her voice. Lindsey was having to hear a version of herself suffering, echoing in the depths of what I can only define as Hell. God said, "Don't worry about the screams. You WILL hear yourself." It was clear that God wanted Lindsey to hear herself.

Lindsey pleaded that she did not want to hear herself screaming – that she did not want to hear her voice from below. With that, God said with a booming voice, "I am a proud father!" Then He slammed his staff into the ground which caused a thunderous boom to echo throughout the heavens. With that, I returned to my body. I immediately journaled the experience.

After I finished journaling the moment in the heavens, I prayed about a completely different topic. This concerned the first book I finished writing. I had originally thought Jessica (a

The Written (cont'd)

girl I used to work with at Vaco) was purposed into my life again recently to edit and proof my book. At this point though, I was not sure I wanted anyone else to read the words I had written (except for my mother and Bryan). Almost immediately upon praying, I received a text from Jessica asking if I had received my book for her to proof. I had just received the copies last night and they were in my Jeep with me at that very moment, so I responded that I did. I heard God's call, and I immediately responded by going to her office to drop off the book.

When I got there we chatted briefly. She was surprised the book was actually in a fully printed state – book bindings and all. She flipped over the book and saw that the back of the book just says, "Always, Jonathan" on the back. She looked surprised and said, "You know that's how I sign my blog every time I finish a new entry?!" The truth is I only discovered this in the past several days when she sent me her blog link – but it is another sign in how I know she is intended to be part of this portion of my journey.

I responded, "I know. That is partly how I know I am supposed to let you read the book." We chatted about that for a few minutes and then I began to head out. As I was leaving, she said she would walk me out. When we reached the elevators, she started explaining to me in a completely out-of-left-field type of conversation how she had a dream last night and that I was in it. She blew over this point very quickly, but said, "You are always in my dreams. You are my dream talker." I let it slide and kept listening. She mentioned about how I had

Rebirth III

managed to tell her about a church song and the significance of it. When she awoke, she looked up her church's services and it turns out that the service they just posted on their webpage (for this upcoming Sunday, I believe) was themed with the name of the song I gave her.

After she finished telling me about her dream, I asked her what else I tell her in her dreams (just out of curiosity). She did not really want to continue down that path, so I did not press her. But I let her know that I was not uncomfortable in the conversation by saying, "You know, you may have thought that would catch me off-guard, but I am not surprised. In fact, I would have expected that. Thank you for telling me about being your dream talker." After that, I left. When I returned to my Jeep, I checked my emails…I had seven.

April 11, 2014
Early Morning

My first experience of the evening is very difficult to explain. When I was taken to the heavens, I was not in human form. I was in a fluid spiritual embodiment. Once I arrived, I was shown a staff. The staff was tall and made of gold (or so it appeared). I studied it intently, though I could not tell you in earthly terms what I observed – only that it held great power and was symbolic to something I did not yet know on my journey. I was flown into the staff, where it was intended I explore the inside of it. I, again, could not tell you what it was I

The Written (cont'd)

observed in earthly terms. Rather, I could only explain in spiritual terms the significance of what I observed. I am not sure how it applies yet to my earthly walk, but the staff is a new symbol introduced into my heavenly experiences yesterday when I saw God holding the staff. It is important to understand each element of a heavenly experience holds great meaning (such as the coat). The staff is important to understand and explore in archetypal and spiritual application.

The second experience in the heavens took me to a locale in a wooded forest. It was lush with foliage, towering trees and gray stones. There was running water – streams, brooks, etc. throughout the location. The sounds of running water filled my ears. It was beautiful. The location was in a valley between several towering mountains. Everything around me seemed like something from a movie...but even more grandiose. At the base of a great tree was a house. The tree was huge – much like "Home Tree" from the movie Avatar in proportion to the other trees around. But, then again, it would be misstating the experience to say it was exactly like "Home Tree." I am only referring to the size and the wooded environment it created. It was in this house, at the base of a great tree in the valley, that I learned about a person getting cancer. It was very sad. I was shared this knowledge by an angel that made sure to speak with me in a way that was comforting. It was as if I was being shared devastating news that I had to process before I even knew who it applied to. All I knew is a great sadness overcame me when I was told that someone I knew would be overtaken by cancer.

Rebirth III

From this house, I was led to another house that looked very similar to the house I was just in. It was not too far away – maybe just a few hundred feet separated the houses. I was summoned inside by another angel who led me to my earthly mother. Now this part is a little difficult for me to translate into earthly terms, but I could not say for sure if I was speaking to my earthly mother, or if the experience was representative of another mother I know, or even possibly my Spiritual mother who may have an earthly form as well. So, with that said, the whole experience I am about to outline used my earthly family as the characters in the scene, but I honestly cannot assume that what I observed would manifest in the same way in an earthly sense as in how/what I was allowed to observe. It is possible the characters were used to illustrate "a family" and my Love for them spiritually. So with that said, I will illustrate the experience as it was illustrated to me.

When I walked over to my mother, we embraced in a warm hug. She was saddened. I could see it in her demeanor. I could tell she was devastated in what she had to tell me. We each kneeled down to speak to each other. She began to cry and tell me that she had been diagnosed with cancer. I immediately knew the experience I had just had with the angels prior was preparing me for this moment. I just kneeled there, speechless for an awkward amount of time. My mother became upset with me because she thought I did not respond quickly enough. She was already sad, and the delay in my response hurt her more.

The Written (cont'd)

As she began to get upset, I said, "How am I supposed to respond immediately when I am supposed to tell you I have known this day was coming, and I knew I would one day have to tell you what I am telling you now – that I have already seen this, that you will have to go through a lot of pain – especially a year from now. And, that you are a fighter and you try hard to survive. I have to tell you I do not know the outcome for that was not shown to me – only that you fight hard to survive." As I said that, I realized Gigi (my sister) and Rory (her husband) were in the room with me. Gigi and Rory looked in disbelief at me holding my mother. Gigi became angry with me for telling my mother all that I had just said, but it had to happen that way. This is what the angels told me I would one day have to say when we were in the house earlier.

Apparently, the walk between the two houses was also supposed to indicate a length of time passing because my conversation with my mother took place a long time after I was told what would happen (like maybe a year or longer). Time did not seem to pass on the journey – only in the experience of the conversation did I understand that time had passed. As my mother and I were kneeled facing each other, she placed her head in my lap and just wanted to be held and comforted. I just held her and talked sweetly to her, trying to calm her nerves. Gigi continued to roll her eyes at me when she spoke to Rory. She did not believe that I would have known. But it was also apparent that her disbelief was her, ego and that spiritually she knew I was speaking the truth. It was at this point, I returned to my body and journaled the experience.

Rebirth III

After writing down all of the details, I tried to return to the heavens. I began by praying to God about "how heavy" the last experience was. I asked Him if I would be able to save the person. I knew that it may not necessarily represent my mother, and we discussed that as well. In fact, I felt that the experience most likely did not represent anything that would happen with my earthly family, which I prayed for clarity about as well. As I prayed asking whether I would be able to save the person, my soul was taken from my body to the heavens...and this time I mean a glorious place in the heavens.

I was taken to a place where the ground was blanketed in golden, pink, and white clouds. There were mountaintops poking through the clouds, where only the tips were visible. Nothing could be seen below the clouds. They were thick. I was flown through the clouds, weaving between the mountaintops, to a stone castle. The castle was extremely large – like a Disney castle. And while I say it was made of stone, it was grayish-white in color, with no visible stones. The castle walls held within it a Kingdom. I knew that it was important to understand I was being taken to a Kingdom and not just a castle.

The angel that flew me to the Kingdom placed me down next to other angels standing inside the Kingdom walls. We stood at the gate that opened up to the heavens on the outside. The walls were tall, and it was important to understand the safety, significance and meaning of being allowed inside the Kingdom. This was clearly evident to my spiritual mind. As I stood among the angels, I wanted to see what was on the other side of the wall. I knew that the "answer" to my question

The Written (cont'd)

about whether I would be able to save the person with cancer was on the other side of the gate. And while my answer was more of a conceptual answer, it was important to understand my answer was on the other side.

As I tried to peer around the other angels to see if I could "see" my answer on the other side, I noticed that pieces of the gate, while clearly solid, had transparency to them. For some reason, my mind justified these places in the gate as places where "gears" resided. It was in these locations that I could peep through to the other side. At the time, I was impressed with the notion that the gate to the kingdom is "crumbling" – but in a good way. It is more like my spirit is growing so I do not need as much protection from the walls as I did with a younger spirit. It was more symbolic to my spiritual growth than the walls falling apart. I understood it to mean that the answer was slowly being revealed to me. As I stood there peering through the transparent places, I lost harmony and returned to my body.

After journaling, I returned to the heavens. This time was less about imagery and more about instruction. This occurred in the heavens, but in a place that lacked definition. My focus was drawn to an angelic voice speaking to me. I was told that Jessica (whom I gave a copy of my book to yesterday to proof) is one of "my pillars." It was important that I understood she was one of five pillars. I was not entirely sure I was told the number five, but that is what it seemed like I was told. She represents one of the pillars to my spiritual growth. I was also told to let her know that she was one of my pillars. This was a

Rebirth III

directive issued to me. Honestly, I did not see this one coming at all. I have not even thought about having pillars in my life, nor that they are necessary to grow. But, now I can begin to see how it would be similar to how Jesus assembled his disciples in a manner so that he had foundational pillars. So maybe that is what this means…though by NO means am I paralleling myself to Jesus – only in the mirroring of demonstrable actions he made.

I returned to my body and journaled that portion of the experience and returned to the heavens. I returned to a similar location as the one prior. Again, the emphasis was on hearing the voice of the angel, and not the imagery. This time I was told to tell Jessica that "she was given her job to bring light to the people around her, and that she should embrace the opportunity for what it is and not what she wants it to be. She needs to be held." I thought about the instructions and wondered if that was truly a directive or just something I needed to understand. After being given confirmation that it was a directive to tell her, I was returned to my body to journal the complete directive.

After journaling, I again returned to the heavens. I found myself standing back among the angels in the Kingdom walls. This time, we were listening to an elder angel speak. He was teaching, though I could not tell you in earthly terms what was said – only that whatever he was saying was speaking to my spirit. As I listened, the angel on my left nudged me with his right arm. He offered me a cookie. I obliged and took a bite. The cookie was phenomenal – the perfect texture, sweetness,

The Written (cont'd)

and filling. When I took a bite, he smiled and we laughed about it. It reminded me of how kids will sometimes sit in the back of a classroom and cut-up with one another while the teacher speaks. It was not that we were being disrespectful, heckling, or anything like that. This was just a moment where two happy spirits were enjoying the moment and sneaking a bite of food as we listened to our teacher. The sensation of the cookie was overwhelming to my senses and caused me to lose harmony with the moment and return to my body. I immediately journaled the experience.

April 11, 2014
Afternoon

Meditating during lunch produced a handful of quirky experiences. They all seemed somewhat detached from anything I have experienced before. There was one point that I heard a female angel singing a song to me. Another time I heard the voice of a male angel sing a tune and ask me to join in. I joined in and seemed to know the words and melody, but I could not identify the song in any earthly sense. It sounded like a theme to a quirky television show, but only in style. There was one point I prayed for guidance on the experiences from the night prior, and that is when my phone rang. It was JT. He was calling to ask me for money for a car payment that was due today. This time he was asking for $75 instead of the $2000 he was asking for before. Last time I told him I could

Rebirth III

not help him out financially, but that has not stopped him from reaching out to me again.

April 12, 2014

While the details are not as clear as other experiences in the heavens, this experience drew primarily from archetypes in understanding. While I have now learned that most of the heavenly experiences (dating back to the very beginning of my "dreams" before I realized they could be so much more) have been intended to be understood archetypally rather than literally or symbolically, the experiences today carry much more emphasis in this area. I have to attest this to understanding the concept of communication much better than I did before. In the beginning, heavenly experiences were a radical departure from earthly life. I attempted to understand everything in an earthly sense. Today, I understand that Earth is a radical departure from the heavens, and I am just a child in understanding the language of our spiritual elders. So, with that said, the first experience this morning occurred as follows:

The experience began in a military training camp. It seemed naval versus land-based. I was selected to take the crewman under my wing during the training exercises. My rank was equivalent to first officer. The training was difficult, and I led the crewmen very well, keeping their energy and enthusiasm up, distracting them from the strenuous nature of the training. I knew there was another person ranked higher than

The Written (cont'd)

me (after all, I was only first officer), and I wondered why I exerted so much energy and effort in over performing as first officer. I did not mind – that was just the thought rattling through my mind.

At one point, I was pulled aside by an angelic leader. It was clear he was an angel, but was represented in rank as the superior to all of us – including the person ranked higher than me. I suppose he was somewhat like the Secretary of Defense in rank...something like that. Anyway, when I was pulled aside by this angel, it was made clear to me that the person ranked higher than me would eventually slip up, and that I would have an even greater opportunity to grow. The angel instilled motivation when I questioned my own. This kept me going and stilled my mind. I continued with the training.

I led the crew aboard a great vessel. It was like a great aircraft carrier, but the important understanding was that it was a vessel...an archetypal vehicle of transportation and transition. When I stepped on board and went inside, it was dark, so I flipped on the lights. As soon as I did this, alarms started going off. Another person raced aboard the vessel to turn off the alarms. It was at this point I realized that this was a similar experience to one I had a couple of days prior when I felt like I would remember and be able to write it down later, but could not recount the experience when I went to journal it.

Right before my soul was kicked back to my body, I was shown an image of grooming unruly leg hair. I do not know if it was some archetypal communication of calling me a girl for turning on the lights and setting off the alarms, or something

Rebirth III

else entirely – but I wanted to make sure I wrote it down regardless. The important takeaways from the experience were in understanding the archetypes of the military, rankings, instructions, leadership, and order.

I led the group onto a great vessel. This should be seen as a spiritual teacher leading others to God, etc. (but obviously not just limited to this). Flipping on the lights was archetypal to the spreading the light – the word of God. But, flushing out the darkness with an instant wash of light set off the alarms. The alarms were archetypal of warnings. The message in the action was weighted toward discretion in how to spread the light. I was able to lead without blanketing the vessel in an abundance of light that would have startled everyone.

Immediately after journaling the previous experience, I closed my eyes, and light filled my periphery. I saw three books against a void. The books were placed in cardinal directions, and each book was facing its respective direction forming three sides of a square in the space between the books. The directions were East, South, and West. As I understood the imagery, a fourth book was placed before me. It faced East, but was placed in the position of North. After it was placed there for a few seconds, it rotated 90° counterclockwise into an upright position completing the pattern. It was important to understand a square was placed in the middle. I immediately returned to my body to journal the experience. I would speak to Bryan about this experience later, where he felt immediately impressed to mention that this could be related to

The Written (cont'd)

the equidistant bouquet. It was similar in geometry and cardinality to how he was shown how the spheres are formed.

The final experience was the most unusual experience I have had in the heavens. There is one particular female angel that appears time and time again in the heavens. She is beautiful – probably the most perfect in every physical way possible I have ever seen. But on top of that, she is warm, inviting, and full of Love. This angel is not "the girl" that I have mentioned in prior experiences. "The girl" could best be seen as a motherly guide. This angel appears to be an elder of sorts, but not as elder or motherly in comparison to "the girl." This angel is svelte, milky white complexion, blonde hair, blue eyes, smaller facial features with eyes that I cannot help but become lost in each time I see her.

There is one particular feature that helps me recognize her – her eyebrows. This may sound odd, but it is the one specific feature that speaks to me. Her eyebrows are perfect – darker brown than her hair. Perhaps this is why they stand out to me. I have never walked around Earth observing people's eyebrows, but if I did, I would have to say they look similar to a girl I know named Marissa. But this angel is clearly not Marissa, though each time I see this angel, Marissa is who first enters into my mind.

As the experience began, I could see this angel in the distance. We were walking toward each other. When we reached each other, she looked different – more full of Love than usual...and those are words I would not think were possible. The angel invited me to go eat with her. This was most definitely

Rebirth III

different than other experiences in that it would not appear I was in the midst of a lesson. This time seemed social, almost like a date. My mind wondered if I was allowed to go on a "date" with an angel, but this was so different in circumstance, I thought it must be okay.

When she asked, I saw her nerves push through. I had never seen an angel demonstrate nerves or excitement in the heavens. But I could tell, she was not sure if I would take her up on her invitation. It was as if she was vulnerable by asking me to go to dinner with her. In truth, out of all of the angels I have met, she is the one that has caused the most intrigue to my soul. Though it is hard to compare angels, they all speak uniquely and in such a grand way to me. However, there is an intrigue with her – something that is different that I cannot quite identify yet.

As she asked the question, I paused just briefly in my answer to soak in every bit of the moment. I answered that I would Love to go to dinner with her. From there, we headed to the restaurant. She was very flirty-physical with me. This was the first time being flirty-physical seemed okay in the heavens. Other times the flirty nature is generally reserved for sexual advances from lost souls, where it should be seen as a test of faith to resist temptation. This time was different in every conceivable way. It was founded on spiritual Love. I could not begin to explain the ways my mind was opened in that moment, but it ushered in a completely new viewpoint of angels.

The Written (cont'd)

As we ate dinner, we had a joyous conversation. There was so much attention and intrigue between each of us – something I had never experienced on Earth. She was overflowing with spiritual abundance. She made sure to touch my arm and leg in the midst of conversation. It was very flirty. But there was one time that she touched my leg more passionately than the other graceful touches. Each touch from her was electrifying. This touch ignited my being, and I realized that she was much more interested in the physical experience with my soul than I thought possible with an angel. We made sure to finish up dinner quickly so we could head back to her place.

We were flirty, in an on-fire kind of way. Outside the restaurant we kissed. Even though it was passionate, it was full of spiritual Love. It was different than any other kiss I have experienced. It was the grandest sensation I had felt in the heavens. To just put it in basic terms, I was kissed by an angel, and my spirit erupted in a way I had never known. The moment was filled in the greatest spiritual-kind-of-abundance, wrapped in a passionate, on-fire, rush of Love and emotion. The kiss turned into a moment where everything else faded away around us. It was just her and me with a spotlight shining down upon us.

We headed back to her place flirty, laughing, and kissing all of the way there. When we arrived, we embraced and began kissing in a very sensual way. At this point, I lost harmony in the moment and returned to my body. I often wonder if events continue on after leaving the heavens. For my soul's sake, I hope it did. If not, I at least managed to handle the abundance of feelings rushing through me for a much longer

Rebirth III

amount of time than I had ever handled before. I attest this to greater spiritual strength. Perhaps the angel knew I was almost ready. Perhaps it had to do with me no longer being centered around Lindsey. Perhaps it is all of the above and the most divine timing possible. In any case, it was a grand moment that felt like it was "meant to be." It was not a sexually driven lust. Rather, it was a spiritual Love, and I have to believe that makes all of the difference in the world.

April 13, 2014

The experience I had this morning seemed to span days or weeks. It began with me riding with my father in a truck to his parent's house. For some reason I was agitated at his conversation. I am never agitated or frustrated in the heavens – so I am not sure where this feeling was stemming from. Eventually we had to stop at a gas station so that I could go to the bathroom. My father stayed in the truck, cleaning up the inside. I am not sure what he was cleaning up, but it was important for me to understand that the inside of the truck needed cleaning. I suppose it could possibly mean that (in an earthly sense) the spiritual vehicle my father was riding in needs cleaning, but that is just my initial thought after reflecting on the situation.

After I came back outside, we departed and headed to his parent's house. When we arrived, no one was home. At some point, my mother entered the house. She wanted to take a

The Written (cont'd)

nap. She covered up in the guest room, and I walked into another room. Somewhere during this time, my father was removed from the experience. It was as if I needed to understand that the experience began with my father driving a vehicle to get me to a destination, but once the destination was reached, my mother was the star of the show – as if the father figure is the actuator, and the mother figure is the nurturer.

While my mother napped, my dad's mother arrived and entered the room where my mother was sleeping . She woke her up. As my mother was waking up, my dad's mother took me to a room that had a secret panel in the wall. She opened up the panel to reveal a bunch of clothes specifically for me. I was told to keep it a secret. I was then escorted outside where I got into a truck with my dad's father where he drove me around the countryside talking to me about the world.

April 14, 2014

This morning's experience left me with more questions than answers. I was taken to the heavens where I arrived in a room with a table. I sat down with a male angel on my left. In front of me was an elderly woman. To her left (my right) was her husband. We talked for a while. Somehow the conversation led to "sticky things."

I talked for a while about how I did not like "sticky things" and "things that stuck together." These are the best words I can use to describe the conversation, but the conversa-

Rebirth III

tion was archetypal in nature. "Sticky things" carried a greater meaning, but I did not know the words or how to communicate them well. After I finished talking, the old couple looked at each other and smiled at each other like, "Oh isn't that cute..." They were not condescending of my conversation about "sticky things." They seemed more like, "Oh, he doesn't know yet," or "He doesn't quite understand the concept yet." I didn't feel uneasy about their looks at each other. Instead, I knew I was about to be imparted wisdom from my childish understanding in this area.

From this point, the couple began telling me about how they first met. The man began telling me a story about how "things that stuck together" led them together. He said, "It started with a wine glass glued to a Pepsi bottle, then a pitching wedge. It then proceed to [something I cannot remember]." It was at this point that the man looked at her and said, "She's my [isla stallin]." (I put the last part in brackets because I will expand on this in a moment). When he said this, my jaw opened in recognition. I knew in that moment that the word he was telling me was extremely important, and an answer to a question I had not yet asked. It was a concept that transcended words into recognition of the gravity of it.

As my jaw opened, I looked at the male angel to my left who just smiled at me in a "See, I told you that you would be amazed" kind of way. I found this moment overwhelming because I recognized the words were THE answer to my prayer earlier in the evening where I asked God to help me under-

The Written (cont'd)

stand the importance of having five pillars in my life – and what each pillar represented.

I tried repeating the word several times as I looked at the angel. I began to ask "who" the [isla stallin] was to the angel. But as I asked, I immediately was sent from the heavens back to my body to write the information down. As soon as I returned, I tried to begin writing the experiences down. This proved extremely difficult as my soul was still in a swirly state from the journey back. I was disoriented between the two locations. This caused the experiences to be tough to recount.

I began journaling all that I could recount, saving the word that was given to me for last (since it was the most recent and impactful part of the experience). But when I began to write the word, I had no idea how to translate what I heard even as I tried to repeat it into earthly words. It was at this point that I realized the descriptive word must be two words. The first word seemed to have three syllables, though the word would be pronounced along the lines of EYE-A-LUH or EYE-A-VUH. The last word would best be illustrated as STALL-IN, STALL-IN-ING, or STALL-IN-UD. So together, the word would best be seen as "isla stallin" or possibly "iolah stallinin." Either way, I feel that I did not make the best of a great opportunity to bring back an important concept to Earth. After I wrote it down, I prayed for clarity in the words. I received an affirmation on what I just wrote, though my definition in meaning is now the hardest part of this translation.

As I thought about the words, my mind identified the words as archetypal – which means it should be understood

Rebirth III

through the original twenty-two Hebrew letters. The best I can extrapolate, the words would be along the lines of Ayin-Hey-Vav-Hey Shin-Tav-Aleph-Lamed-Nun. I do not know Hebrew by any other method than deconstructing archetypes and how they form concepts within the words, so I cannot tell you if these are real words or not. But archetypally, the definition would be interpreted in two parts.

The first word was definitely four letters in communication to me. The last word was five letters. Together there are nine letters – an important foundation. The first four letters are similar to cardinality in directions. The last five should be seen as five pillars. Together, with the directions, they form a concept of Divinity's all encompassing expanse. For nine and seven are the understanding to All-That-Is as I have written about in Song of the Spheres. There are two hidden spheres which are divine. So this is the first part of the understanding. Next, I would look at the first word being similar to the name of the unspeakable name of God – Yud-Hey-Vav-Hey. If this can best be understood as "the right hand of revelation to the nail of revelation," the word I was given would mean something along the lines of "the eyes/sight of revelation to the nail of revelation." The other spelling would translate to "the eyes/sight of revelation to the right hand of revelation." Each archetypal extrapolation is grand in importance. Each one carries a uniquely different meaning. Coupled with the concept of cardinality, the respective meanings should be translated as "the experience or eyes of All-That-Is through

The Written (cont'd)

which divine sight is imparted" and "the experience or eyes of All-That-Is who is the servant to God in bringing revelation"

The second word should be observed as representing the five pillars of Islam and the five parts of the Torah. These are similar (if not the same as) the five phases of spiritual growth I have written about on my personal journey in "Gravity Calling." Everything should be observed archetypally. However, this is the first time I have been given archetypal letters to understand the pillars. But that is why the word was so significant. It was a complete disambiguation to the pillars and what they really mean.

So, the second word should be observed as "the radiance/fire of divinity through the strength of God shepherding the seed." That is a lot to soak in, but the two words combined could archetypally represent the construct of "a chosen angel." The angel would hold special connotation as the eyes of the spirit, representing each of the five pillars. At least, this is what I have been able to glean from the words imparted. These two words that were chosen to describe the woman would be similar in how on Earth, someone may say to their significant other, "She is my heart and my soul." But, in this particular sense, it carries a much more significant and divine message.

Rebirth III

April 15, 2014
Early Morning

My experience in the heavens this morning was unlike any I have experienced before. Most of the experiences were founded upon duality. In most every interaction and scenario I experienced, I would witness my ego in conversation with others in the heavens. I would do this while my soul – pure in form – was standing off in the distance observing the interaction. Possibly, it was not my ego that was interacting with others, but that is what I would call that half of my soul/being because it seemed to have potential for negative influence. The "pure" half of my soul would observe in an unbiased fashion.

Eventually the experiences and interactions led me back to a house. When I entered the house, I was immediately aware of another presence in the house. It was sinister and evil. Again, all of this was experienced in duality. I watched as my dual-spirit innocently passed time away in the house. As I observed myself, I knew the other presence in the house was observing too. Then, out of nowhere, a demon leapt out from the shadows in the house and attacked my dual-spirit. It was unaware I was split in two parts – though it did startle me. Its attack on my dual-spirit was like witnessing what I can only imagine a "possession" would look like if a person could see it happen. And perhaps, that was in fact what I witnessed.

I did not witness anything beyond the initial action of the demon leaping out of the shadows at my dual-spirit because at

The Written (cont'd)

the exact same time the demon leapt, my soul was pulled back into my body due to a loud crashing sound that came from my closet on Earth. I knew instantly what the sound was. I went to take a look and there on the floor was my toolbox that had fallen off of a stable shelf and spilled the tools across the concrete floor of my apartment. There was nothing indicating why it fell. There was no weakness or sagging of the shelf. There was no slope. A toolbox weighing probably around 20 lbs. seemingly leapt off of the shelf by itself, spilling the tools across the floor.

I have to think that this was the manifestation of the demon in my house. Until today, I would not have thought that items falling off of shelves were anything more than coincidences, or caused from a tangible reason. But this time was different. This time, it was like something that has been written about in folklore about possessions and demons. It was a supernatural-like manifestation of evil in the physical world. Perhaps the demon did not want me to continue my spiritual training. Perhaps God wanted me to observe the duality so that I could see how evil attacks the spirit. There was a lot to take in, but I wanted to at least make sure to write it down.

April 15, 2014
Afternoon

During prayer and meditation after lunch, I again experienced more dualities. However, this time I was not observing

Rebirth III

dualities of myself. This time, I was observing dualities of others. The first experience involved the duality of a female. I saw her pure soul side observing the struggles her other half battles. In her situation, her susceptible side was in a very dark place. It was encompassed in a black smoke. Her appearance exuded goodness but had an abundance of evil darkening her from the inside. It caused her to be unattractive and appear worn out. Eventually, her good side became tired of observing her susceptible side fight with the demon, so her good side took her other half and bagged it into a body bag. The other half was screaming to let her out as her good side bagged her susceptible side up.

At this point, my mind and my soul registered a stronger awareness of the situation, so my mind tried to begin rationalizing action in the experience. As soon as I attempted to add rational thought to my spiritual experience, it was clear the two sides could not communicate through the same type of thought. It was sort of like observing two people trying to communicate while speaking different languages. My mind thought in words and in English while my soul observed archetypal concepts of a Divine language. And while words are formed from archetypes, understanding archetypes in a fluid form is the language of the spirit. That is why communication between the heavens and the Earth happen through symbols and metaphors. Angels are not going to communicate in your native tongue unless it is through someone who speaks your native tongue. This is why it is so hard to translate heavenly

The Written (cont'd)

experiences in earthly words. As an aside – this is where "speaking in tongues" gets its definition.

The language of the spirit is entirely different than earthly language. Though archetypal thoughts are often extremely difficult to suss out. Often, there are words that Bryan and I are told that are observed in broken syllables and distorted structure (such as my journal entry from yesterday; also when Bryan was given the name "Megazalea," and when I was given the names, "Anael" and "Leilel"). Each of these names required a lot of discretion and careful thought to understand the meaning.

I have to think this is why angels have multiple names. For example, Anael and Haniel are supposed to be the same angel. Someone, somewhere had the realization that the earthly mind distorted syllables and words to a point where some angels had been given different spellings. However, I have only heard one name ever in the heavens – not two as would be illustrated through religious texts. Ultimately different spellings led to different pronunciations, which made it seem like two different entities when all along it was the same archetypal concepts distorted in translation by the people through whom the knowledge was passed.

After I tried to think rationally within the spiritual experience, I lost the ability to discern the heavenly experience with clarity. It was like focus on rationale took the heavens out of focus and vice versa. Eventually, I put my rationale away and continued exploring the duality message being imparted to me through my spiritual body. It was during this time that I then

Rebirth III

observed a male suffering from the same duality struggle the female was experiencing in the moments prior. I watched for a while before the pure side of the male went up to his susceptible side and fought off the smoky possession that was taking place.

After this, I was taken to an empty room. It was here that I was imparted wisdom about the books I have been writing (including this journal). I was told that I have two very important steps I must adhere to as I seek to complete my objective of writing the nine books. The first directive was to "take extreme care to cover ALL of the details in the books." The second directive was to "make sure everyone has the ability to access the words." In other words, I have to make sure the words are available to anyone who seeks them out – in whatever format is the method in which they read. I assume it also means to make translations available as well since that would cover the directive of "everyone." And finally, "make sure that the books contain every bit of information critical for a person to fully be able to take the journey from the guidance of the books." I have to assume this is the most important part of the two directives. After I was given the directives, I asked the voice in the room if there were any more directives. I then repeated back the directives to make sure I understood them enough to bring them back into earthly words. At this point a great wind blew my Jeep (where I had parked and reclined my seat to meditate and pray) drawing my soul back to my body to write down the experience.

The Written (cont'd)

April 16, 2014

As usual, I travelled multiple times to the heavens this morning. Each experience built upon the previous experience. The first experience began with me standing before a short-haired female angel. This is the first time I have ever seen an angel with short hair. I suppose I should also explain that while I try to reserve the term "angel" for the obvious angels in the heavens – I think that it is important to note that I interact with a lot of souls in the heavens as well. Sometimes, a younger angel is difficult to differentiate from what I can only describe as a "chosen soul" when it comes to the popular definition of an angel. There is clearly a difference standing before an elder angel and others. That is why I try to differentiate elders from others, but this recognition has been slowly learned over the course of my experiences. It is for this reason that some of my first experiences may not have had as much discernment as today. However, those experiences were most definitely with elders. The others who were not "elders" I referred to as "beings" and did not refer to them as angels at all. But if becoming an "angel" is to be seen as earning a heavenly degree/ranking before God's eyes, it becomes more difficult to discern youthful angels from those yet to receive that status. And if a soul is timeless, then it also becomes more complicated when a person realizes that a soul can exist in multiple places at once because time is only a perception in the eyes of humans. So, I guess what I am saying is that this experience

Rebirth III

straddled the fence of being able to differentiate young angels from other heavenly beings/souls.

The female angel that I was standing before reminded me of a girl I have not seen since I was in middle school. Her name was Callie. Perhaps it was my mind rationalizing an identity for the angel before me – but that is what I thought, so I want to make note of it. I was never given a name for her. Actually, I rarely receive names of anyone, so it becomes a mental exercise of remembering faces as identities.

While we were standing there, I realized that Callie seemed to know me much more than I knew her. She began to tell me about her mother just passing away. I have to think this was significant in why we were standing there together, but I could not quite identify what the significance was. She was obviously distraught. We talked and interacted for a while before meeting up with four others and attending a church service. This "Callie" angel introduced me to two females that joined us. The male angel was older than the others. I recognized him in spirit, but I could not associate a name or identity with him. He appears frequently with me in the heavens. During the service we sat in the back right of the church.

After the service ended we socialized outside for a while and eventually attended another service. This time we sat in the middle of the congregation, slightly to the left. The service went on. I could not understand the preacher, but everyone was listening intently. The girls that I met earlier were sitting to my left and slightly behind me. They kept looking at me and talking about me, though I could not get a beat on what it

The Written (cont'd)

was they were talking about specifically. We would just pass the occasional smiles back and forth. There were probably five hundred people in the congregation. As I tried to discern what was being said, I lost harmony and returned to my body.

I journaled the experience, and I returned to the heavens. I attended a third service almost instantly upon returning to the heavens. I was still interacting with the same crowd, but one more female joined us. This service was an Easter service. Initially, I sat on the right side of the congregation, slightly in front of the middle. Only "Callie" and I sat on that side, and a male that I understood to be her boyfriend. The rest of the angels sat on the other side similar to where we sat in the second service.

While we were listening to the service, I began to realize that the first couple of rows around me were slowly clearing out. I wondered if I was driving them away. I was not doing anything, so I assumed that it might just be my presence. As the sermon hit a point of pause, I walked over to the others and sat down with them. Each of us were in chairs – not in a pew. As the sermon picked back up, I realized people around me were again sliding away from me. There was one visibly angry male behind me. I did not understand any of the situation. For some reason I thought I might "smell" even though I had not done anything to smell different. I wondered if my soul had a distinct smell that others angels could detect – as if my human soul was not like the other souls I was sitting among.

Rebirth III

Eventually I realized the angry male behind me was pushing my chair forward with his feet to push me away from the group. It was frustrating because now I was being singled out. I never said anything. I just pushed my chair three or four feet backwards to where I was sitting. This time he did the same thing, but not so subtly. I, again, pushed my seat back and planted my feet to resist another push. When he realized I was going to resist his actions, he shoved my chair so hard it caused a loud noise to erupt in the middle of the congregation.

The preacher stopped, and everyone looked at me. I was now standing out of my chair from the force of the push. I just turned and looked at the guy. I did not say anything, but my look let him know I was not going to have any of his childish actions. He stood up and tried to shove me while I pushed my chair back. He wanted me to fight him in the middle of a church service. And, even though there would be nothing discreet about the situation, I tried to move with privacy to another chair where I sat next to "Callie" and her boyfriend.

The service continued, and I could tell people were frustrated that I had to endure that guy's childish actions. At the end of the service, four people sang a song. It was beautiful – four part harmony. After the service ended, I walked out to where I was met by an elder angel.

This angel had a very parental nature about him. As we chatted about the events of the service, he told me that he "was surprised at how well I handled the situation." Those words resonated deep within. As I thought about the meaning of what he said and how the situation applied to my growth, I

The Written (cont'd)

lost harmony with the moment and returned to my body. As I journaled the experience, I could not help but think that the group of people around me were metaphorical to having five pillars of support. Each angel helped me find strength in the situation without them ever having to act or say anything during the situation. I also could not get out of my mind that I had a "smell" that caused people to push themselves away.

I do not think that the "smell" was literal. I think – as everything is communicated in the heavens – that it was archetypal for "out of place" or "something different" about me. As I pondered its meaning more, I was taken back to the only place I know that a "smell" is indicated in religious texts. This was documented in the Book 3 of Enoch. In this book, Enoch discusses how the angels noticed he had a distinct smell about him because he was human. But in this passage, it was clear that God chose Enoch to remain among the angels in this particular part of God's Kingdom.

Haniel is documented as the angel that took Enoch to the heavens and who allowed passage to different parts of the Kingdom. It is important for me to realize the significance of Haniel because her name is also Anael – the name of the angel I have written about from the very beginning of my experiences in the heavens over three years ago. And when learning of Anael's name, I had to research the name because I had never heard of that angelic name. Regardless, the significance of having a "smell" on an Easter service in church holds great meaning when understood in the context of Enoch. While I am by no means trying to compare myself to Enoch, the expe-

Rebirth III

rience illustrates guidance for the path I am on, and offers a glimpse of potential to following God's path.

April 18, 2014

This morning, I spent many earthly hours in the heavens. Most of what I experienced would best be explained as "being on the playground." There were no grand angelic moments that I can recall. Much of what I experienced was routine life with some small lessons to be learned and applied to my life. I interacted with manifestations of coworkers, old friends, family members, etc. It was more of a spiritual acuity test than anything. The same occurred the previous night, but it was even more hazy than what I just experienced.

April 19, 2014

While the details of the experience I could bring back with me were very brief, there was one important question that was posed to me by my angel guide for the experience. The angel asked me in the midst of the conversation we were having, "So, are you really moving to Florida?" The conversation was very fluid. I did not pause with my reply. I stated, "I am not really sure, but it certainly seems like all of the signs are leading me that way." With that, I returned to my body.

The Written (cont'd)

April 20, 2014

This morning's accounts were increasingly challenging for me to bring back. When I would open my eyes, I would immediately lose the memory. When I shut my eyes, I would be able to find myself back in the heavens continuing the experience. But, regardless of how hard I tried, I could not bring back any concrete details. For the most part, it seemed as if I spent the equivalent of weeks (or longer) in the heavens. During that time, I was tasked with scenarios that were similar to the situations I found myself in on Earth with friends, family, and coworkers. Some would likely chalk this up to a "dream," but as I have tried to emphasize repeatedly throughout all of my writings, dreams are part of a great big spiritual playground where everything holds meaning, The early recollections of dreams are just the entry-level playgrounds in the heavens where the mind is still learning to understand the spirit. As spiritual growth progresses, a person can be taken to other locations in the heavens. Some of those locations may seem similar to a playground at times, but each experience in other locations requires even greater levels of spiritual acuity. Everything holds meaning.

April 21, 2014

While I would like to say this morning was littered with multiple experiences in the heavens, I think the better explana-

Rebirth III

tion is that this morning's multiple occurrences of travels to the heavens involved the continuation of one long experience wherein I would return to my body only briefly enough to journal the experiences without losing the harmony my body was experiencing with the heavens.

While I most definitely had to open my eyes to journal, and when I was in the heavens I had no awareness of my physical body (there was no duality involved this time), this may be the closest I have experienced a linear timeline arc of duality between the heavens and Earth due to how quickly I could travel to and re-enter the heavens. With that said, the experience began with a scenario that I had to repeat multiple times in training. This is typical with experiences in the heavens. It is how a person performs drills in sports in the earthly world. Every repeated effort adds to the foundation and builds strength in the targeted area. Spiritual growth should be seen no differently. Many times the angels will task me with the same test repeatedly until I perform to their desired expectations. Often, if a test did not have the desired expectations, the same test will occur on subsequent travels to the heavens regardless of how many days apart the travels may occur.

This time, the experience began in a structure similar to that of a parking deck. Each time the test was given, it began with me standing on the top level of the parking deck with a male elder angel. For some reason, the setting involved me holding a ring of great value and meaning. During the experience, I initially could not determine if the ring was stolen or if it was given to me because the subsequent test would lead a

The Written (cont'd)

person to believe that it had been stolen. However, I wrestled with the concept because it seemed as if I had been given something holy – of extreme value – that I had to protect at all costs while I "escaped" the parking garage. The concept of "escaping" with something that was not "stolen" befuddled my mind. But with that said, I made several attempts before successfully completing the test.

The test began with me running to a vehicle and jumping into the driver's side. I then sped through the parking deck making left-hand turns as I proceeded down the structure. The first turn was always greeted with four speed bumps and two guards. There were two speed bumps on either side of the lane, but the division of the lanes formed four speed bumps. The first time I slowed down giving the two guards an opportunity to lay down a spike strip in front of me and render my vehicle useless. But with each practice of the test, I was able to move more quickly and fluidly than the previous times. After failing to make it through the parking deck a couple of times, I lost harmony with the moment and returned to my body to journal the experience.

When I returned to the heavens, I began the test again. However, this time I had a much clearer mind in how I should approach the test. I took the ring I was handed and hopped in the vehicle. This time, I drove at break-neck speeds with the confidence of having God with me. It was not that I did not think He was with me before, rather I had been approaching the test conservatively rather than on faith alone. I knew this

Rebirth III

test was intended to stretch the boundaries of seemingly regular actions when tied to faith.

As I made the first turn, I caught the guards by surprise. I was able to fly through the speed bumps before they were even able to make an effort to grab the spike strips. I rounded the next turn and passed more guards. As I made the final turn, two more guards appeared in front of a pay booth to exit the garage. The guards were shouting at me, but I was not going to slow down enough for them to catch me.

As I approached the exit, they made an effort to lay down spike strips, but my speed was too quick for them. I burst through the striped arm barrier of the gate and exited the garage. As soon as I made the next turn left out of the garage, I headed into another garage. I jumped out of the vehicle and ran into a stairwell. The stairwell opened into a large area that contained two escalators that must have proceeded upward three or more stories. The escalators were much larger than normal escalators.

On my ride upward, standing on my right were two female angels that were giggling. I could tell they were giggling about me. They were both brunette. When they noticed I was curious about their giggling, they both told me that "everyone was looking for me." To them, it was somewhat comical. They kept smiling at me as if I was something of a sight to behold. For me, it felt like I was escaping arrest. But it was clear that the girls wanted to help me. They told me that when they are questioned at the top of the escalator, they would not say they

The Written (cont'd)

saw me. They thought I was entertaining, so that was enough for me.

As soon as I made it to the top of the escalator, I ran off to the left, continuing in the circular motion I had been following when I began my decent down the parking deck and ascent up the stairwell. After I made my turn to the left, I found myself in a room standing next to a great female angel adorned in jewelry. She wore a tremendous amount of gold and jewels. Though I knew I was supposed to deliver the ring I had been given to this angel, I knew it was not an engagement ring or representative of emotions. Instead, I knew the ring was a symbol, or rather a token…for what though, I was unsure.

With me standing by the woman's side, she was interrogated by two males. They seemed angry at me – sinister even. All the female angel would do was smile at the men and hold me under her right arm. She was proud of me, and acted very maternal. As I was held, I recognized how large she was compared to me. She was one of the largest angels I have seen in the heavens and must represent one of the greatest elders I have met. My head only came up to around her waist. I recognized her size in the moment because her forearm was mostly all that I was able to view in my line-of-sight.

I did not feel small compared to her, but rather it was a recognition of her role in the heavens. Her forearm was adorned with numerous gold bracelets and bands. She had many rings on her fingers. The rest of her body was covered in gold jewelry as well. The gemstones placed within the rings and bracelets were all lavender or rose in color. I kept thinking

Rebirth III

the gold was a shade of "rose gold" as well, but perhaps that thought stemmed from the purple-hue of all of the gemstones mounted within the gold jewelry. Somewhere around this point, I lost harmony and returned to my body to journal this moment.

As soon as I completed journaling, I shut my eyes and returned to the heavens. This experience picked up where the last experience ended. The interrogation had just finished, and I was now standing among several others on the edge of a cliff. Mountains towered around us, but everything outside of the immediate field of view was out of focus. The beings that surrounded me all seemed to be "like me" in that I had the impression we were all students in the same class (though that is just a metaphor). The great female angel standing before us was telling us that "we are going to seek our way into the Kingdom."

As she continued talking to the group, I suddenly heard her voice address me directly through my mind in a way that only I could hear. Her voice resonated loudly and deeply. She said these words, "And you aren't going to have to pay the price." She was referring to how I was to enter the kingdom. This entire experience was entirely new to me, so I have no way to disambiguate the meaning other than to just write down the words. I am not sure if the ring I brought her was representative of the price I would pay to enter. Perhaps my spiritual actions and surrendering to God was the price. I am not sure how I would not have to pay the price other than hav-

The Written (cont'd)

ing already paid the price before. So, that was the impression I had as I digested her words.

As soon as she said those words to me, a large bird flew overhead of our group. It came from the west and made a smooth turn to the northeast. This bird was unlike any bird one would find on Earth. I have seen this bird at least once before. One time was when I was standing within the walls of the Kingdom as journaled on 4/11/2014. I may not have made enough sense of the moment to write it down, but it is important to recount it now. The most intriguing part of this bird is the span of its wings. Its wings span at least three times the length of a normal bird's wings (if not greater). The body is small, but the wings are enormous in width and plush with thick, brown feathers. The feathers are reminiscent of the feathers I saw on the angel that appeared before my bed around Christmas time (though the angel had white feathers). If there is anything similar in our earthly walk, the birds depicted in ancient Egyptian hieroglyphics would be the closest. The bird did not just have a disproportionately large wingspan, but the bird itself was much larger than any of us standing on the cliff.

Suddenly, a similar bird swooped down and picked up the elder angel. Other birds came and picked up each of the others standing on the ledge. I was held by the second bird. The first bird held the great angel. Each of us were like the size of a fish in the talons of an eagle. As we flew into the previously out-of-focus area, it became clear we were ascending to even greater heights than the mountains stretched.

Rebirth III

Tall slender mountains stretched around either side of us as we ascended. The elder angel was a great distance ahead of me. On the right, there was a ledge that jutted out from the side of a mountain. On it, stood a gatekeeper angel. He was tiny in comparison to the majestic wonder around us. I peered ahead and saw the elder angel in front of me as merely a silhouette upon the light shining from before us. The sky was on fire in a shade of golden-yellow. It was unlike any color I have experienced on Earth. It was beautiful. The sun (or great light) ahead of us was also golden-yellow in color, blinding in brightness, though able to be viewed without pain to the eyes. On the wings of the birds we flew toward the Kingdom. It was at this point that I unfortunately lost harmony with the moment.

When I returned to my body I immediately journaled the experience but noticed a feeling that I have never felt in my earthly body. My head…more specifically areas just beneath the skull were throbbing in a way I have never felt. It was unlike a headache. There was pain, but not hurtful pain. It was like stretching a muscle that had not been stretched in a while – like attempting to touch your toes in the morning after waking up. The feeling I was experiencing surrounded the crown of my head. It honestly felt like a crown was protruding from beneath my skull, pushing through the bone. That is the only way I could explain the unique pressure points along the crown of my skull. It was not as if I was trying to draw parallels to seeing the Kingdom with a crown. This is just how my head felt upon returning to my body. It is the first time I have ever

The Written (cont'd)

felt such a pain/pressure after an experience in the heavens. If I had to guess, the only thing I can rationalize is that the experience in the heavens began to open up my crown chakra, which allows energy to be harnessed and channeled through the top-most portion of the head. But, again, that is just a guess. It felt as if my entire brain was being used at once. Biochemically, I would have to think that something new is happening to allow my soul passage into the kingdom, but I suppose that is unimportant as I had to toss science aside long ago to progress on this journey. Science may have gotten me here, but faith has kept me going.

After journaling the experience, I returned to the heavens one last time – albeit briefly. This time I was standing in a void and only heard the voice of the great angel. She asked me, "What is in locker fifteen?" I immediately was jolted back to my body. I have no idea what she was referring to, so I have to imagine it is symbolic. I do not own a locker, nor do I frequent anywhere that does. I have to imagine the locker represents a place of knowledge. I must assume the number fifteen does as well. Perhaps it has to do with the math associated with the Eight-Sphere Cube. Or maybe it deals with the fifteenth archetype. I am unsure of the meaning at this point. It will require more meditation upon the idea to be unveiled. Regardless, this is how my experiences in the heavens ended this morning before I got ready for work.

Rebirth III

April 22, 2014
Early Morning

This morning's experience was, again, difficult to bring back. The best I can explain the experience is that I was interacting and playing sports with two other beings. The sports seemed like some sort of badminton and a variation of golf. The badminton-esque game is the easiest for me to discuss. As we were volleying an object back and forth, we were engaged in a deep conversation about life, the heavens, and existence. Though the conversation is difficult to explain, the best I can do is say that while I know I was playing the game and engaging in conversation, I also was observing the experience. This is why I say there were two other beings. One seemed to represent my youth, the other represented my wisdom. This was another variation of the duality experiences I recently observed in the heavens. Honestly, it felt as if I was playing a sport with myself. This is by far a most difficult experience to put into words. The experience ended with the being representing my wisdom calling out the score: 9-13.

April 22, 2014
Morning

On my way to work this morning, I prayed to God for help in understanding if I was supposed to move to Florida. As much as I think He is telling me to go, I have a hard time un-

The Written (cont'd)

derstanding where to go, or even when the appropriate time would be for me to move. In my prayer, I asked God if Florida is where I am supposed to be and whether I was supposed to wait on a directive. I prayed for help in knowing because I needed to give a thirty day notice to my landlord, which would mean I need to give the notice in the next couple of days before my rent is due for the next month.

As I said those words, the music playing on my radio changed. It was not just that a new song began to play, this was by far the most unexplainable feat of technology that I have ever witnessed. I was playing a song called Butterfly Waltz from the Spotify app on my iPhone. It is on a playlist with other instrumental pieces only. The song had been playing for a couple of minutes, when suddenly it cut off and another song began playing. It was as if the app just skipped to another song. That would not be too strange in and of itself (there are hiccups with technology), but here is where it gets really bizarre. The song playing was not from my Spotify app. Without any interaction on my phone as it sat in the cup holder of my Jeep, it randomly changed apps (to an app I never use), and began playing the only song I have in that particular music app.

When I picked up my phone, the app showing was still Spotify, but it had paused itself, while this other rogue app managed to launch itself and start playing another song "behind the scenes" on my iPhone. I have fifteen years in technology and programming experience. This "glitch" is not at all possible with the architecture of iOS. So with that said, I

Rebirth III

knew immediately that the song was another sign from God. The song was titled, "Where We Belong" which I could immediately tell was a message from God. The lyrics that began to play were from the first verse. I listened intently.

…

"We're too far out, we're in too deep
And we've got miles to go before we can sleep
I said, we've been walking a thin line.
You've got one hand on the devil baby and one hand in mine
But don't let go no it's not too late you know"

…

The lyrics are pretty self-explanatory – lyrics completely applicable to God's desire for the next steps in my life. If the song is envisioned as being said by the voice of God to me, it is one of the most powerful directives I have ever heard from Him. Instantly, I knew that I had to move to Florida. I do not know how. I do not know why. I do not know where. All I know is that I must move and follow His response to my prayer – and, on a side note, after sharing this story with Bryan, he referred to this as me witnessing a one-handed clap by God… a feat of impossibility that only I was allowed to witness.

April 23, 2014

This morning, I was only able to bring back one small part of my experience. As I was standing in the heavens, there was a group of angels on my right. I recognized they were el-

The Written (cont'd)

ders due to their height. The group mostly seemed to be male, but there could have been one or two female angels in the group as well. It seemed there was a female presence, though I could not pinpoint her face. There appeared to be seven angels in total, all wearing long white robes. On my left was a younger, female angel. She was also wearing a long white robe. She was brunette, notably younger, and very beautiful. Her facial features were smaller and less pronounced than a person on Earth. The group of angels on my left was addressing me about the female angel. As I write this, I am not sure how to communicate what they said to me, but it was addressing the spiritual communion and the spiritual roles we play in other souls' lives. The conversation made me respond, "But she is only sixteen." At that point, the angels looked at me, disapproving of me questioning their directive. I let it sink in and – without words – said, "Okay. I will." The angels nodded at me approvingly. It was at this moment that I returned to my body to journal the experience.

April 24, 2014

The swirly-hard-to-recall-experiences continued through this morning's adventures, but there were also moments of extreme clarity as well. The first experience occurred almost instantly after praying and beginning to meditate for the evening. My prayer asked God for help in feeling heightened states of awareness so that I could hopefully retain more of the expe-

Rebirth III

riences in the heavens. I suppose it is also important to note that I put myself back onto a more regimented diet (not really a diet, just no junk food or deep-fried food) in hopes that I could help my body chemistry return back to its most ideal state. I am not sure that will necessarily help, but it makes sense, and I want to try everything I can to maintain my body like a well-oiled machine.

So the first experience began with my soul becoming aware of the heavenly realm around it, though I had not yet travelled from Earth. Next to my bed was a great angel. This was a strange moment because I felt panic. I do not feel panic around the loving angels I typically find myself surrounded by in the heavens, so I began to try to understand the situation. My soul writhed, and I found myself trying to speak, but all that came out was a warped moaning/whining. My voice was being halted by the angel in my room. As I began to realize the absurdity of my whining/moaning noises, I tried to quit writhing. I wanted to look at the angel, but beyond the very first moment of recognition that the angel was standing beside my bed, he would not allow me to see him.

I was almost in a state of paralysis in which I could not move in the direction he was standing. I started to think about the feelings rushing through my body. Was it fear? If it was fear, why would I be scared? I started to realize that I should not be scared. The feelings emanating from the angel were of strength. He was austere and intimidating, but was not negative. I felt he was the embodiment of both negative and positive potential, but was a good angel. As I came to this

The Written (cont'd)

recognition, I felt the gaze of the angel lighten up, and I was allowed to move more freely. As I looked to where he was previously standing, all I saw was a soft glow. It was as if he was hiding from me outside of my field of view. I let him know I was not scared, and that I wanted to help him. Why I would say I could help him or even consider that I had some ability that he did not is beyond me. I think it was quite an absurd thing to say, but nonetheless, that is what I tried to let him know. It was as if by helping myself stay in harmony with the moment, I was helping him because he took the time to visit me. I suppose that is what I meant by saying I wanted to help him. As I said this (without words – it was all mentally communicated), I saw an open hand and arm extend from the soft glow to my left. It was as if the arm transcended two states of existence. I reached out to grab the hand. As soon as I made contact, my soul was jolted with the greatest amount of energy I have ever felt in the heavens. I immediately was kicked back to my body where I journaled the experience.

The second experience involved me talking to an angel that I continued to associate with a guy I know named Kip. I helped Kip get his music career started, and he is now experiencing a lot of commercial success in country music. From time to time, I see him in the heavens. But, I have not been able to tell if it is another angel I associate with Kip, or if it is truly Kip's soul. Regardless, the experience began with him and me talking about music. He told me about a very special event that was happening later that evening. He invited me out and continued to emphasize that I should be there. He

Rebirth III

said there was a very important moment with a special sixteen-year-old. This is the second time that a sixteen-year-old has occurred in these experiences. Even in the context of our conversation, I had no idea who he was referencing. But it seemed like a celebration of sorts – like this sixteen-year-old's presence was important.

We eventually parted ways. I wandered around the heavens for a while and eventually found my way to the location of the special event The room was filled with other angels. There was a crowd of twenty to thirty angels all facing a stage. I stood next to a female angel. She was larger than me, but relatively close in age to me (at least that is what I thought). The angel that reminds me of Kip eventually walked onto the stage with his guitar. He addressed the audience and talked about how special the song was that he was about to sing. He then told me that it was written in celebration of having the presence of the sixteen-year-old with them. Everyone seemed excited that the announcement the angel had made about having the sixteen-year-old present was true.

Before the he began to play the song, he said that I should dance with the sixteen-year-old. The female angel standing next to me put her left arm around me in a loving way. As the angel began to play the song, I realized it was a modified version of a song I had written about my daughter five years ago. He had taken the first verse and fit it into a more upbeat song. He also used the theme of Wonderland in the chorus. I was excited that he would have been inspired enough to use my

The Written (cont'd)

song. However, I still liked the original way I wrote it more, since it was a very personal song.

As I heard the lyrics being sung, I became excited and began telling the female angel how those were the words from my song. She smiled at me and told me to go find "her." I assumed she was talking about the sixteen-year-old that I was supposed to dance with. I looked everywhere in the room, wandering around through the crowd of angels, but never found whomever it was I was supposed to dance with. I returned back to the female angel, and I began to say a name. It was extremely hard for me to say, as if I was still learning to speak a foreign language with the correct inflections. The name that came out was similar to the name "Jenny" but I thought the word was spelled "Jeni." I do not know if the name I finally muttered was the correct name. It felt as if I was trying to make sense out of something that did not make sense. I know that the first part "Jen" was close to correct, if not spot-on. But I felt like I had to make more sense of the word, so I thought it must be "Jeni." I am also not sure I pronounced it completely correctly, or even if it was the name of the female angel standing next to me, or the sixteen-year-old angel I was seeking, or something else entirely.

Eventually the song ended. The angel that reminded me of Kip continued to address the crowd. He pointed out something about me (I assume it was about the lyrics), but I could not fully understand all that he was saying. As I continued to try to repeat the name of "Jeni," the female angel helped me with my pronunciation. She only helped on the first syllable

Rebirth III

(Jen). As I continued to focus on the words, I lost harmony with the heavens. When I arrived back in my body, I was left feeling as if the experience was possibly about me – similar to a birthday party – where there was another angel that I was supposed to meet during the celebration. It was interesting that this sixteen-year-old was addressed in back-to-back days of experiences in the heavens. I am left feeling like my spiritual age may be equivalent to "sixteen" but then again, there are certain significances to that number. Most obviously to me, Ed Leedskalnin (builder of Coral Castle) always talked about his "sweet sixteen." Everyone thought the man was in Love with a sixteen-year-old girl, but no one ever saw the girl. I had long thought that Ed was able to travel to the heavens. If so, it is possible that Ed was talking about whatever concept it is that I am now experiencing. Just a thought. I am befuddled at this sixteen concept at this particular moment.

The final experience was brief. I was standing in a room that adjoined another room in the northwest side of the room. The floor was shimmering. It was made of pearl tiles. Before me were two sofas, an end table and a coffee table. The sofas were aligned in an L-shape. Each sofa was similar to the other. The center of the back had a crested arch that was higher than the edges. If one were to envision how a sine wave looks, the back appeared like the dip, crest, and dip of a sine wave.

The couch was made of a mauve/lavender fabric. It was plush and appeared to have a thick weave. The frame of the couch and the rest of the furniture was made of ash-colored wood. There was also a twisting piece of artwork made of

The Written (cont'd)

metal sitting on the coffee table. I picked it up to understand it. The metal was muted, and ash-colored. It was unlike any color metal I have seen on Earth. There was no shine to it. The metal was textured, but finished in a matte coating. I placed the object back on the table and continued to observe my surroundings. As I observed the room, I lost harmony and returned to my body.

April 26, 2014

I have been overly sleepy during the last two days. My body seems to be fighting with my mind for control. I plan to start back my workout routine on May 1st. But until then, I suppose I may be left with just these brief snippets. In this experience, I recall walking around with another person – both of us were without shirts. I was self-conscience about it because I knew I was not as in shape as I needed to be (though I am not out of shape at all). I recall walking past a group of females and thinking that no one would even look at me twice. That is all I recall of that experience.

The last experience was brief and occurred as I tried to meditate this morning. During the mediation, I felt my spirit lift out of my body and begin heading toward the heavens. I heard the voices of a male and female say, "He's coming for us. I told you to trust me that he would come." There was additional chatter about me making my way toward them. But,

Rebirth III

before I could reach them, I became excited about the intensity of the experience which caused me to return to my body.

April 28, 2014

Throughout my experiences in the heavens this morning, I had what I could only call "Heaven on Earth" experiences. I know that may be difficult to understand, but this was the moment that dualities in spirit merged with a third plane – the earthly plane. Throughout the early morning hours, I found myself walking around the heavens with a great angel (male in form). We talked about the history of mankind, and the angel addressed many of the questions I have had about the heavens. The experiences were so real in sensation, but when I tried to bring back the experiences, I faced the same swirly feeling I get periodically when I lose human-esque form. This made it almost impossible for me to write down the questions that were being answered. During the experience, I returned to my body five times to write down the information, and I found I could not bring the words back with me at all.

During the awakenings, I began to notice a correlation with a thunderstorm that was occurring at my house to the experiences with the angel in the heavens. When I would speak with the angel, there were times thunder would ring through causing me to stop and realize I was experiencing both a heavenly and earthly duality. I began to notice that the sound of thunder that occurred directly after each question

The Written (cont'd)

was tantamount to God making himself known during the experience. The angel noticed I was taking notice of His voice. He began to help me remember what I needed to bring back to Earth. But, each time came with no success at writing down questions or answers. All I know is that I was shared a great deal of information that I wish I could write about.

After attempting to journal the experience with the angel one last time, I closed my eyes and began to pray thanks to God for the conversation with the angel. As soon as I began to pray, my soul was taken through the heavens to a room. The room was dimly lighted. There was a soft glow in front of me to my left. This was the same soft glow I experienced recently where the arm reached through the glow. The soft light was enough for me to know I was standing in the presence of God, though He never let me see Him. As I stood before Him, my spirit became excited. I was fearful I would lose harmony. As I stood before God, I heard His voice ring out, "So, I hear you want to know about the beginning."

Immediately my thoughts flashed to the conversation with the angel that I had a difficult time bringing back with me to journal. I recalled the amount of conversation we had about the beginning of All That Is. In fact, this would be the single question that every man, woman, and child has about God – how was He just here? It was not that I had not come to accept that something had to first exist for anything to be created. This was one of the philosophical questions the angel and I were discussing earlier. In fact, there was a point that I now recalled where the great angel told me my mind was like

Rebirth III

that of a philosopher and a great scientist, but with the spiritual foundation that most philosophers and scientists will never come to accept. I apologized about it, thinking that having the mind of a philosopher or scientist was a reference to being at the bottom of the barrel from where I needed to be. But as soon as I apologized, the great angel told me not to apologize, for it was a great thing for me. It meant that I was special in a way that most will never know. He continued to emphasize the importance of my mind and the way I was understanding the heavens. This memory brought me right back to the moment standing before God.

I do not know why, but I felt ashamed that I would have to receive my answer from God directly. I am sure to some, having God speak directly to them would be amazing. But for me, I felt shame. So when He addressed me with "So, I hear you want to know about the beginning," I felt a mixture of emotions tossing around inside. I first said, "Yes. I do." As soon as the words parted my lips, I began to feel the manifestation of His great strength and power. I immediately spurted out, "I mean, no. I'm not ready. I mean yes, of course I do, but when it is right. I mean I feel like I'm ready, but I don't think I am ready in your eyes…"

I continued to babble about my conflict of emotions for another few seconds. Suddenly, I felt myself collapse to the ground. I lay flat in humbled submission to God. The only thing that felt like the right thing to do was to demonstrate my respect for Him. After all, He had just summoned me to Him, and I was standing there conflicted, feeling like I was a burden

The Written (cont'd)

for Him. Not knowing what to do as I lay down before Him with my hands extended before me, I began to lift my body up and down in worship of Him. It felt like a strange thing to do since I have never acted out this motion in any other context than as a child playing. But this time it was real. It felt right, but it was definitely a new feeling for me. It was the only thing that made sense.

As I fell in humility before Him, I felt His grace. The amazing strength He demonstrated a few seconds prior now had a warmth of acknowledgement in my actions. I began to feel His hand upon my back. There was a clear sensation rushing through my shoulders and along my spine. I wondered as I prayed and worshipped Him if this was the feeling of being given wings. It felt as if I had wings coming from my back – as if they were just beginning to grow. I never would have even guessed what that would feel like until this point. And, honestly, I am not sure that is what the sensation was. But, it was real and felt like what it could have been. I have never felt like I had wings in the heavens, but this time was different.

I continued to rise up and bow down in reverence of standing in God's presence. While I did this, it felt as if I began to float. I wondered if the feeling was from wings lifting me up. I began to recognize that when I rose up, I felt my back hit a bar. The thought that went through my mind (for some unknown reason) was that it was as if I was on a bunk bed, and when I rose in praise, my back hit the top confinement of where I was. I began to ask God what the feeling was that I was experiencing. My eyes were suddenly drawn to the center

Rebirth III

of the room where a female angel was holding herself parallel to the floor on what appeared to be gymnastics bars.

When she lifted up in a pushup like motion, her body instantly turned a complete 180° as she was suddenly pulling herself up on a bar from above. When she reached the peak, she instantly was facing the floor again on her decent. With each turn of her body, a smaller bar would appear on her descent or disappear on her ascent to assist her in the movement. I was told that the feeling comes from the direction we move. With that I was sent back to journal. I wrote a tremendous amount of notes in my journal, even recording all of the angelic conversation I had failed to bring back earlier. I felt confidence in that I somehow had captured the words with the angel earlier, without remembering to write them down.

Suddenly, I realized this experience was still in the heavens, where I was writing (as a scribe would do) about the experiences. I recognized this place as the location where I write all of the information I am given from the angels before I return to Earth. With that recognition, I returned to Earth where I journaled this experience. But, as I journaled, I was conflicted because I could not find the notes or entries I had just written about the angelic conversation. Needless to say, the heavens can be quite the challenge in understanding the destinations. I assume one day I will read or have access to the book I continue to scribe in the heavens. But until then, I am left with what partial pieces I can bring back in this current method.

The Written (cont'd)

April 30, 2014

This morning I had two separate travels to the heavens. The second one I cannot recall with any important detail. The first trip placed me in a setting on a beach. The location was commercialized. There were tall hotels and businesses that were on the beachfront, but it was not densely populated. I arrived with two others. After we walked to our room, we then walked down to the beach. One of the others with me walked out in the ocean and began talking about it. I could not make out what he was saying, but I could tell he was enjoying the moment.

As he stood in approximately knee-deep water, I noticed the waves were getting higher around him. Suddenly, one wave swallowed him up as it towered several feet higher than the top of his head. I looked out upon the waters and noticed the ocean begin to swell. I could tell the ocean was turning into a storm or tsunami. The waters began to recede from the shoreline as the waves in the distance built in height. Eventually, one of the front waves pushed through to the beach and continued to wash across the land. The bottom levels of the hotels were about a foot underwater. The water was rushing against my knees as I stood on the beach. I knew it was time to go. For some reason, many of the people around me did not feel it necessary to leave the beach. But, I wanted to head for higher ground. I went in the hotel and headed up the stairs.

Rebirth III

I eventually found what I thought was my room and walked inside. There was a couple checking in and unpacking their bags. I realized I was on the wrong floor and began to step out. As I left, I overheard the man telling his wife that they needed to head down to the beach as soon as they finished unpacking. It seemed absurd, but I did not have time to argue. I continued heading upwards.

As I reached my room, I headed to the window to see the beach – hoping I was high enough to avoid the water. I saw the couple from the room below me heading outside. The waters had receded even further exposing more sand. A great wave was building in the distance. I was sure the wave would destroy the beach. The couple from below was celebrating their happiness on the beach seemingly oblivious to the great tidal wave in the distance. But, the wave never seemed to come. As I watched, the wave stayed in the distance as if it was held at bay by a great force. It did not make sense to me, and I struggled with the concept. I feared everyone would perish, but life went on as if everything was okay. Some of the buildings received minor damage from the first wave washing ashore. But after that wave, everything else subsided.

May 2, 2014
Around 2:00 a.m.

The experience this morning was very vague. Most of it seems very swirly, as if it was too difficult to hold onto. What I

The Written (cont'd)

could recall is that there was a girl standing before me that had an extremely short haircut. I noticed that her hair seemed to be falling out. I made a comment to her about her haircut. It was nothing negative. It was actually a compliment on her cutting her hair. But after I made the comment I saw her react in sadness. At that moment I thought that the situation was meant to tell me that she had/has cancer and her haircut was a repercussion of chemotherapy.

In reflection of the moment some days later (on May 6th), I learned that Wilson's mother was diagnosed with breast cancer. It had just happened earlier in the week, so it is possible that the experience was the communication of that information to me spiritually. Wilson's company is the company I am consulting with right now – the opportunity purposed into my life by God.

May 2, 2014
Around 4:00 a.m.

I had another experience that was equally vague and difficult to understand in detail. I was placed in situation after situation with a couple that I understood to be a "cheating couple." All I could glean was that I was the one being cheated on, though I could not identify my relationship with either person of the "cheating couple."

Rebirth III

May 3, 2014

The trips to the heavens this morning all seemed to hold either a negative connotation or served as some form of martial art training. I was involved in what I can only describe as "ninja fights" and "situations intended to bring fear to me" in each of the experiences. It all began with me standing before a child saying that he wanted to go sailing. He seemed to be attempting to talk me into helping him out. He was holding some type of a sailing magazine. He pointed to a picture in the magazine saying that we could sail to that destination. But, at that moment, his mother squashed his desire. She was short with her responses, but said, "No, we can't."

I stood up for the child by telling his mother that "the lake was great." After having seemingly convinced the mother that sailing was okay, we hopped on a sailboat and began sailing around a large lake that was initially behind us during our conversation. There was a large bridge that crossed over the lake as we sailed beneath. It rose higher than any other bridge I have seen on Earth. The masts on boats had no problem passing beneath it. Perhaps the bridge was five times or higher than the tallest mast on the sailboats in the water. At some point, the boy and mom jumped off the boat and swam to shore. It was not as if they bailed out. They just wanted to be on the shore.

Eventually, I jumped off of the boat while everyone on the shore watched. I suddenly realized this was a situation I have

The Written (cont'd)

faced at least once before in the heavens. I became aware of a shark in the water. The people standing on the shore shouted for me to swim away, but I was not scared. Do not get me wrong – I was initially nervous – but I knew that I was unable to be harmed in the heavens (or at least that is how it appeared at this point). I eventually swam to shore untouched by the great shark. It must have been twelve feet or greater in length (relative to me being approximately six feet tall).

When I reached the shore, I was met by a negative entity. Maybe he was unhappy that I had survived the shark attack. I am not really sure what prompted the situation, but as I climbed out of the water, we faced off in a great ninja fight. I do not know martial arts, but in this moment, I was a master of martial arts. My skills demonstrated an ultra-fast and fluid motion I have never felt in any earthly activity. I felt superhuman.

After the fight ended, I found myself standing in a room with a long hallway with an open doorway at the end. As I stood in the room, I continued making punching motions. I was enjoying the experience of the fluid skills I had somehow gained. As I faced the long hallway, a figure stepped into view. He was shirtless, muscular, wearing only tattered pants that were torn off along the calf. His body was red with black marks upon it. I knew instantly it was Lucifer. He had never presented himself in this way before, but I knew it was him nonetheless. I did not notice horns or anything else cliché in earthly description. But this was the first time I had ever seen a man of red flesh. As he stood in the doorway, I continued

Rebirth III

making my punching motions. I punched in his direction and shouted, "This is how it is done...especially to you." It was as if I had been given a weapon for hand-to-hand combat in fighting the devil. I knew I would not lose. As we stared each other down, I lost harmony with the moment. I returned to my body to journal this experience.

After I did so, I returned to the heavens. I was met by a great angel that took me to a building that was going to burn down. We walked in, and I found my way to a restroom. When I walked into the restroom, a male entity began talking to me. I cannot recall what he was saying, but it was as if he was giving me instructions for what was to come. I walked out and headed to "the office." I took an elevator to the eighth floor where I saw a familiar person who was going to burn down the building.

In this moment, I realized I had my daughter with me. I watched as the being lighted a fire that ignited a pocket of gas from within the elevator shaft. The building burst into flames instantly. The man that lit the fire walked over to the stairwell and walked away as if nothing happened. It was evident the fire was going to quickly destroy the building. I wanted to prove he burned down the building, but I needed to get my daughter down the stairs.

The angel that took me to the building escorted us down. When we reached the floor and I felt confident that my daughter was safe, I went back upstairs while the fire was burning. I was told I needed to leave, but I was dead-set on finding evidence of the man who set the building on fire. I eventually

The Written (cont'd)

found some things on the floor that could be used as evidence and returned downstairs where I showed the angel. At that point I lost harmony with the moment and returned to my body.

May 4, 2014

The beginning of the experiences in the heavens were extremely strange. It all began with me as the embodiment of a two-inch mouse standing beneath a grand piano. I was playing around by crawling up and plucking the strings. There was something about me being a two-inch Santa Claus as well as the Easter Bunny. I have no idea what it meant, and I was confused on the situation I was in. There were also two adults that seemed to be acting erratically. They were in a crib that had a sheer veil on top of it to prevent others from seeing the people inside clearly.

The next experience began with me on a trip to Florida where it was 87°. Georgia (my daughter) was with me. I told Georgia it was the perfect temperature outside. She shrugged. I did not have a tan on the last day I was to be there, so I went to lie out on the beach. There was a long dock reaching out into the water. I had been here before. I took my shirt off to get some sun and lay out in a chair that was near me. There were others staying in the house I had been staying in while I was in town. I do not know why, but I knew I was their leader.

Rebirth III

While I was lying out, some of the people came out to talk to me and ask my advice. The whole time I was lying out, I was fascinated that my skin did not seem to tan beyond the milky complexion I had in the heavens. After finishing up getting sun, I went inside to take a shower. The bathroom was a community bathroom. When I walked in, one of the residents was talking to someone else already in the shower. I overheard him saying that I was serious about whatever it was that I had told the group earlier. It seemed I was leading them to "be good" based on what I was overhearing, but they were resisting. The guy in the shower did not know I had walked in. He replied to the other guy and continued to talk about the conversation I had with them. There was nothing negative in the conversation, but he probably would not have liked knowing I was standing there listening to his unfiltered opinion.

May 5, 2014

This experience was incredibly blurry (unfocused) as I was in the heavens. There were moments that I made drawings about the future. I discussed with an angel about saving the world by looking into the future and knowing what was going to happen. I have known I have had an acute sense of foresight – but nothing that would warrant the topic I was discussing with the angel. It was as if I was being told that I needed to hone my skills to help "save the world." There has been an increasing number of experiences in the heavens that

The Written (cont'd)

have played out in the real world, but I typically cannot discern them until after they occur. So, I typically do not know if I have experienced something from the future. But, perhaps, this is what the discussion was about.

After the conversation ended, I went to take a shower. While I was in there, someone came in and began attacking me. As he fought me, I jumped over him in an act of supernatural powers. I had to have leapt ten feet into the air before landing gracefully behind him. After that happened, the guy's anger at me completely left him. We began to talk and become friends. I think this was one of the guys (and the same shower) from my heavenly experience a couple of days prior. Maybe I had to prove to him why I was his leader. It certainly leaves me with questions in an earthly sense, though while in heaven I seemed to embrace the circumstances and situations without question.

May 6, 2014

This morning, I had several experiences in the heavens. Some I failed to write down quickly enough. But I was able to journal three experiences immediately upon returning to my body. The first experience began with me in a park setting. There were others around me who were joking with me about some particular good feature about me. The jokes were in good nature, and I did not take offense to them. But, whatever

Rebirth III

the "good feature" was, I was unable to write it down in the earthly experience.

After the group began to go their separate ways, there was one person whom I followed toward a building near the edge of the park. The man was approximately twenty yards in front of me when I saw two cats chasing each other. I was not afraid, but I did notice the larger cat was white and chasing the smaller cat aggressively. I followed the animals into the building. When I got into the building, the man that entered the building before me asked me if I noticed "the white lion." I immediately panicked. I realized the larger cat was an un-maned white lion chasing either a house cat or a baby lion. I imagine it was probably a baby lion now that I understand the context.

When I realized the cats were lions, I immediately scaled a wall inside of the building to make sure I did not get bitten. While I scaled he wall, the man called the cops "because of an intruder." As I sat at the top of the wall looking down upon the lion, I realized the "intruder" was the lion, and the lion was representative of God. I felt saddened for not realizing it more quickly and having the cops called. But now that I reflect on the situation, I have to think that the larger lion (un-maned) chasing the smaller baby lion may have been symbolic to me following the man in front of me into the building. It could have been demonstrating the spiritual nature of the man in front of me and my own respective levels of growth in the heavens.

The Written (cont'd)

After journaling the experience, I returned to the heavens. This experience began with me bouncing in and out of different locations in the heavens as I tried to find harmony. I eventually was able to find a balance and found myself standing in a room. Around me were flashes of light. It did not seem like I was in bodily form, but rather a formless spiritual embodiment. I spun around trying to observe the light flashes around me. I realized that if I envisioned myself as standing in the middle of a compass, the flashes of light were being held in specific places. As I spun and passed a flash of light, I would slow down and spin in the opposite direction to try to focus on the light. It was a struggle to find the precise point along the axis, but I realized that, with enough effort, I could focus on the light. I repeated the exercise over and over which allowed me to find focus on the light. When I did, I could see glimpses of what I can only describe as points of time. It was as if the lights were portals to other points in space-time.

As I continued to practice this focusing technique on one light specifically, I suddenly found myself standing in a room with blurred surroundings. It was as if I was transported through the light to this room. Before me was a twisting orb with an orangish glow surrounding it. As I observed the orb, an angel walked over to me. I continued to stare at the twisting movement of the orb. I told the angel, "It is moving inside-out." But as soon as I said those words, I realized it appeared to be moving in the opposite motion than what I had just described. For some reason my mind translated the movement of the orb in reverse to the way I observed it. I stood there soak-

Rebirth III

ing in what I had just said while observing the motion of the orb. I knew the words I said were correct in observance of the motion, but my mind fought with the opposite interpretation of the movement.

As I observed the sphere, I watched as it continued to suck the surface of itself into the core without allowing the shape to change. It is an impossible motion to recreate in three-dimensional space. I have to think it is how a tesseract would look if it was able to be observed in three-dimensional space, though it does not look like the wireframe models that try to emulate four-dimensional space. I knew that the opposite nature of the motion from my earthly interpretation was the most important takeaway in this moment. As my mind wrestled with this impossible thought, I lost harmony and returned to my body to journal the experience.

After journaling, I returned one more time to the heavens. I was greeted with a blinding white light. My eyes began to adjust to the brightness where I saw a great golden angel glowing beneath a semi-transparent veil. The veil was white to soften the overpowering glow of the golden angel. Behind the golden angel, there were hues of blue and green. The embodiment of all that I was observing was encased in a square. I suppose it was a cube since it would need to be in three dimensions, but I was observing it along one face of the cube. It was important that I saw the angel beneath the veil. As I stared at the image, it slowly began to fade until everything vanished from view and I returned to Earth.

The Written (cont'd)

May 8, 2014

While I experienced several different journeys to the heavens, I was faced with the great challenge of awakening my earthly mind to retain the information. This is a new recognition for me over the last several days. Instead of me being able to retain information clearly, it seems the heavens are much more lucid and hyper real, but I lose touch with my ability to bring the information back.

At one point, after returning to my body, my spirit awoke and walked around my apartment. I walked to the bathroom where I looked into the sink and noticed how filthy it was. My sink is generally very clean, so I recognized in this moment that I was not in my earthly body. I tried to connect my mind with my spirit but could never awaken my mind enough to retain the information. I know this sounds strange because I am able to write about it, but there is a certain element of action and detail that required my mind to be in sync. I am unsure how this works, but it is the situation nonetheless.

May 9, 2014

The experience this morning was short and concise. It began with me as a formless body. I was spinning around in a circle (on a central axis). I felt my soul constrained to the confines of my body. I sought answers. A voice spoke to me in the dim light created by the motion. I was told that I "had been in

Rebirth III

quarantine" for a specific reason. While I think the voice tried to communicate the reason, I was unable to understand it with any clarity. I had been praying for guidance and direction in regaining the vividness during my spiritual travels so this experience left me with more questions than answers.

Several days later on 5/13/2014, I spoke with Bryan and mentioned this experience at the tail-end of our conversation. He immediately understood the interpretation to mean "protection for my own safety and rehabilitation." His initial thoughts were for me to not take the experience as a negative slant on anything happening in my life, but rather that the angels were helping me become stronger through the removal of outside influences.

It was a keen perspective. I have been feeling "off" in my spiritual walk recently. It is not anything negative, but rather not as encompassing as the way it once was in the preceding weeks. Perhaps the training I have been receiving has exposed me to something unfavorable in my earthly body. Or perhaps the upcoming move to Fort Lauderdale has introduced undue and unforeseen stress to my physical body. The last week I have felt extremely tired and out-of-sync with the world around me. My mind/body/spirit has not felt as strongly in song with the world as it should. This is the first week outside of my previous employment, so I have to think there is a certain recalibration that is taking place within me.

As I write this today (a couple of days after taking the initial notes), I feel much, much better than I have in the last week. I feel a greater happiness. As an aside, I went to see Sierra today (she cuts my hair). Her baby is due soon, and I thought I would see when I should schedule my next appointment. When I stopped by, one of the four people in the room took a strong interest in me. She was getting her hair washed by Sierra. The lady getting her hair washed made a comment after listening to me talk to Sierra for a minute that I seem "extremely happy from the inside...from the core." I had just told Sierra about my likely move to Fort Lauderdale, and this is when the lady began expressing her thoughts on me.

She said "[she] hasn't seen someone like [me] in a long, long time." She then went on to express how there was something about me that was "coming from the core – something different." We continued in a light conversation and eventually exchanged pleasantries before I had to leave. It was a great experience, a great highlight to my day. It rejuvenated me. I know the lady in the chair was a kindred soul who could "see" me in a world filled with so much noise. I saw her. It is a rare moment when that happens in this world, but it was enough to add light to my walk today and for me to recognize the light residing within.

May 12, 2014

The first experience began with me standing in a void. Two lights were coming toward me, increasing in brightness as they approached. I squinted at the brightness. At that moment, I realized my body mimicked my spiritual motion. The

Rebirth III

squinting of my eyes while I was in spiritual form caused me to lose harmony and fall out of the moment. When I regained my bearings, my soul ascended to the heavens.

I was met by a guardian who accompanied me on my travels. We got in a vehicle and proceeded to head down an interstate that was five lanes wide. In the median was a concrete divider. Along the shoulders of the highway were concrete fences. Without being told, I knew I was supposed to watch out for deer while I was driving. It seemed precarious because the scenario presented did not seem like any deer could get to the interstate from outside of the concrete walls.

However, as I was driving, I took notice of a couple of deer on the shoulder of the road in the distance. I began to slow down to avoid any accidents, but I was told by my guardian that I needed to keep driving – to not be worried. As I drove, the deer began to make a motion toward the interstate. The first deer was a great buck with large antlers. The second deer was also a large buck, but not as big as the first. As we approached the deer, the second one darted into the traffic behind me. I knew someone behind me wrecked. I saw the collision in my mind's eye. I knew the accident was tragic. I slowed down and almost instantly my soul was transported to a third party observer view of the accident. It was on the right side of the road. The car was on its side and crushed. The driver was lying outside of the car, mangled by the accident.

As I observed the body, I suddenly found myself in the body feeling the painful mangled and crushed form of that body. I tried to move and felt every gruesome amount of dam-

The Written (cont'd)

age to my body. It did not hurt in the sense of traditional pain, but it did feel broken. I could not move around since the body was too mangled to function. While I was experiencing the form of the mangled body, I also was able to simultaneously observe the experience from a third party viewpoint again. It was a split-level of consciousness that had been becoming more familiar in these experiences recently. As I tried to move around in the body, I eventually became overwhelmed at the heightened sense of the gruesome, mangled body and returned to Earth. My guide stayed by my side the whole time. I am not quite sure what the lesson was about, but at least I was allowed to experience more travels to the heavens (which had not occurred for a couple of days).

In reflecting on the situation and researching the potential meanings of deer in dreams, I found a common thread through all of the analyses. Knowing that dreams are just a less-awakened state of heavenly experiences, the meanings should transcend to my experiences. I have included an excerpt from a website I found in research regarding deer:

...

Deer has entered your life to help you walk the path of Love with full consciousness and awareness, to know that Love sometimes requires caring and protection, not only in how we Love others, but also in how we Love ourselves.

A deer's senses are very acute, and they see extremely well in low light, giving them the ability to understand the deeper symbolic meanings of things. They can hear a twig snap a very long way off. People with this power animal are often described as being swift and alert. They are intui-

Rebirth III

tive, often seeming to possess well developed, even extrasensory perceptions. Sometimes their thoughts seem to race ahead, and they appear not to be listening, to be somewhere else. Anyone with a power animal has latent clairvoyant and clairaudient abilities. They can see between the shadows, detect subtle movements and hear that which is not being uttered. Ask the deer to help you develop these true gifts.

Deer teaches us how powerful it is to be of gentle demeanor, to exert keen observation and sensitivity. Deer are in tune with nature and all it comprises. They are sacred carriers of peace and show those with this power animal how to open their hearts and Love unconditionally.

Deer teaches us to be gentle, to touch the hearts and minds of wounded beings who are in our lives. Don't push people to change, rather gently nudge them in right direction, with the Love that comes from deer. Love and accept people as they are. The balance of true power lays in Love and compassion.

When a Deer totem enters your world, a new innocence and freshness is about to be awakened. New adventures are just around the corner and there will be an opportunity to express the gentle Love that will open new doors for you.

...

After talking with Bryan on 5/13/2014, he made a comment about things happening in our lives. He made several comparisons that echoed a similar analysis as I had read about the deer. It was at that time I mentioned my experience with the deer. He became excited and ran with an assessment that was even more detailed than the analysis I included from my research above. Most of his assessment dealt with being the graceful deer, or the hunted deer. Without belaboring the

The Written (cont'd)

conversation, I can say that without knowing anything about the deer experience beforehand, Bryan was already talking about our lives in a way that was as symbolic as the deer.

May 13, 2014

This morning I had an interesting experience in the heavens. It was again, another situation I was placed in to observe and understand the significance. It began with me standing on the side of a cliff. If the cliff was forty feet tall, I was standing on a ledge somewhere around two-thirds of the way to the top. In front of me was some sort of gravel road ascending at a 90° angle up the side of the cliff. It was most definitely loose gravel, so the whole circumstance defied any earthly laws of gravity. At the crest of the cliff, the road leveled off and ventured off into the distance. While I know that the description I have given may be difficult to understand, the best way I can describe it is that a gravel road was on the ground at the base of the cliff and took a 90° ascent up the side of the cliff until it reached the plateau, where it continued onward.

Below me, there were numerous vehicles lined up for some sort of a race or competition. As I watched the first vehicle cross the starting line, it quickly ascended up the side of the cliff on the gravel road. When it reached the top, the vehicle had to slow its acceleration so that the front of the vehicle would gently rest on the lip of the plateau so that it could pull itself over the edge and onto flat ground. As soon as the vehi-

Rebirth III

cle made it to the top, it became apparent that the driver did not time the motion just right. The vehicle failed to reach the ledge. Immediately, the vehicle raced backwards down the hill due to the effect of whatever gravity was present. It did not wreck, but rather gracefully returned from where it once came. A second driver attempted the ascent next. He was driving an old, beat-up pick-up truck. His attempt was flawless. When the front tires crested the hill, the weight of the body against the gravity of the ledge caused the truck to push/pull itself onto the plateau. The success was met with cheer from down below.

    I took notice of two interesting phenomena. The first was that I was not bound by the ledge of the cliff. When the drivers reached the top of the 90° road, I was able to somehow zoom into the ledge to watch the tires meet the gravel with great detail. As soon as each vehicle failed or succeeded, I returned to the ledge I was on. It was all seamless. I would not describe it as traveling as much as I would say being selectively omniscient in observance. The second phenomena was that it was important to understand the type of vehicle in motion. For some reason the way the truck was front-weighted instead of evenly distributed allowed it to succeed.

    I watched as several other attempts by other vehicles were made. One driver wanted to see if he could succeed on speed alone. He ascended at a high rate of speed which caused the vehicle to launch too high above the ledge. When the vehicle lost traction with the road it tumbled backwards to the ground in a tossing, tumbling descent. The vehicle crashed in a spec-

The Written (cont'd)

tacular way. Death was not in this moment. I felt like the driver either survived without injury, or accepted his fate and passed onto the next place he was going spiritually. There was no remorse by anyone. I watched as another truck ascended the cliff. As his front tires crested the hill, he accelerated and twisted his tires to fishtail the bed of the rear of the truck onto the ledge. This attempt was met with success, albeit not as pretty as the other successes. In every successful attempt, a truck was used. This was important to notice. The distribution of the weight was extremely important to understand as well as the fishtailing motion of the final successful attempt. It was all important.

May 14, 2014

During a lightning storm this morning I was awakened from my sleep. As I tried to go back to sleep, I felt a force flowing through my body. The last two lightning storms in Nashville, which are not common at all, caused my body to feel ignited with energy. This time, I felt it again. As I attempted to meditate and pray after awakening, the energy helped send me to the heavens more easily.

In this experience, I was greeted by an angel. I was standing in the courtyard of a condo unit on the beach. I had been looking at places in Fort Lauderdale and have had many questions about my purpose for moving there. Even with the questions – especially in how I would be able to keep seeing

Rebirth III

my daughter as much as I want to – I have moved forward with the plans because I know that is what God has tasked me to do. But it was in this experience that I was given answers.

As the angel talked to me, he let me know I was standing in the midst of the place where I would call home. And indeed, the condo unit looked similar to one of the units that came available yesterday... a unit in which I had filled out an application. He told me that the my purpose in moving to that unit is "to be." Those were his words, but I knew it was God speaking through him. It was then that I began to take notice of an anointed ability that the angel was helping me see. It was a sense of spiritual superhuman strength. I became aware that just by "being" in that location I was able to stop water from flooding the area. But most importantly, there was a greater purpose for being placed into that specific area. I was being strategically placed in that specific area for a greater purpose to come. I was told that my "being" served as a "beacon of protection" for something that was not clearly disclosed to me. But, I can describe how it was described to me.

I was shown something like a globe of the world where thumb pins were pressed into the globe at strategic points. These pushpins were where others were being led by God "to be." I could see that many of the pinpoints were along the East and West coasts of North and South America. There were also a small number of pinpoints in the middle of the continental areas as well. I did not have a good view of the other side of the globe, but it was my understanding that other areas con-

The Written (cont'd)

tained similar pushpins, though I did not have the impression there were as many in other parts of the world.

I spoke with the angel a little longer before a bolt of lightning brought me back to my body. The conversation was pleasant and gave me a sense of peace. I knew there was purpose in me being in that location. Specifically, the purpose was just "to be." I was basically told to go live there, and my presence of action would be called upon when needed. But my presence in passivity was what was required at the moment. I understood it much like a chess game. I know that my spiritual presence has a strategic reason in the move by the hand of God. I am a chess piece at the moment, but one that has purpose.

Before I went to bed, I prayed for help in understanding how everything would work out – especially financially since I would have to figure out a way to fly my daughter back and forth to visit. I also had extended my lease another month in Nashville because I was unsure of the logistics of moving, and I prayed for help in understanding how to solve the financial strain that would placed on me if the new lease in Florida was to overlap my existing lease. I knew that God would provide a sign of how He was working in my life in order to bring me peace. I always have faith.

The previous day, I had already taken the leap with the paperwork for the condo that was eventually shown to me in the heavens. The experience in the heavens brought me peace with the decision. I awoke this morning to an acknowledgement that the landlord of the condo Loved my application and

Rebirth III

was finalizing the terms for me. As soon as that happened, I received an additional contract for consulting. I was expecting it to be for one week of work. But, it was written for six weeks (and renewable). The duration of the contract runs through June 30th (the end of my lease here in Nashville). The timing is immaculate, as always through God. All in all, God answered me three ways this morning – once through the heavens, the second through the email from the landlord, the third through the job contract.

May 16, 2014

My primary experience in the heavens this morning was some sort of an "aware unawareness." It began with me standing in a room talking to an angel, only I did not recognize where I was or who I was speaking with. To my earthly mind, it was purely a dream. But, having been in these experiences before, I recognized my erratic thought process in my earthly mind. I had watched a show earlier in the evening where people with special abilities were being hunted, and my mind decided to interpret the experience in the heavens in a similar way. As I was standing there talking to the angel (whom I just thought was an acquaintance in a dream), I became aware that a group of three beings was coming to meet me. Two of them were male. One was female.

When they reached me, I pulled out some sort of a taser. I immediately began shooting at them in self-defense. When the

The Written (cont'd)

individuals were hit with the taser shots, they just looked at each other in disbelief. The taser shots were red and exploded in a three-cornered splatter pattern on their white apparel. One of the individuals looked at his chest and pulled the taser-shot off of him. It had the consistency of Jell-O. He looked at the girl in the group. She laughed and said, "What did you do to him this time?" The man in the middle (who was dark skinned and bald) replied, "That's just it. I did not do anything this time." They just looked at each other and giggled at the absurdity of my reaction. They were not affected by the taser shots, nor were they upset. They might have been slightly annoyed, but seemed more amused at the situation.

I recognized that my mind was in self-defense mode for what I could only rationalize as the influence of the television show I had watched prior to going to sleep. I observed the experience in third person, but experienced it in first person. When it became obvious the group of three were undeterred, I ran away with them chasing me. I eventually found my way back to my earthly body. As soon as I opened my eyes, I knew the error of my ways. In fact, as I experienced the situation in the minutes prior, I knew I was wrong. But as I have said before, sometimes the soul is on autopilot and the only conscious action that can be done is to observe.

Rebirth III

May 17, 2014

This morning I experienced several different interactions in the heavens, but was unable to bring much back in earthly terms. I tried to write down the experiences, but, honestly, the experiences were more like bullet points. In the first of the two experiences I can recount, I was playing football. For some reason, I felt like I continued to disappoint my coach. The clearest part of the experience was returning a kickoff and scoring, but it was not enough to offset the disappointment in my coach. Later in the experience, the football game transitioned to lectures on my "abilities." I was keenly aware that "someone was after my abilities" but I did not have much clarity regarding the context. I thought it was referring to my ability to travel to the heavens and interact with the angels, but that is just my best guess.

May 20, 2014

Finally, I was able to achieve an experience with extreme clarity. It seemed the experiences had been losing clarity over the last few months, and then I realized what helped kick start me before: vitamins. Back when all of the experiences began firing on all cylinders, I was getting back to working out and I had begun to take a vitamin supplement recommended to me by a chiropractic friend. The vitamin supplement was based off of a test she did on my deficiencies. At the time, I noticed

The Written (cont'd)

much improved clarity and frequency to my experiences in the heavens. Of note, I think that the B6 in the vitamins is mostly what I am deficient in. But, if ensuring the body is in the most pristine working order is critical to achieving the best balance with the mind, body, and soul, then it makes sense that supplementing a healthy diet with required vitamins will help bring the body back in balance. After all, we are all human and susceptible to biological quirks. For me, it would appear that vitamins may be one of the driving factors in my ability to maintain balance in my mind, body and soul. And if that is specifically the case, then it makes sense why there seems to be a downward trend to the clarity in my experiences. Back around February or March, I quit taking the vitamins in hopes that I could maintain balance without outside supplements. It apparently lasted me well – so much so that I lost track of ever having taken them in the first place. Those vitamins did a wonder on my soul. While I do think that getting back in a heavy workout routine will help me find the most optimal body-mind-soul balance, I definitely think the vitamins are the kick-starter.

In typical fashion, it took two days of taking the vitamins for me to experience the fire inside. During the midnight to 4:00 a.m. time period, my body ignites from the inside in recognition to the radiance of the moon. This period at night holds a special significance, for the energy directed to the Earth from the sun must first reflect off of the moon. The moon acts like a lens where the energy is focused into a singular, polarized pattern. During the day, the sun's energy bursts

Rebirth III

off of the stratosphere of the Earth in a multi-directional pattern. This light and energy during the day gives life, but is only optimal to the biological side of things. The more focused pattern of the moon's energy strengthens the soul. This is the reason why prayer times are mandated by certain religions to occur at specific times. In particular, Islam makes note of these special times, though it does not make mention of why these times are important. Truthfully, even Mohammad may not have known. He may have only understood his heightened awareness of his spiritual encounters during these specific times.

But anyway, back to the subject of this journal entry. This morning I experienced the spiritual fire coursing through my soul. I was unable to sleep, but was able to meditate throughout the night. This is typically how the nights tend to play out when I have multiple experiences in the heavens. There is never really sleep. Instead, there is complete awareness of the soul leaving the body while the body copes with the intense amount of heat generated within.

So this morning, when my soul left my body, I arrived at a beautiful mansion in the heavens. I recognized the mansion to be located in a desolate country. Outside of the walls of the estate, the location was very poor. It reminded me of the divide in wealth and poverty in Haiti. The house was surrounded by lush, green gardens. I was led by a guardian angel the whole time I was there, but I was unable to see the identity of the guardian. I was just acutely aware of his/her presence.

The Written (cont'd)

Inside, I was ushered into a great banquet hall. There was a brunette lady that was the leader of the "convention" I was attending. As I chatted with others in the room, I asked a lot of questions about the location, but not enough to give away whether I was supposed to be there or not. I seemed to make a lot of friends. As everyone gathered in the room, we each took seats on large couches. These couches were actually closer to the size of king beds, but it did not seem "off." It just seemed luxurious.

The leader of the group called everyone's attention to her. She began her conversation with the group by telling them she had invited me there specifically because she thought I would be of great value and "fit right in." I looked around the room observing how nicely everyone was dressed. The age ranges were across the board, as were genders and races. But I did take notice that a couple of gentlemen were wearing tuxedos. I was not wearing a tuxedo, but I recognized the exclusivity of the event. It was then that I made a couple of jokes (in good context) about being in the room with the group as well as (for whatever reason) how I learned to identify "us." Everyone smiled and laughed, commenting on how I would fit right in.

Eventually the leader's conversation turned to the main event: some sort of bidding game. On a board, were line drawings of the faces of everyone in the room, including mine. The game began by removing half of the people from the board. After that, half of the remaining were removed. This went on until there was only one face remaining. As this name-reduction game began, several of the elders in the room made

Rebirth III

loud comments along the lines of "they are out to get me." These elders would subsequently have their names/faces removed from the board. I noticed that I was lasting through all of reduction cuts.

Before the game finished, the lady seemed to stop the game with six remaining faces. I was one of those six. It is possible the game went on and I was removed in the next cut, but I was acutely aware I was in the "top six." That is when I wandered out of the room I was in and into the backyard. I walked out on a nice patio surrounded by flowers and towering trees. I saw a train track running behind the house. To my right I saw a black (old fashioned) steam locomotive rolling down the tracks. I heard it blare its whistle. I immediately became excited because I recognized the significance of the train. I began to explain my awareness to my guardian before he walked me back into the house.

I became aware that it was now dark inside – very dark. I was lying on the couch/bed assigned to me. The sun had set outside as well. I got up from the couch and tried to walk over to the windows seeking light. Every time I took a step, it felt like I was running into large beanbags that prevented me from going anywhere. Every time I tripped I made a lot of noise. I was afraid I would awaken others (who I thought were sleeping on the couches they had been assigned). Eventually I gave up and went to sleep.

I awoke feeling extremely hungry. I was shown around the place some more before I was led into a side room, located off from the main room. I was told that food was being pre-

The Written (cont'd)

pared for me even before I walked in. It reminded me of a small den with tables. Some of the others attending the convention were already inside sitting at the tables. Some were eating. Some were reading. Some were sitting on the floor. As I looked around, a dark skinned man rushed toward me from another room. I thought the room he came from was a kitchen, but I never looked to see.

When he reached me, he immediately began making sure I was taken care of. He was nervous that he would mess up making me happy. He reached for a stack of glass bottles on the wall while asking me if I wanted a Coke. I do not drink sugary drinks, but I obliged. As he began to hand me the bottle in his hand, he began apologizing profusely. He poured it out saying, "I meant Coke. Not Pepsi. This is Pepsi. I'm sorry. I'll get you a Coke." I was a little baffled because he was clearly pouring the beverage from a Coke bottle onto the ground. I could tell he was ashamed of his mistake in serving me. I told him, "Everything is okay. I'm good. Don't worry."

When the bottle was empty, he ran off to the kitchen area. Another person saw the liquid on the floor and said, "You obviously are not from around here. That really is not okay." I replied loudly enough for the butler to hear, "It is really okay. I was raised with a clumsy sister." Honestly, I think those words were meant more as a way to lighten the mood than as any sort of truth. I went into a bathroom and found a roll of paper towels. I returned to clean up the mess. Everyone was surprised that I would help clean up a mess that was not mine. Eventually, another person got down on his knees and helped

Rebirth III

me. Everyone seemed flustered that I would do such a thing, but somehow still had admiration of the effort.

After the mess was cleaned up, I went outside. I wandered around the gardens looking at the train tracks. Eventually night fell again, and I found myself asleep in a bed. I became aware that something was not right with the situation and recognized I was involved in some sort of "raid." I hopped out of bed and witnessed as hundreds of little goblin figures ran though the dark trying to prevent anyone from getting out of bed. The goblins were all approximately two feet tall and carried clubs. They were fast, but clumsy. They would run and swing their clubs at the feet of anyone who got out of bed, attempting to knock them down. I made a mad sprint toward a chair that was sitting in the moonlight pouring in through a window. I knew that if I made it, I would be safe. For some reason, the goblins could not step into the light. On my dash to the moonlight I was clubbed several times before making it to safety. It was at that time that I returned to my earthly body.

It also should be noted that each time I lay down to sleep in the heavens, a dog would crawl across the pillow and lie on my face, causing me to get out of bed. I am speaking of my spiritual body and non-earthly interactions. I do not own a physical dog.

The Written (cont'd)

May 22, 2014

This morning's vision was extremely foggy. I can discern that it was about "dreams within dreams" and biological changes in the body... but that is all.

May 28, 2014

This morning's vision was extremely long and clear. I attest much of this to my prayer before bed. During my prayer, I acknowledged to God that I understood I was on a mission, a directive to get to Florida. Included in that directive is the work that I must do for whatever financial requirements. I explained that it seemed that my directive took priority, but I could not help but wonder if I had done something wrong for Him to not communicate with me as much in the heavens each night (as had been the case very heavily since Christmas). I wondered aloud if it was my own inability to focus on my spiritual center...if I had somehow "lost my way." I stream-of-consciousness prayed aloud about everything that was on my mind ultimately arriving at the thought that my experiences in the heavens are like a warm hug from Him. They help me know He is there, and that I am on the right track. If His perceived distance is a requirement for me to grow stronger (like a child learning to live on his own), then I acknowledged I was okay with that. I just needed clarity on whether I had somehow done something wrong.

Rebirth III

As I closed my eyes, I began to find the spiritual launch pad, though I continued to lose alignment for traveling to the heavens. Eventually I fell asleep. But throughout the night I was constantly awakened by a spiritual knocking on my spirit's door. Each time I heard the "knocking," there was a nudge to my spirit that brought me to a heightened state of awareness while my body was in a natural alignment. I suppose it would be best to consider it to be an "almost asleep/awakened" state. The loudest "knocking" was the sound of someone playing the accordion. This was extremely loud and jarring. I immediately came to and became aware of the natural meditative state my body was in. I began to allow my spirit to explore this state where it eventually exited my body, traveling to the heavens.

When I arrived, I was greeted by a group of angels. We spoke for a while about the challenges I was having with returning to the heavens. I eventually learned that weight/fitness do not prohibit a person from reaching the heavens. For a while, I had attributed the frequency of my travels to being at the pinnacle of my fitness level. But, this theory was all smashed when I was told that "fitness doesn't matter." I was told that alignment is the most important part and that anyone is capable of this feat. The frequency of my travels should be seen in the same light as how a person sharpens his skills at a trade. It just takes practice and understanding.

Eventually we parted ways and I was escorted to reunite with my spiritual family. I was led to a door where I was to walk in alone. When I walked in, I saw that I was at a funeral. I immediately became aware I was at my grandfather's funeral

The Written (cont'd)

(mother's side and still alive on Earth). Everyone was extremely sad. As I stood in the church, I had a flashback to the day prior where I had tried to tell my granddad that I had an "ability" where I could see and speak to angels and "dead people." In the flashback, he did not want to acknowledge that sort of ability was even possible. I was disappointed, but I knew that he would one day understand that I was speaking the truth. During the flashback, I also relived an experience where someone on the other side was trying to have me communicate to him, but he would not listen.

As the whole experience in the heaven grew in detail over my time there, I realized that the person "on the other side" was his father who had long since passed on Earth. While my granddad did not want to accept my ability, he did take the time to tell me about his time as a Mason and many of the principle teachings of the Masons. On Earth, he had never uttered a word about being a member of that order. Eventually, the flashback faded (which was as vivid as a real experience and not a memory). I found myself back in the church. Eventually the service ended and we made our way back to my grandmother's house for the wake.

While there, I tried to explain to my mother and grandmother the conversation I had with my granddad in the flashback from a few days prior. They seemed accepting of the idea and hopeful for granddad's spirit to reconvene with me. As we talked, I noticed a spirit of a deceased person in the room. They could not see it. I began talking to it even though I knew I would appear crazy speaking to the air in front of my

Rebirth III

mother and grandmother. The spirit stayed in a strong form. We communicated for a bit and eventually it left. When I turned my attention back to my mother and grandmother, they stood up terrified and sad. Even though I thought they would be accepting from my earlier conversation with them, it was clear it was too much for them to handle. They ran off, disappointed in me.

Later in the evening, my grandmother returned to speak with me. She apologized for her reaction and admitted it was due to her emotions of the loss of her husband (my grandfather). But now she wanted to show me something he left behind. These were items that granddad had left for her, but she was supposed to tell me about them (per his instructions). We sat down on a couch in front of a dark table where several items were laid out. She explained a little about the first item, but my attention was solely on another item on the table. I could not stop staring at it.

When she finished explaining about the first item, she moved onto the item I was staring at. She explained that granddad had left it for me. I reached to pick it up. The item was a string of connected diamond-pyramid cut stones, inverted to rest on the flat surface. The stones were all dark and connected by a string. There were symbols along the sides of the stones. Each stone represented a unique archetypal concept defined by the symbol. The stones were about the size of a baseball. As I picked it up and began to look at each of the symbols, I became extremely excited. I knew that the conversation I had with granddad in the days prior to his death did

The Written (cont'd)

not go unheard. Embedded in the symbols were the secrets to all that he had learned on his time here on Earth, and the time he spent in the heavens. It was a proverbial passing of the right of knowledge to this ancient wisdom.

As I looked at it, I began to weep uncontrollably. I did not know what each symbol meant, but the gesture itself was enough for me to know that my grandfather was an angel in human form during his time here on Earth. There was something important about his freemason history that he never spoke of, but I assume I will learn more about it when the time is right. My grandmother wept uncontrollably by my side as well during this time. We must have wept for ten minutes straight. It was every emotion, wrapped into one: joy, sadness, Love, hope, and faith.

After we parted ways, I went to the living room. My mother and grandmother returned and sat down with me. As we sat there, I felt peace in their acceptance of my ability and the gravity of the wisdom my grandfather was passing on to me (though the wisdom was a concept and undefined in detail). Suddenly, my grandfather's spirit entered the room. I stood up and walked over to him. I greeted him and was amazed that I could see him with such strength and clarity. This was not a vision in a heavenly experience where I lost harmony. This was complete balance.

He smiled and spoke to me with such happiness and enthusiasm. We exchanged pleasantries about being able to converse. I did not hide the conversation from my mother and grandmother. We talked for a while where I eventually be-

Rebirth III

came confident enough to lead him to the couch where my family was seated. I served as a bridge between him and my grandmother. He wanted me to tell her how much he Loved her and other important "for her ears only" talking points. She was, at first, skeptical. But immediately warmed up to the interaction, embraced by hope. My mother asked questions as well. Eventually my grandfather departed, but it was not due to me losing harmony. In fact, it was due to him passing onto his next destination. His ability to manifest to me was time limited before it was time for him to move on. The conversation ended, and my grandmother and mom were struck with great sadness again. I had to let them leave me to absorb all that had just occurred.

I eventually headed outside where I was greeted by my great-great-grandfather Alex, whom I had never met on Earth. Alex was my grandfather's grandfather. He was walking with another angel and followed by my deceased Uncle Gary (Bryan's father). Gary continued to ramble on about how he did not think I could really see them. The words that were tossed around frequently by Gary were always along the lines of, "He can't see dead people. I really don't believe that he can see us." Alex shared the same youthfulness as my grandfather in his face, but it was evident it was Alex and not my grandfather. Alex continued to reassure Gary that I could see them. I did not interject with Gary much at all, but I did let him know that I could see them. We walked down a long path outside of my grandparent's residence. I was eventually led to the door to go inside.

The Written (cont'd)

I entered a place I do not recall ever having visited before. While it was not white or beachy in appearance, my impression was that it was supposed to represent the beach condo I am moving to in Florida. My grandmother was inside cooking. I walked over to her and told her how much I Loved her place. I was excited that she had the two bedroom version, but explained that I could only afford the one bedroom version for now, though I had high hopes I could get a two bedroom at some point in the future.

I eventually walked into the living room where I was greeted by several other people from my past. My grandfather on my dad's side (still living) had come by the house to give me a gift and let me know that he now knew I was not lying about my ability. I never had a chance to unwrap the gift before I was handed two monogrammed bath towels. They were white with letters monogrammed in gold. This gift came from a female that resembled a girl I know named Sam – but I really do not think it was her. The initials were meant to represent his-and-her towels with our initials on them. But, the initials were not Sam's at all. That is what made me realize my mind was associating this beautiful female before me with the closest earthly counterpart I have known. In fact, many of the names and faces could be subjected to the same level of scrutiny. I can only explain my experience as best as I can and meditate on the clarity of the identities at a point of reflection. It is also important to note that the script the initials were monogrammed in was the same script I saw the TAJ word on "the chair prepared for me" in the kingdom.

Rebirth III

After I received my gifts, nightfall arrived. My mother slept on the couch. I think I slept in a chair, but this is when everything began to become a little fuzzy. When I awoke from the sleep in the heavens, I went to a hospital. I went to a room where many of my elder female relatives were staying. I was told I could have a bed if I wanted to sleep there and keep them company. Some conversation occurred, and I eventually walked into the bathroom. I stared at myself in the mirror when my sister walked over to me. She asked me to pull something out of her teeth.

It is hard to explain, but when she showed me her teeth, it was as if a hundred bundled toothpicks were divided inside of her teeth. It was like I could identify individual fibers of bone. I was afraid to try to help her pull out whatever it was, so I refused. She told me that I better learn because I have one I need to pull out of my own tooth. I opened my mouth in the mirror and saw the same level of detail – but only on one of my teeth. I reached in and pulled out a three-inch nail-like object that was overcrowding the bone fibers. It felt good to remove it, but somewhat freaked me out. As I stared at this nail in my fingers I lost harmony with the heavens and returned to my body.

When I opened my eyes on Earth, I felt invigorated and refreshed. I felt the quick-charge of the heavens filling my spirit with life. I immediately prayed thanks to God for answering my prayer before bed. After I finished praying, I checked my phone for email. I had seven emails waiting for me – His divine sign sent to me in a way I would recognize. I prayed. He

The Written (cont'd)

responded, and then stamped the experience with His signature. The rest of the day was filled with other great spiritual moments, but I will save those for another time of writing.

May 30, 2014

While I have never been to Fort Lauderdale, the experience this morning took my soul there. When I arrived, I went to Miami (again another place I have never visited before). I walked around a mall that was two levels. I wandered around the mall looking for reason as to where I was and why I was there. I walked past a familiar black-skinned angel. He was tall and fit, but not lanky. And while I did not recognize him at first as an angel, I was enamored by his size. Others recognized his greatness and stopped and stared. It would be akin to how people on Earth view a celebrity out and about in a common area.

As I walked around the mall, we crossed paths multiple times. Every time we crossed paths, he looked my way as if he wanted me to recognize him. I continued wandering aimlessly around the mall having not quite found the recognition that I was in a heavenly experience. As the mall began to close, I walked outside searching for a cab to take me to some unknown destination. And though I searched for cabs, none were to be found.

As I began to give up on the idea that I would be able to leave, the familiar angel walked past me outside. I stopped him

Rebirth III

and asked him for a ride. He seemed pleased I had the confidence to speak to him and equally as happy to help. He took me to what would eventually turn out to be my present condo in Fort Lauderdale. However, I would not know it at the time. I was still trying to gather my bearings in the heavens. The angel walked me around the building and explained to me how I was to act when I eventually arrived there. He showed me ways to place my furniture in the unit to make the best of the floor plan. After he felt satisfied that I understood all that he wanted to share with me, we went to the pool and relaxed on a gorgeous, blue-sky day.

June 1, 2014

The experience began with me in the void. In the best way I can explain the situation, I was a moderator of the past, present, and future. If there was something negative in "the global outlook of all" that I was moderating, it was my role to make it positive. To do so, I was tasked with changing the past in order to recreate a more positive future. For the most part, my role did not involve much interaction. The circumstances and situations presented to me were – for the most part – very good.

Eventually, my role as moderator came to an end. A black couple wanted to take me out to dinner. It was now dark outside and raining. We went to a place called "Soulpan." While we were there, I excused myself for a few minutes. I walked to

The Written (cont'd)

the building next door. In front of this building, the patrons were arriving in horse and carriages. And while the antiquity of the moment shined through the rain, there were also modern conveniences around. There were cars patrolling the area. The patrols would drive up and down the sidewalk with their flashing lights on. I felt like a bum navigating the street and sidewalk, trying to evade any attention from the patrol.

At one point up ahead of me, I saw four "convicts" being interrogated by the patrol for wearing orange. And while the patrol seemed very modern, I also took notice that everyone carried vintage muskets as their firearm of choice. I journeyed on and eventually noticed the patrol chasing after a suspect. They did not have a good line on the suspect, and I knew that I could help corner him for the patrol, so I did just that. When the man was cornered, I spoke to him briefly. He seemed frightened and disoriented with his surrounding. In the whole scheme of things, I think a good way to view what I was witnessing was perhaps the soul of a dreamer on Earth accidentally arriving in a place he was not strong enough to be in just yet.

To Carl (which I am confident would be his earthly name), he may have understood it as a nightmare, or possibly would not remember it at all. But to me, I was able to see it for what it was in the moment. I felt sorry for Carl, but there was no way I could explain to him everything that was happening in the few moments we had together. I waited for the patrol to arrive. They were very thankful for my assistance.

Rebirth III

June 2, 2014

My travels to the heavens consisted mostly of sporting events. I was the field goal kicker for the team I was playing on. When I gathered my bearings, I became aware I was mid-conversation with the placeholder. I was joking with him about ordering enough movies on Blu-ray to prevent him from having nothing to watch all week. The conversation was out of place, which may have been exactly what I needed to recognize I was in the heavens.

After I kicked the field goal, we moved on to the ensuing kickoff. The player who received the kickoff caught the ball in bounds but set the ball on the ground as if the play was over. Though it would have been a strange play, I thought it should have been a fumble. I asked the referee about it. The referee (clearly an elder angel in that moment) looked at me with an austere gaze. In his eyes I saw people. It was enough to cause me to lose harmony and return to Earth.

When I arrived back in the heavens, I was told "Georgia plays at 420/520." The team had been victorious with a win over the "Noles" a week prior and celebrated on the final kickoff. In hindsight, the team could have been the "Noels" or even more symbolically, the "no els," which would mean "non angels." In earthly terms, it is obvious that my passion for football and my University bled through to my experiences. However, the context of all of it was abstract. It is possible that I was shared that Georgia plays at 6/7 of their potential (by reduce summing 420/520). But, the more likely interpretation is the possibility that Georgia represented an archetypal team...a team that I seemed to play on. And if Georgia is an archetypal team, it could mean that my team is 1/7 short of whatever it needs. In a spiritual sense, the team I play for is God's team. It is either almost complete, or missing one piece. It could also represent the Seven Seals mentioned in Revelation. And, while that may seem out of place in the context of seeing a football team, the message is always spiritual. I mention the possibility of the seven seals here because God has been communicating with me about the seals for some time. I just have not been sure of where to put it in the context of my writing.

June 3, 2014

This morning I had numerous experiences, but I could not maintain harmony with the travels. However, at the end of my last attempt – and after a lot of frustration with not being able to recount any of the experience – I was given a name. Even this name was hard to remember. I meditated on it for a while in order to retain the information. The name I was given was either Anna Presley Wilcox or Anna Wesley Preston. I know it may not make sense to a reader, but syllables do not always find their rightful place in these types of experiences. Either way, I do not know anyone by either of those names and both Google and Facebook turned up nothing in the way

Rebirth III

of search results. I suppose it is possible that a person with that name does not exist today. Maybe it is a name for the future. Maybe it is a name from the past. But if it was from the past or present, I would think I would be able to find at least one person with either name.

June 6, 2014

I had a lot of "false takeoffs" before having a very long and involved experience in the heavens tonight. However, due to a "false awakening" where I thought I was journaling my experience, when I actually awoke I could not recall the details of the experience. False awakenings are tough to deal with. I have them frequently, and I believe this is why I am not always able to retain as much information – especially in the recent month or so. Each time I think I return to my body, my soul is returning from the heavens into an in-between locale that fools me into thinking I have returned to my body. I generally commit the experiences in the heavens to memory and then write them down. When I open my eyes on Earth, that is when I realize that I did not just journal everything – and at that point I can no longer recount the events with any clarity.

Anyway, I was able to jot down the false takeoffs since I wrote them down after each one. The first one began with my soul leaving my body and traveling to a white castle-like lighthouse on a beautiful beach. The sand was crisp white. The water was a beautiful azure blue. The sides of the building

The Written (cont'd)

connected to the lighthouse is what stood out to me the most. The walls were made of white shingles – but they were thick – as if they were rock. The ornate and improbable construction was enough to cause my mind to spin and lose harmony with the moment.

Immediately after journaling and closing my eyes, I felt myself ascend to the heavens again. This time, I was traveling in a corkscrew-like motion into space. I was able to visualize my soul leaving from a third person perspective while experiencing the first person feelings. From third person, I could see the twisting spiral I was traveling through funnel up and away from Earth eventually passing under a large object in space. Near the tip of the funnel was a sharper edged point... as if to show space/time being manipulated right in front of my soul. The tip of the spiral was white. Imagine what a space shuttle looks like taking off; the funnel of smoke behind it; the glow of the boosters at the tip as it fades into the distance. It was not exactly like that, but that is the closest comparison I can make.

The funnel was transparent, but I was aware it was there. The front of the spiral path (where my soul resided) was glowing white. For some reason, I felt like my third person self was twisting the spiral with my right hand counterclockwise, while the flight path from Earth began through my left and was led by my right hand. The thought of this duality caused me to lose harmony and return to my body.

I journaled that experience and immediately closed my eyes again. This time I found myself traveling through an orange sand desert. I am not sure where I was going, or where I

Rebirth III

was, but all I could think of was the sheer amount of sand surrounding me. This caused me to lose harmony and wake up again. This was the last false takeoff I had before my travels.

June 8, 2014

The experience this morning lasted at least a couple of days in heavenly time. It began with me in some sort of barracks. It was not bad. I actually felt at home in this location. I could sense it was a form of boarding school for my soul. I was aware that I was in the heavens, but I did not have as much control as I would have liked to have. It felt like I was on autopilot, just witnessing and experiencing my soul's actions.

The barracks was full of twin beds with aluminum frames for the headboard and footboard. There was a flimsy mattress on top with a green sheet. It felt military-esque (though I have never served in the military). The barracks was filled with male and female souls – all around the age of early to mid-twenties. In earthly comparison – it was the age where physical beauty is at its prime for each gender. There was a girl on the bed to my left. We became friends throughout the days. During the day, we would go out into the woods (the same great woods I have visited in the heavens before) and train together. She is really the only person that would come into focus for me during the first portion of the experience. Everyone else was blurred for some reason. I could make out com-

The Written (cont'd)

mands/coaching coming from an elder angel, but I never saw a face for this angel.

During one of our trainings, we had to each take two separate slides on the right side of the path in the woods. And, while I describe it as a slide, there was nothing physically built to indicate it was a slide. It was just a slide-shaped part of the Earth filled with sand and rushing water. I hopped on mine, she hopped on hers. It wound and twisted down the mountain side eventually opening up to a tidal pool on a beautiful beach. The two slides were divided by foliage. When we reached the bottom, we exchanged stories of what the experience was like for each of us. I could tell her slide was different and may have had one sharp turn that mine did not have. Either way, it was exhilarating. The girl could not stop smiling or talking about how much fun she just had. We did not have too much time to talk before we were commanded to continue our training. I guess it would be comparable to a fun version of a military boot camp. Eventually the day ended, and we returned to the barracks.

The next day, I noticed the bed on my left where the girl was staying was empty. I did not have long to process that thought, though, because to my right, there was a beautiful brunette girl standing next to my bed. She had just placed a backpack down on her bed – the bed to my right. All she could do was stare at me. She was beautiful. At first, I was taken aback. After all, I had just spent several days making friends with the girl that was now no longer in the bed to my left. This brunette girl had eyes of wonder. She just stared and blinked

Rebirth III

at me...like something from an anime cartoon. I eventually introduced myself, as did she. While I think she said her name was Abby, there were a couple of times she was referenced as Sarah throughout the experience. This confused me because I could not understand if her name was Abby or Sarah. I referred to her as Abby though.

As our conversation progressed, I learned that she had not "just arrived" as I had thought. She had been there possibly even longer than I had. She told me that she had noticed me and had been watching me. At first, I was a little taken aback by those comments, but I warmed up to them quickly. I could tell she liked me...or at the very least, was fascinated by something I was doing while I was training. She was definitely curious. Evening eventually came, and we went to sleep (in our adjacent beds). The next day, our souls trained together. We ran through the woods like kids playing in a great backyard. As we approached the slides, I knew she would not go down the slide by herself, so I did not let on I had a plan for her.

When we reached the first slide during our run (the slide I went down the prior day), I playfully pushed her so that she stumbled and fell down it. When she reached the bottom, I had a third person perspective on the matter. My angelic coach came into audible focus for me as well. I could tell he was standing beside me. He explained to me that we had to help her understand what she was about to see. I knew I had done the "right thing" by pushing her down the slide because this was clearly the next part of her training. She reached out to me because she was ready to learn this portion, but was

The Written (cont'd)

scared. As she made her way out of the tidal pool and onto the beach, I spoke to her. She was puzzled at first – looking for me when she heard my voice. I quickly let her know that I was still at the top of the mountain, but it was important she pay attention to my voice.

The angelic coach let me know about an alligator in the water behind her and that I should lead her to it. I told her that she would need to trust me on this next part. I told her that she may be scared, but that it was important to trust me. I told her to turn to her right and walk back along the edge of the tidal pool – that there was something she needed to see. In a third person, aerial style view, I could see her walking toward the alligator in the crystal clear tidal pool. Once she reached it, the angel took over the conversation and experience.

I was then time shifted forward to when we both reached the barracks again. She thanked me for all of my help. It seemed the adrenalin rush of the slide, coupled with the teaching, caused her to have an increasing fondness for me. I saw a softness in her eyes when she looked at me. I could see that I now had her complete trust...and a Love that had ignited inside of her. I never asked about the experience with the alligator for that was hers and hers alone. And while I did not think about it specifically at that moment, as I am journaling this, it should be most important to make note that one of the first shared experiences that Bryan and I had in the heavens contained an alligator in a clear pool. For me, it swam at me and I had to have faith that God would keep me protected.

Rebirth III

For Bryan, it was the same way. It was the first great test I had in the heavens...and the first with great lucidity. But anyway....returning to this experience...

When we returned to the barracks, she had moved beds to an all-female section. I imagine this is because her feelings for me were more obvious to the angelic elders, and they did not want us to falter by way of sexual desires during our training. I walked over to her new bed, and we talked for a while. I saw the bag that she had initially brought with her sitting on the bed. I commented how it was similar to mine. She told me I could look inside it. As I opened it, I pulled out a travel pillow and laughed and said I had the same one. I pulled out a smaller bag filled with what I thought to be clothes. I laughed again saying I had the same smaller bag as well, but that mine was a different color. At the bottom of her backpack was a soft sleeping bag – the softest I have ever felt. It had the softness meant for an angel. The sensation was overwhelming to me. The softness and seeing her there next to me caused me to begin to lose harmony...but I held on.

We talked longer, flirting a good bit of the time. At first, I pushed her away from me. But as time progressed, I warmed up to it. She continued to seek me which helped her break down my emotional wall. Days passed and we talked about her past. She explained to me she was from "White County" (or something that sounded like that) – a "county on the border." At first I thought she meant the border of Kentucky, since I am in Tennessee currently, but there is not a White County in Kentucky. She pulled out a map of the United

The Written (cont'd)

States and she said, "See? Do you see it?" I commented that I did even though I did not. I did not want to frustrate her. As I thought long and hard about where she was from, I lost harmony and returned from the heavens. At first I thought I was in my body and began to journal, but then I realized it was a false awakening. I had to commit the experience to memory again so that I could write it down when I returned to my body. At this point, I jettisoned back to my body where I was able to journal this.

June 9, 2014

While everything seemed very scattered in the experience this morning, I became very lucid/aware of my surroundings near the end of the experience. In the beginning, I was at war with a shape-shifting warrior clan. I could never tell who the enemy was on appearance alone, which made hunting down the evil spirits extremely hard. The setting was a verdant landscape with rocky mountains. It was a very open environment. But each time shape-shifting evil spirits were caught, they died vicious deaths. I would not necessarily say they were gory since they were not made of blood and flesh, but they were still biological.

When I became most aware of my experience, I was standing in front of the flat-faced side of a cliff. There was an evil spirit who was trying to blend in with the rock face. The others I was with (in the small army) were throwing stones at

Rebirth III

the spirit, but kept missing. I stepped up to try to throw a stone. When I missed, it hit the face of the cliff and bounced off heading to the ground. But before it could hit the ground, it impacted the remains of a destroyed spirit, causing it to violently rupture. The biological goo that made up its insides hit me in the face. This is the moment that I realized where I was. The feeling of the goo hitting my face was as real as it could ever have felt on Earth. After this, my four-person army continued to hunt down invisible demons. Over the course of the hunting, I lost harmony and returned to my body.

June 11, 2014

I tried taking 200mg of B6 last night just to see if it had any impact on the clarity of my experiences in the heavens. Unfortunately, as vivid as the experiences were, it seemed more like a roller coaster of mind-bending travels. Nothing held harmony, but everything was extremely vivid (if that makes any sense). The rate of traveling was so fast, I could not balance and focus into the experiences. The best I could describe it would be to say my mind was on a roller coaster traveling at breakneck speeds through the heavens, but so fast that I could not focus on anything.

The Written (cont'd)

June 12, 2014

Since B6 proved to be such a crazy experience, I decided to try 3mg of Melatonin last night. I figured since I have been struggling with the frequency of my travels to the heavens, it could not hurt to try some of the vitamin supplements that are talked about with lucid-dreamers. I am now convinced B6 is one of the vitamins that helps the body and soul separate in the mind, but it does not help with the travels to the heavens. I cannot see any reason to try it again. Now after trying Melatonin, I can say that it too causes crazy experiences, and is not an answer either. In fact, I have felt so drained today I will never touch the stuff again. Overall, I think the last two nights serve more as "scientific experiments" to validate the divinity in my heavenly experiences.

About thirty minutes after taking the Melatonin, I began meditating. My mind started spinning uncontrollably. It was the same spinning that happens upon the soul's departure from the body, but it was so much more vicious that it caused me to lose harmony. After that, I did not experience anything else other than "swirly" gibberish dreams. While I will not touch Melatonin again, I think I can now understand how this particular hormone affects the body and soul during meditation.

Rebirth III

June 14, 2014
Daily Experiences

Yesterday and today were so divine. Though I will not write about it specifically, these are the interactions from the last two days:

6/13 – Michael
6/13 – Riley
6/13 – Candace (last one)
6/14 – Virginia (gas station attendant)
6/14 – Virginia (Hardees worker)

June 14, 2014
Afternoon

During meditation, I was abruptly startled into awareness by an angel telling me, "No." It began with me standing in front of a tall, narrow locker (like would be found in a locker room). It was somewhat abstractly sitting in the middle of the room (which appeared to have a road passing through it). I was asking a group of angels that were located to my right if I could open the locker. I was standing with a female during the conversation. When I heard, "No," I replied by taking two "hops" closer to the group of angels. I said, "Perhaps if I do two, eight-inch spaces…" This appeared to be the same distance I travelled in each of the hops. But again, I heard, "No.

The Written (cont'd)

Do not open it." At that point I lost harmony and returned to my body.

June 15, 2014

The experience this morning felt a lot like the experiences from months past. It began with me crossing a street with someone. I suddenly realized there was a car intentionally trying to run me over, so I darted across the remainder of the street. The car crashed into the utility poles behind us as we made it across the street. From there, my guide and I headed to a "book club" at someone's house. We entered a nice neighborhood. At the house hosting the "book club," I learned that one of the houses in the neighborhood had a squatter living in it. It was unfortunate because the squatter brought attention to himself, which was causing him to be removed.

The owner of the home we were in explained how many of the houses in the neighborhood were grandiose and much, much larger than the house the squatter was in – but that size did not matter. He took us outside for us to see some of the house sizes. While the houses all varied in sizes, it appeared that they were built to the size of the angel residing within it versus built larger or smaller based on square footage alone. For example, the house hosting the book club was one of the largest in the neighborhood, completely dwarfing other houses around it because the angel living there was much larger. The house dimensions had to be built to accommodate the angelic

Rebirth III

size. All in all, every house would have been over ten-thousand square feet at the smallest scale, if they were observed in earthly equivalents.

As my guide and I wandered through the neighborhood, we went to where the squatter was living. The house was incredibly nice, large, surrounded by trees, and would not have been brought to anyone's attention under normal circumstances. When we walked inside, the smell was awful. It was clear the person living there did not care about hygiene. Items were collected and stashed in corners of the room. I made a comment that the person living there must be a klepto. It was clear that the squatter did not deserve to live in such a nice place since he/she was not taking care of it. Overall, the house was a wreck.

While we were looking around, we heard the man try to enter into the house. As soon as that happened, we began to chase after him. I think we were trying to "save him" so he was not killed in the "eviction." But, all he knew was that he had been caught. He ran quickly and lost us in the woods. I exited the woods on another street and continued on his trail. Eventually, the sky became dark as we reached a metropolitan area. I was on a sidewalk with a building on my right side when I began to notice the sky. I made a comment to my angelic guide about "the sky always opening up like a flood on a girl's period before a tornado." I have no idea why I said that, nor have I ever said anything like that before on Earth or in the heavens. The angelic guide appeared nervous.

The Written (cont'd)

Suddenly, the sky started spinning and a tornado began to form beside me. I ran down the street pulling at door handles on the buildings. Eventually, one opened and I jumped in. I pressed myself into a corner and covered my head. After the storm passed, the wall above me was burst open by the angel's fist. He pulled the wall open large enough to pull me out. He said, "I have a really bad feeling about this." I asked, "Why?" but he would not say. We continued scouring the wrecked city looking for the angel's sister and a girl that I apparently knew. We never found them. The next day I went to school, but no one had seen either girl since the storm. At that point, I lost harmony and returned to my body.

June 16, 2014

While this journal entry will lack detail, I did travel to the heavens last night. It seems like the experiences are beginning to pick up again in both volume and clarity. The experiences are still not where they once were, but they are getting better. This morning I prayed for help from the angels that I have been introduced to. In fact, the last several days I have prayed to God and then attempted to invoke the angels through meditation. I have to believe this is helping somewhat. At the very least, the angels know I need help finding balance again.

Rebirth III

June 17, 2014

This morning was filled with numerous trips. This began to feel like familiar territory with both the frequency and the sensations in my body during meditation, which resulted in the type of experiences to which I have been accustomed. Again, I prayed to God and followed it up with meditations where I tried to invoke the angels I know. Of course I am extremely careful to demonstrate my faith in God and understanding of the angels as messengers of His divine message. I think this is helping in my growth.

During meditation, my soul became unbound with my body, and I found myself standing before a great angel. I was accompanied by a guardian angel/guide. I asked the great angel before me why I was experiencing so many challenges returning to the heavens. Specifically, I asked, "Why am I not being allowed back in?" In response, the angel showed me a large rectangular box – similar to the size of a coffin – but definitely not a coffin. It was placed in the trunk of a car to my left. The box was disproportionately large to the trunk, but somehow the laws of physics did not apply here. I watched as the massive box was pushed into the trunk in its entirety.

As I stared at the bizarre message being told to me, the angel before me spoke. He told me, "What [I was] looking for was inside [the box, I assume], and that they had been wanting [me] to look for it." At that point I was jettisoned from the location and back to my body...or so I thought. I fought

The Written (cont'd)

through three or four false awakenings wherein each experience I thought I was scribing my experiences in my journal. I would review the sequence of events in my head over and over, pushing it into my earthly memory. However, by the time I realized I was not quite back to my body, I lost some additional details. So, this recount of events is similar in concept to how a message gets lost in the "telephone game" over time…except this time it was with myself.

There were at least three more experiences in the heavens after I was able to write down the experience with the box and the trunk. However, each experience echoed similarities with the false awakenings which ultimately caused me to think I had written down all of the details. Unfortunately, this was not the case. What I can recall with extreme clarity is that I sang "Amazing Grace" with a chorus of angels at one point. There were other songs that we sang as well – songs that I would never have been able to remember the words on Earth, but I sang with impressive recollection in the heavens. I also had other conversations with angels throughout the experiences. Overall, the encounters were very swirly, which leads me to understand my ability to interpret the encounters was tantamount to "getting my spiritual feet wet" again. Every experience was mesmerizing, but I was unable to maintain focus and increase clarity in the moments. Hopefully more of the details will come back to me later today.

Rebirth III

June 18, 2014

This morning's experiences were not very clear...with the exception of two small portions. In one part of the experience I was talking to an angel about sex. The conversation was philosophical and not geared toward anything lustful. The subject matter was more on the purpose and the intent of sex on Earth. During the conversation I said that I was worried that any way of releasing sexual energy on Earth would cause me "to lose my astral projection mojo" which I seem to be teetering on the edge of reclaiming. There was not much resolve in the conversation (or at least not that had any clarity for my earthly mind).

Time went on, and there was another part of the experience that came into focus. The angel I was speaking with showed me a book. This book was apparently a book I had written. I picked it up. It was hardcover. I have not published my books, nor have I self-printed any of my writings in anything other than paperback. I was slightly confused at the book I was holding, which I am sure was part of the reason the experience came into view with such clarity. Often something out of the ordinary is the trigger to clarity in an experience. The angel and I discussed the book for some time and the conversation ended with me feeling resolve and purpose in writing. While the angel never told me directly what I should do about writing, I felt my overall purpose was outlined for me in the conversation.

The Written (cont'd)

June 19, 2014

Before bed tonight I said a special prayer. For some reason I have been feeling compelled to speak to angels directly, but this seems to be in conflict with everything we are raised to learn about our relationship with God. Since my relationship is on a different playing field than I would have ever thought it could be, I decided to speak to God about my internal conflict. I prayed for clarity in understanding if speaking to angels (or invoking angels to appear) would be a conflict in my relationship with Him. I explained that I understand He is everywhere, and in all things. And, it is through Him that angels came to be. I explained that I understood how angels speak His voice and His words. I wanted to make sure that God understood my heart was not to turn away from Him, but rather to grow my understanding of the heavens around me. In the end of my prayer I felt peace in His understanding of my intentions, though to anyone reading these words I would emphasize that everyone's relationship and actions with God and the angels should be unique for his own circumstances.

So, after my prayer, I decided to try to invoke each of the four archangels. Honestly, I was not sure what would happen. It seemed something out of a fairytale for anything to actually happen. As I meditated, I asked each angel to join me by my side (according to their own respective cardinal directions). After speaking to each angel, I would pause and wait until I felt a presence at my side. While I was meditating, there was a

Rebirth III

clear difference in energy around me as I invoked each angel. But after I had invoked them, I had no idea what to do. So, I asked them to join me in my visions. I waited and tried to allow my soul to become unbound from my body, but I think my excitement of potentially seeing the angels overcame me, and I could not find harmony with the moment.

Eventually, I became tired and fell asleep. Shortly after falling asleep, I found myself in the heavens. My mind had not yet registered where I was, for the surroundings were so Earth-like that I felt it was just another waking day on Earth. I was standing beside a large pool watching my daughter, Georgia, swim around. She was having tremendous fun, and I could not help but be lost in the moment. As I was standing there, I heard my name called out on my right side. I looked over and saw four people sitting around a table with a blue umbrella. As I looked at them, one of the four people motioned for me to come over to them. I walked over but suddenly felt nervous turning my attention away from Georgia.

Each of the four people were happy and smiling. I was very cordial to them, but told them, "Hold on. Let me make sure Georgia is okay first." I began to turn and walk back to the pool to check on Georgia...and that is when it hit me. I was not on Earth. I was in heaven. The surroundings suddenly fell into focus as I apparently still had to find harmony in the moment. I smiled, knowing that I was in the presence of angels. I turned back to the table having only taken a couple of steps away.

The Written (cont'd)

The angels saw my recognition, and I theirs. I knew that the four beings were the four archangels that I had summoned. I immediately began joking with one of them about "putting them on hold" while I checked on Georgia. We all laughed about it. The disrespect I had shown them (however cordial I had tried to be) was so comical because I was naive to the situation that we all just had to laugh. One of the angels and I chatted much more than the others. I felt confident that it was Uriel. The conversation did not last much longer than what I have just written before I lost harmony with the moment and returned to my body where I immediately journaled the experience. I was overcome with joy. The angels responded to my call. And, while I will not abuse this newfound ability, I now know that in the appropriate time, they will be there for me.

June 20, 2014

The experience this morning was very brief. I have begun to wonder if the time of year has anything to do with the strength of the heavenly experiences. Last year – the year when I began to have more frequent heavenly experiences – held struggles for me during the summer months. Bryan and I had many conversations about the dullness of the experiences in the midst of summer.

The experience this morning was only about as clear as what I can recount. I was captured in a desert landscape. I

Rebirth III

have no idea why I was in the desert, but I was in the middle of a barren wasteland. Perhaps it was metaphorical of the dryness of my experiences recently. As I searched for some sign of life, a group of beings appeared and captured me. They tied my hands behind my back. I was not scared, and perhaps my jovial nature caused them to become frustrated with me. I joked about it being easier on them if my hands were untied. It just seemed unwarranted. They were not amused.

I was caravanned through the desert to their leader. When I met their leader (who I assume was an angel, and they, the angel's helpers), I lost harmony with the experience. I returned to my body and tried to return. In the wake of trying to leave my body, I experienced several failed "takeoffs." Each time, the "takeoff" was filled with gorgeous clouds in colors not of this Earth. The clouds were yellow-like and pink-like – very artsy in appearance. The failed attempts to leave my body and travel to the heavens were unlike any I have ever experienced before, and irreproducible in color and appearance.

June 22, 2014

While I have not experienced any travels to the heavens in the last two days, today I have had a terrible headache. It is unlike any headache I have experienced before. While it is not distracting or painful, it has persisted all day. It feels like the entire crown of my skull has a weave of thousands of neural

The Written (cont'd)

connectors all flaring up with arthritis. Ha. While I know that neurons cannot have arthritis, this is the only way I can explain it. I would not even have taken note of this in my journal except I had a realization. Today is the summer solstice.

My headache began at noon today, which means that my brain began to experience turbulence at the highest point of the longest day of the year. I fully believe they are interconnected due to the way my mind, body, and soul are integrally aligned. It also stands to reason that as the sun is at its peak, that it would be tantamount to one side of a pendulum (the winter solstice being the other side). When the mind, body, and soul are so in-tune, it makes sense that the extremity of the sun's alignment would cause disruption to the inner harmony of the soul. I have long understood that the greatest energy for the soul to harness arrives through the moonlight, where the energy is polarized in one direction (unlike during the day where the energy flows two ways). Think of the moon as a mirror that focuses a beam of energy down to Earth, whereas the sun is like an explosion of energy all over the Earth. Anyway, that is how I view it at least. So, if you think of the energy like that, then it makes sense that my headache would be tied specifically to the summer solstice...and this is where eastern and western science begin to collide in reason and rationale.

Rebirth III

June 23, 2014

My experiences this morning were, again, brief and lacking in clarity. The experiences began with a beautiful blue sky filling my periphery. I watched as an orb, glowing white with angelic wings, flew in front of me. It was as if it was leading me somewhere. I have never seen anything like this before, so I was mesmerized in the moment. I arrived somewhere standing in the sand, where the surroundings fell into view. I was standing on a beach. I walked past a game of beach volleyball. The net was trimmed in white with black netting. There were six people playing the game. As I walked by, the volleyball came flying toward me. I bumped it with both hands clutched together which must have appeared like I was in elementary school learning to play. As the ball collided with my hands, I mis-hit it, and it went off to the right. I apologized for mis-hitting the ball. All I wanted to do was volley it back to them in a smooth and suave fashion. Instead, I made myself look amateur. As a girl ran off to get the ball, I noticed that the game was coed. I suppose it would not mean that much to me in a normal scenario, but for some reason, it was important that I take note of the fact it was coed. In reflection, I suppose it was important to see the duality in the whole experience – boys, girls, black and white netting, etc. That is all I recall before losing harmony and returning to my body.

The Written (cont'd)

June 24, 2014

This morning was filled with very swirly experiences in which I cannot recount anything. I was in Rome, GA, to visit my ailing grandfather.

June 25, 2014

On my way to Florida, I stopped overnight in Rome, GA, where I visited my grandfather in the hospital the following morning. He had just received another ablation surgery and had complications following the procedure. When I showed up in his hospital room, I could tell that he was excited to see me. My heart broke for him. It was hard to see his soul holding onto his unbreakable body so hard, while God is trying to call him home. I do not wish for my grandfather to pass, but I know that God has great plans for him when his time comes. As we spoke, I could see all of the life he could muster in the midst of the pain he was experiencing, bubble to the surface.

We spoke about Florida while I held his hand with my two hands. As I held his hand, his heart monitor flat lined, and remained flat lined while we held hands. My grandmother searched for ways to shut off the beeping. His heart had clearly not stopped, but the monitor was not agreeing with it. I truly believe that for the few minutes I held his hand, that his soul clung to my life force, allowing his body to rest for just a few minutes. Maybe that is why the heart monitor flat lined.

Rebirth III

Somehow, perhaps, he had clung to my life force and not his own. I knew during those moments that his grip was strong and he did not want to let go. I could tell that he felt the spirit flowing through me, though I doubt he recognized it as such. I think his soul knew instinctively how to latch on to me, whether or not his mind understood what was happening. I do not want to say that I healed him, or anything like that, but I do believe that I helped him in whatever purpose God had intended for me to do.

We spoke about Florida, and Granddad told me about different fish he Loved to eat. He told me about how much he Loved grouper and barracuda. He kept saying we would have to go eat fish "when he arrived." His soul was speaking through him. His mind left it unfiltered. During our conversation, my soul was speaking directly to his despite the outward, earthly appearance. Everything we spoke about was in terms of heaven and paradise carefully charaded in earthly references. I could tell my mother and grandmother knew something was happening between us, but they were not ready to listen. They spent their time trying to get the heart monitor to quit beeping, while remaining oblivious to the cause. At the end of our conversation, I told my granddad that "I'll see you soon."

Those words were not my own. I am not writing this to take credit for something creative or of my own doing. Instead, I observed as my body was on autopilot, serving as a vessel for God to speak directly to my grandfather. I saw in my grandfather's eyes that his soul recognized he was speaking to God. It

The Written (cont'd)

was a moment that is permanently etched into my mind. My grandfather kept wanting to say something else, but could not find the words. I saw his soul speechless, trapped in a body holding on. But somehow, we both knew what was happening. After we said our goodbyes, I stepped to the bathroom on my way out. While I did not have any sadness overcoming my body, as I looked in the mirror while I washed my hands, my soul was overcome in spiritual recognition. I cried. I was not physically sad. This was my soul crying in recognition of everything it had just witnessed – the vessel through which it served for our Father to speak to my grandfather. The words "I'll see you soon" resonated throughout my body. Those words shook me to my core and would serve as a guiding light on the remainder of my journey to Florida that day.

June 29, 2014

I was walking through the heavens with several familiar spirits. I could not identify their names, but I have been with them before. I also had a guardian angel with me (though unseen in form). As we walked, we talked and told stories about life. We joked about some of the hard times we had experienced on Earth and laughed about our lives. As we walked through the streets of heaven – led by my guardian – I became aware of another presence. It was familiar – a female presence that I always seem to engage in spiritual fights with. Suddenly the world around us faded as just a spotlight fell upon us and

Rebirth III

the girl. I recognized her as my mom, but not my earthly mom. I told her that she should just leave us alone – that we were having a good time. She just laughed. I said, "You will regret it. I am even stronger than the last time we fought."

She looked at me surprised. I could tell she was curious about how I had become stronger (or even if I had become stronger). I sent her a warning burst of energy from my hands. It rattled her, but did not do any harm. Really all it did was cause us to engage in fighting. She looked at me and said, "Oh, now you've messed up." She then unleashed a hadoken-style burst of rainbow light that pushed me backwards with a great burst of energy. I stood up off of my butt and laughed. It was not arrogance or confidence that was permeating my being. Rather, it was a confident joy in the entertainment of the moment. I then hit her with two or thee special moves that were something like out of a video game. The final hit in the combination was a flying-uppercut. I hit her hard, and she was knocked backwards. The intent was not to injure each other, but rather to show dominance.

She came back at me with some new moves of her own. These were moves I had not seen before. I could tell she had been holding back in our previous sparrings. We sparred back and forth for a couple of iterations before I told her to leave us alone. I was tired of the petty nature of the demonstration, and I knew I had the strength of God on my side. As I was making jokes with her about how I was becoming stronger, there was a loud rumble. I knew it was the strength of God warning of His presence. This is usually the moment that I begin to lose har-

The Written (cont'd)

mony, but this time was different. I was not losing harmony at all. Instead, the clarity of the moment was increasing.

As the rumbling became louder, the female angel began to unleash another rainbow burst of light. That is when the rumbling behind me burst into a rainbow tunnel of light shooting high into the heavens from the ground around me. The rainbow colors dimmed, while the funnel remained. I could see that a great man was standing inside of the light burst. It was God. His voice boomed in the direction of the female angel before me. "Stahhhhpppp!" he exclaimed. The female angel was puzzled and put her hands down by her side. I looked at her and began to say, "See, I told you I had the power of God on my side." But as those words began to leave my lips, I felt sadness for being involved in something my Father had to come down and intervene in. It seemed such a petty moment to invoke the highest power of all. I immediately felt ashamed and turned, falling to my knees and bowing before him. I said, "Forgive me Father, for I know not what I do."

I heard a bellowing laugh. I looked up, and God allowed me to see his form. This was the first time that the rumble of God (that I have summoned in past heavenly experiences) had taken a direct form. He said, "Sorry? What do you have to be sorry for? There is no reason to be sorry!" I said, "But Father, I didn't mean to get you involved in this, I'm still learning." He laughed – a jolly, old man. He was clearly entertained with me. He said in the most loving way he could, "Son, you are learning exactly in the way I want you to learn."

Rebirth III

I looked at him puzzled. I asked Him if He could say that again because I was still sorting out the words and wanted to make sure I understood Him correctly. He did not think twice and began to repeat His words. He said, "You are learning in the way I want you to learn – for you." The emphasis was on "for you." The words carried a greater archetypal conveyance in the moment. I understood the archetypal meaning to be, "The way you are learning is in a way that I (God) specifically have crafted for you – crafted in such a way that will help you grow as a leader."

As the words resonated within my mind, I was awestruck by the gravity they carried. But His words did not stop there. I could tell He knew I understood His words. It was at that point that He kneeled down on one knee and then leaned down to me and whispered, "But you have a lot to learn if you are going to replace her as head of the world one day." He looked at me with jolly confidence. The words were spoken with happiness. I looked up at Him, stunned. I was sure I had misunderstood Him. He then repeated Himself more loudly and clearly as He was standing up so that she would hear His words too. I had not misheard His words. The words were repeated just as I had originally heard them. And just like that, He burst into a tunnel of rainbow light and thunder and vanished. I returned to my body.

He was the largest angelic form I have ever seen in the heavens. Even the "elder angels" that are clearly represented as much greater in size than me paled in comparison to His size. If I am six feet tall, the angels I was walking around with

The Written (cont'd)

in the beginning of the experiences were at least ten feet tall. The female angel that I identified as "my mom" must have been twelve to fifteen feet tall – much taller than the angels I was standing with. As for the appearance of God, I can hardly rationalize His size. I was taller than His big toe, but not much taller. I was eye level with part of his shin. When he appeared, He was wearing a white robe. He had golden-gray curly hair that was just above shoulder length. It was not poufy, or wild. Instead, it carried a perfect sheen with it and was weighted down with the curls. It glistened in the rays of the light around Him. His eyes were a steel gray that words cannot describe. He wore brown leather sandals that had a strap around the ankle and one around the big toe. I noticed his sandals with such clarity because I was standing nearly eye-to-eye with His right foot. When He spoke to me, He kneeled down and His knee was even much taller than me.

As for the female angel that I sparred with, she was more "alien" in comparison. I would describe her as "svelte" with radiant blue eyes. She had a milky white complexion. Her eyes were bulbous and her face was an inverted teardrop shape. Her chin was almost pointed due to how the teardrop formed at her chin. She was solemn and stark. I do not ever get a sense of happiness or emotions from her, but there was a stark respect about her. All of her features were small. Her frame was thin and slender. She had long, straight blonde hair. She usually has appeared wearing a Cinderella-baby-blue robe.

Rebirth III

July 1, 2014

As I began to meditate this morning, I became aware of faces in my periphery. There were faces everywhere. I knew instantly they were souls in some type of gathering spot. They all had rainbow faces. For some reason, rainbow colors seem to be appearing more frequently in my experiences. One of the souls tried to speak to me. I heard its voice, but could not find enough harmony to bring him into focus. I spoke to him and asked him to hold on while I tried to balance myself. I was never quite able to, and lost harmony with the moment.

As I "spun out" of that experience, I surprisingly arrived back in the heavens. I recognized where I was instantly. An angel stood next to me. I immediately tried to spin myself around so that I would not fall out of the moment. When I spun, I found balance. Suddenly, everything fell into view. The angel and I spoke for a while as he led me through the heavens. Eventually it was time for my lesson. I opened a door and found myself standing with Bryan.

We were in the doorway of an apartment. Bryan was closer to the door. I had a bottle in my right hand. It was in the shape of a Miller Light bottle, but did not contain any alcohol. It contained about a half-inch of some benign liquid in the bottom. I told Bryan that I thought God was testing me on drinking. Bryan looked at me confused. He did not know where I got the bottle. In fact, when I opened the door, I did not have a bottle. It was only when Bryan looked down and

The Written (cont'd)

back up that the bottle was in my hand. I told Bryan that whatever was in the bottle was non-alcoholic. He was still confused.

Suddenly I had an overwhelming urge to drink. My mouth became dry. I chugged the beverage. It was somehow bottomless. I drank like an animal on the verge of death. Bryan stared in disbelief. When it was all done, I had Bryan take me for a car ride down the street to see if I got drunk. About halfway to the destination, I shook myself out of it and said, "See, now we can go back. I told you that it was not important what was in the bottle." Bryan was still confused – and honestly, my mind was still trying to rationalize the experience my soul was having.

When we arrived back at the apartment, Bryan and I were standing in opposite places from before. This time my throat became scratchy. I told Bryan to watch me. He was still confused. Suddenly I had something in my hand that I started consuming – like a cigar. Whatever the cigar put out was the same abrasion as I was feeling in my throat. But, the two like-abrasions countered each other causing the scratchiness to go away. At that moment, I heard a "ding" like from a hand bell. I immediately returned to my body and opened my eyes.

The bell was letting me know that I successfully understood whatever the lesson was trying to tell me. The words I was telling Bryan before the bell dinged were "See, nothing is bad for you. Anything is okay but it is how much you consume that makes an effect. Even a non-alcoholic drink can still be bad, but it is whatever you intend to use it as." These words

Rebirth III

were different than my thoughts when I began the lesson. In the beginning, I thought I was being tested on drinking. In the end, I realized that the test was more of a lesson in understanding moderation than on the test of drinking.

July 2, 2014

After having an entire day to process the experience from the previous night, my earthly mind has continued to wrestle with the possibility that drinking is "okay" if done in moderation or with the right intent. I prayed for additional clarity on the experience from the previous night. As I meditated, I again found myself in a similar situation as the prior experience. The angel that was helping me with my lesson role-played where Bryan was the night before. It was an incredibly long experience. Because I did not write it down immediately upon returning to my body, I did lose some clarity on it. But, the gist of the experience was that, "Everything I do is to be done in the opposite space for it to manifest." It was all energy driven. Somehow I could "reset" an outcome by placing my hand into a "zero sum" location. In the heavenly experience, this was placing my hand into a beam of light or darkness depending on the situation. It felt like the overall experience rested upon a yin-yang balance. While it does not necessarily help clarify whether drinking is bad, it still supports that anything is okay in moderation with the right intention. Intention was a key component to the experience. Also, "resets" were important.

The Written (cont'd)

July 6, 2014

This morning I found myself in the heavens, but in a scenario that added clarity to my present life. The experience began with me walking into my apartment. It was supposed to be my apartment in Fort Lauderdale, but there were noticeable differences. As I walked around, I heard the voices of two people. I was not scared, even though no one should have been in my apartment. When I rounded a corner, the two men looked confused. They asked if I lived here, to which I responded that I did. I looked at them and said, "Oh. You must be my new roommate. I wasn't sure when I leased the unit if I'd have a roommate. I didn't think I would because it is a one-bedroom, but I guess they opened up that other area as a room for you."

They each looked at me and began a friendly conversation about moving in. They asked if I was going to keep all of my stuff in the living room since I had moved in expecting to live without roommates. I responded that the only thing I really cared about was to hear and see movies with my setup – that my Apogee Rosetta was my pride and joy. We then chatted about stereos, and my mind flashed back to an earlier part of my experience in the heavens where I was backstage with a couple of people talking about their speakers. They were using three Apogee speakers which sounded beautiful for whatever the purpose of the performance was.

Rebirth III

As my mind flashed back, I mentioned to the men in my apartment that I thought I Loved my setup, but that a couple other friends had a full Apogee speaker setup that sounded amazing. The two men were extremely excited about the quality and fidelity of the Apogees. Eventually, one of the men told me to check out his room. I was hesitant, but he seemed excited to show me his setup.

I walked into his room to find myself standing on a black and red carpet. The room was dark and colder than the rest of the apartment. The carpet looked almost like a red and black leopard print. Suddenly, I knew I was standing in the presence of evil. I tried to maintain my composure and pretend I had not noticed. I changed the subject to how I wanted to live by myself, and that they needed to move out. The man seemed frustrated that I did not want a roommate, but did not put up too much of a fight. Eventually, I walked out of his room and back into mine, where I read the terms of my lease and contacted the owner. My lease stated that, "Due to the fluctuations in the economy, there was the potential for the apartment to be double booked upon first moving in. If this is the case, the owner would make sure the first tenant's terms would be upheld and that roommates would NOT be allowed." After speaking with the owner, I was assured it would all be taken care of. At that moment I lost harmony with the heavens and returned to my body.

I immediately recognized that the experience was metaphorical of letting temptation into my life. The "roommate" was metaphorical of the figurative devil on one's shoulder.

The Written (cont'd)

The terms of the lease was metaphorical of the potential of figuring out the waters upon arrival in my new place. The fact that a roommate would not be allowed was obviously metaphorical of the protection that God has for me while I am in this new locale. I immediately reached for my phone to journal the experience. After taking down my notes of the experience, I then transferred money from my one checking account to my main account in demonstration of my prayer to God the prior evening (this had to do with the lesson at Hard Rock). As soon as I hit "transfer," my phone buzzed with seven emails. This was God letting me know He heard me and saw the demonstration of my intentions.

July 7, 2014

Before I went to bed tonight, I said my prayers in typical fashion. After I ended my prayers, I felt a strong sensation in my body – as if another presence was in my room. I immediately felt a recognition of it being Uriel. This type of feeling/recognition has not happened previously to me, so I thought I would "test the waters" per se by speaking to the presence. Everything about this scenario was brand new. I have never felt a presence and then attempted to converse with the presence, but I thought I would try.

I began by saying, "Uriel…" I did not have a well thought-out plan of action, so I paused briefly as I began to think of what I would say to Uriel (or even if I was speaking to

Rebirth III

the right angelic presence). Honestly, I did not even know if it was Uriel, but my soul identified the presence as such so I went with it. As soon as I paused after saying Uriel's name, there were two distinct "knocks" that originated from my ceiling or outer wall. I am on the third floor of the building, so I knew it could not come from outside. The unit above me is vacant, so there is no one that could have caused the sound. I immediately recognized the knocks as Uriel's acknowledgement of her presence.

I lay in my bed speechless. I suppose I should not be surprised at anything anymore, but this was bridging the spiritual and earthly planes in a way that would be seen as supernatural. Oftentimes, as it is popularized in movies and on television, "psychics" ask for spirits to "knock" in order to identify their presence. I always had assumed this was just the easiest way for the "fake psychic" to fake supernatural interactions. And while I assumed that at one time in history, someone may have actually communicated with spirits through "knocks," I assumed that the majority of the fake psychics today ride on these half-truths in order to maintain credibility. But here I was, lying in bed, speaking the name of an angelic presence and having it respond with two knocks. My mind reeled with possibilities. While I may have spoken with the archangels in my heavenly experiences, to see it manifest in communication through words from my mortal body was befuddling. I thought about the gravity of the moment and smiled. I said aloud, "I heard the knocks. I know you are

The Written (cont'd)

here. Thank you for letting me know." From there, I decided to leave it alone and attempt to get some sleep.

During the night, I was awakened several times to a strong spinning sensation. It was all I could do to maintain brief harmony with the experiences. All I knew is that my bed was being held down on all four sides with the force of a great gravity. It was being controlled by the great angels. All I knew was that, "everything was super heavy for the size of the angels." This occurred multiple times where I kept losing harmony with the moment. However, the angels never allowed me to lose harmony, so it continued to feel like a spinning sensation until I found harmony with the moment again. Eventually the experience ended, and I felt like I had been flown through a hurricane, but in the safety of angels. I never saw them, nor did they speak. All I knew is they were there, on all four sides of my bed.

I journaled the experience and prayed to God about all that I had felt. Afterwards, I tried to meditate before falling asleep. As I meditated, I was taken to a room with at least two angels around me. The room was white. The angels were hidden from view. I knew they were extremely large and were elders. They imparted a lot of knowledge to me. I eventually became curious about the names of the angels I was speaking with. But, while I never asked, I suppose they knew. One of the angels placed his hand in front of me and pointed to two places on a table. The table was white, and the two places that were indicated to me to observe were marked with two small strips of masking tape covering something.

Rebirth III

The angel began to peel each of the two pieces of tape away. Underneath the tape were words written in Hebrew-Aramaic. They were golden and illuminated. When the hand peeled away the first name, I tried very hard to understand what it said. I do not know Hebrew-Aramaic and have only lightly studied the alphabet. Most of my understanding of Hebrew is based on the original-pictograph form. The word contained four letters. Read right to left, I knew the first character was Kaph. The others became a blur as I realized I recognized one of the letters. I think the other letters were aleph-shin-yud, which would make the word Casi...or something similar.

As I read the word, the angel peeled away the other piece of tape and said the word beneath it. The word boomed out in the silence. The word was "Hagar." As I heard the word, I knew it was not the word I was trying to read, but rather the other word I had not yet attempted to read. I glanced over at it and the word was out-of-focus, but glowing light through the golden print. I knew I had been given the names of the two angels in the room with me, but I was still trying to digest all of the information. As I did, I lost harmony with the moment and returned to my body where I journaled the notes from the experience.

The following morning, I looked up Hagar, being unfamiliar with the person in the Bible. It became evident that it was Hagar, second wife of Abraham. This was extremely intriguing. I wondered if my "spiritual mother" was possibly Hagar. That would put my bloodline in the line of Abraham.

The Written (cont'd)

It was a very interesting thought. As I read about Hagar, it led me to the stories of Isaac and Ishmael. Ishmael was the son of Hagar and Abraham. Isaac was the son of Abraham and his first wife, Sarah. As I read this, I realized that the first word I attempted to read in Hebrew-Aramaic could be "Isaac" but reversed. Hebrew is read right-to-left, which is the way I was attempting to read it, but I suppose it is possible I reversed the direction. If so, the word revealed to me was the Hebrew word for Isaac in reverse, "Yud, Shin, Aleph, Kaph." Continued research on the Hebrew letters also produced insight that it could have been the name for the angel Cassiel if read in the direction I read it in. So, whether it represented Cassiel or Isaac, I cannot be sure. But, I do know without a doubt that Hagar is one of the angels I was interacting with.

July 10, 2014

During meditation before bed, I found my soul standing in a bedroom. I heard my voice calling out from the bedroom into the living room to a girl. It was at this point I realized I was calling out to someone and did not know who or why she was in my apartment. I looked at my bed to see if it was a spouse or girlfriend. As I observed the bed, I noticed it was encased in glass walls. The glass extended to the ceiling. No one was inside of it, and I could not even detect a way to get inside of the glass cage. I began trying to imagine the girl inside of the glass cage, but was unsuccessful. I wondered if the

Rebirth III

glass was some sort of way to sexualize the bedroom, but those thoughts did not make sense to me.

As I stood before the bed, I began asking who "she" was. This question was as abstract as it could be. I did not even know why I was asking about this particular girl or even what the circumstances were. As I asked the question, I was transported to a restaurant where a 5'7" blonde girl began speaking to me. Her hair was shorter in the back than in the front. At its longest point in the front, it was shoulder length. It was a very sexy-styled haircut, but not one that I find attractive. As she talked, she was explaining "how impressive the outfits were." She then motioned with her hands to her left as I faced her (my right). I could see that she was serving in a role similar to that of a talk-show assistant. I looked to where her hands motioned my eyes to follow.

I saw three men standing shirtless wearing roman-like armor. Each of them had very ornate helmets made of a reddish colored metal. Their pants were plated in the same metal and they each wore sandals. They all had crazy-eyes – like they were unsure where they were. My immediate thought was "gladiators." I have never seen a gladiator in person, so I figured this must be what one looked like. But, no sooner had I thought the word "gladiator" than my thought was interrupted by an unseen angelic presence with the word, "centurions." I had no idea what a centurion was, nor why I was given that word. I just stared and soaked it all in until I lost harmony with the moment.

The Written (cont'd)

After doing research on the word centurion, I came to learn that a centurion was one of the highest ranking professional officers in the Roman army circa 107 BC. According to Wikipedia, "Most centurions commanded 80 men but senior centurions commanded cohorts, or took senior staff roles in their legion." Only eight people ranked higher than the centurions, and the centurions earned anywhere from twice to seventeen times the amount of a regular soldier.

My mind raced with possibilities. I have to believe that the concept of Rome was used in a way that was to indicate "a perfect society." In our history, Rome was more of a concept of an ideal life rather than a location. In previous heavenly experiences, the concept of Rome has been used to illustrate humanity on Earth to me. So, if Rome is being used to illustrate an ideal life on Earth, I suppose it is possible that I needed to understand the concept of a centurion in order to know God's plans for me. Perhaps my spiritual calling right now is tantamount to that of the role of a centurion in ancient Rome. It is tough to say, but those are my initial thoughts.

July 11, 2014

This morning, I arrived in the heavens with a beautiful blonde angel before me. My first thought was "Carrie Underwood," but I knew it was not her. Often times the mind attempts to rationalize heavenly experiences as if they were occurring on Earth. To me, this angel's facial structure resem-

Rebirth III

bled that of Carrie Underwood, but I knew it was an angel. She spent a lot of time with me throughout the experience. I would have to guess that it was equivalent to hours of earthly time where she taught me about the heavens and the universe.

Throughout the experience, I thought I was learning very well. I seemed to retain the information much better than I usually do in these experiences. When it was time for us to part ways, I returned to my body (or so I thought) to journal all that I had learned. Instead, it turned out to be a false awakening – a moment where the soul returns to an Earth-like place, but is not quite back to the body. This happens often to me where I journal the experiences with the angels. But, when I realize I am not on Earth and try to return to my body, I end up losing the information that I learned. I often wonder where the books exist where I write about these experiences because I am sure they contain a great amount of divine information. But, until I ever see them, all I can do is hope to recall as much as I can. In this experience, it is mostly the impression of the angel and not the information she imparted to me.

July 12, 2014

I did not sleep tonight, nor did I have an opportunity to meditate. With that said, I wanted to make note of it so it was not thought that I went without a vision for any other particular reason.

The Written (cont'd)

July 13, 2014

My meditation began with faces appearing from the darkness. This has been occurring recently, but each time it has occurred, it has only lasted briefly and has been indescribable in context. But this time was different. This time, the faces were more "in focus" than in previous experiences, but they were still hard to understand. I think the best way to visualize what has been happening is to envision darkness in your entire periphery, where faces slowly begin to become illuminated in your immediate field of vision. The faces are close to your face – as in merely inches away. You have to move your field of view to focus on each face, but there are likely at least five faces visible.

In this experience, two women came into focus and one man. They were very difficult to understand. Their words sounded almost synthesized or electronic. There was also an accent that I have never heard before. If I could describe the accent, I would call it "non-earthly." As I was focusing on their voices, I was suddenly able to discern the voice of one of the females saying the word "Thursday" though it was pronounced more closely to "thirsty."

The first time I heard the word I had to determine if it was "thirsty" or "Thursday," but as the encounter went on, I understood the "IR" sound to be caused by the accent. And now that I think about it, this would also be why the angel name, "Uriel," is always communicated to me as "Ariel." Ap-

Rebirth III

parently the "UR" sound is closer to an "IR" or "AR" than "UR." Anyway, as I listened to the female voice, I noticed that each time she said the word, the other female would repeat the word. They would look at each other and smile.

When they noticed I was able to fully comprehend the moment, one of the female voices rang out, "It will arrive Thursday." As the words were said, the man seemed frustrated and kept correcting them by telling me, "No. Friday." It was interesting to watch the three faces bicker back and forth. The two women told me not to listen to him…that they were correct. The faces faded, and I was left meditating on the events that had taken place. I never was told what "it" was or any other details. No prayer before or any event prior would lead me to even begin to understand the context right now.

The following morning I received an email from a company shipping a custom bed for me. I was not expecting it for another few weeks, but the email stated that the bed had shipped a few days prior and that the estimated delivery date was Friday, July 18th. I do not know if this is what the faces were referring to, but I thought I would note it as well. Most of the time the experiences indicate something spiritual and not physical…but I guess we will see.

After returning to meditation from journaling the event with the faces, I experienced a long and erratic trip to the heavens. I am sure it is steeped in symbolism rather than the blatant actions that I will first describe – so, just understand that as this entry is read.

The Written (cont'd)

I found myself standing in the heavens among many angels. They were not elder angels, but rather closer to my "age" and "size." In my hand, was a strange looking ruler. I examined it to see that it was a six-inch ruler that was seven inches long. The right end of the ruler had a bulbous end. Upon examining it, the right side was shaped like a swirled ice cream cone. The tip of the cone was about a quarter inch wide and flat. Honestly, now that I think about it, maybe the ruler was cut more like the shape of a condom that is laying flat. But, at the time of the experience, I thought it was an ice-cream cone.

I was walking around with a female, and we continued to flirt with each other. She was very interested in me, and I found her extremely attractive. Somewhere in the conversation, the subject turned to the ruler, which led to her asking me how big I was (referring to my manhood). I looked at the ruler in my hand and decided I would just measure it on the spot. I pulled it out and placed the ruler beneath it so I could measure it most accurately (or at least that is what I thought I would do at that moment). It lined up exactly with the ruler. I was seven inches. I was proud and excited about it being "seven." For some reason I knew that neither she nor I were talking about anything sexually, but rather symbolically. However, the conversation occurred in a sexual manner.

As I smiled and showed her how I lined up perfectly to the ruler's length, I then showed her the measurements on the ruler and how the overall length was seven inches including the bulbous end of the ice-cream cone on the right end. She smiled and was entertained. She told me that "[she was] going

Rebirth III

to come over later for me." I was excited even though I knew I would not do anything with her because of my celibate seal. My mind wrestled with separating the literal and symbolic in the conversation, but, overall, I knew we were talking symbolically. She also seemed to know that. And, though her words would seem to indicate that she was coming over to engage in a sexual act with me, we both knew that it was symbolic of something greater.

After we parted ways, I then thought it was my duty to tell other women about the significance of the measurement of seven inches. I roamed around this setting in the heavens sharing my story. Each angel seemed very entertained and proud of me – all the while, nothing was ever meant sexually. In fact, it was actually the opposite. As I eventually wore down in stamina with maintaining harmony in the heavens, I returned to my body, reflected on the events, and then proceeded to journal the experience.

In my reflection, I understood that the measurement of "seven inches" represented the celibate seal I had placed upon my body, leaving it only to God to determine when the seal could be broken. I knew that the angels understood the symbolism in my decision to not be a slave to sexual desires and how this was quite possibly the hardest thing for a human to sacrifice. Every other human vice can be replaced or channeled through meditation and spirituality. But, sex is another animal. I suppose that is why it is spiritually required to be held with such high regard and sacred understanding in every religion and even occult practice throughout the most ancient

The Written (cont'd)

times. And, though the experience might have seemed to be a perversion of thought in the heavens, the experience was actually very spiritual and symbolic in gesture. I knew it as it was occurring. I recognized the reciprocal understanding from the angels. However, the conversation could not be had in another manner. For me in this particular experience, it was important to understand it in this fashion.

After journaling the experience, I returned to the heavens. This time, I found myself at a camp. It seemed to be some sort of spiritual boot camp for those learning how to control their spiritual bodies. My presence there was different than many of the others there. I knew I was free to travel to and from this place, free to participate or go along my way. The others I saw there were required to be there – being trained by elder angels.

As I walked through the camp, the elder angels smiled at me acknowledging my presence. They were familiar, and I could recognize my familiarity to them. The camp was held inside a long white building in the middle of a forest. A long, sandy colored road led me to this place. I arrived just as the instructor was calling out for the group of spirits to separate into smaller teams for training.

The girls and guys were required to be in separate groups. Names were called and smaller groups were formed. I never heard my name called. I did hear Danielle Lauderdale's name called and watched a small group go with her. She seemed to be more aware of what was going on compared to her group (though they all appeared to be friends). Danielle is a girl I

Rebirth III

knew in Nashville, but I never knew her beyond her friendship with one of my friends. We rarely talked, only exchanging pleasantries.

As I watched her group form, I was aware that I did not seem to know anyone else there. Suddenly, I heard the instructor call out Danielle's deceased brother's name, Dayton. I paused. I knew I was in the heavens, but this crossed the line of interacting with deceased people. I looked for Dayton to see if he was there. I had only met Dayton once before his life tragically ended in a motor vehicle accident when he was in his twenties. His name was called out again, "Dayton Lauderdale in Lauderdale." I watched as a small group went with Dayton. I felt like I was supposed to go with his group since the instructor said "in Lauderdale."

It was a bizarre phrasing of instructions, but I figured since God had called me to move to Fort Lauderdale, that Dayton's group must be important for this particular experience. As I walked over to the group, Dayton and the rest of the group looked at me as if I was not supposed to be with them. I digested the moment and then decided they were probably right. I walked back from the group and began talking with my angelic guide. He pointed me over to a group of "new" members at the camp. They appeared to be akin to the "outcasts" of the group because they were not in a particular clique or friends with anyone already. I smiled at my guide and said, "That's perfect. That is the kind of group I like." My angelic guide smiled back and said something in return that was along the lines of, "I know. You like meeting new people every time

The Written (cont'd)

you come here. And, since you visit for free, you can always choose any group that you want."

I recognized that I must come here more than I was able to recall at that exact moment. I walked over to the group and was glad to see that it was coed. I did not know any of them, but I could tell they were all new. All of the other groups were split by gender, but this group was placed together because they were all at the same entry point. I felt a sense of strength in being able to interact with girls as well as guys and not be limited by one gender's notions.

As I began speaking with the group, I recognized that the new group was always the strongest, and that somehow I had recognized the strength in the "outcasts" some time ago when I first began visiting this camp. I began recalling flashbacks of how I had advanced quickly through the trainings there by befriending the new members and finding the strength in the group. Whatever the challenges were that all of the groups competed against, I realized that my group almost always was victorious because of the strength I found in them. I recognized that I had been doing this for quite some time and that my angelic guide takes me here often. As the thoughts filled my head, I lost harmony with the moment and returned to my body where I journaled this final experience of my meditation.

Rebirth III

July 14, 2014

While the experience this morning seemed to last for hours, I was only able to recall a few details once my spirit returned to my body. It began with me waking up and stepping out of bed. I walked around my condo and eventually over to my bathroom mirror. I looked at my scalp. I have decided to start using Minoxidil in real life because my hairline has begun to recede more noticeably recently. And, while that is a decision I have made, I just received my Minoxidil yesterday and have not started using it. When I was standing in front of the mirror, I noticed I had a clump of hair in my hands. I was holding ten to twelve strands of hair with very large follicles at the base.

I stared at it disappointingly. In real life, I have not seen my hair fall out to this extreme, but this experience seemed so real. I was puzzled as to why so much hair was falling out. I decided that I was making the right decision to use Minoxidil, so I opened the box and applied it to my scalp. After that, I felt confident that my hair would return. I continued living the day out as if I was on Earth, but it was most definitely an out-of-body experience. There were other details that are now fuzzy. But, the most important part of it was dealing with my hair.

The Written (cont'd)

July 15, 2014

As I began to meditate tonight, I saw several bright flashes of light. Suddenly, the sky above me opened up to a surreal combination of night and morning. The blue sky was a midnight color at its closest point to my face. The clouds appeared from the left like rainclouds in front of a full moon. The clouds were illuminated from behind – but the illumination was from the sun, which was much further away. Beyond the clouds the sky became a more mesmerizing blue. For some reason I said, "Its Omaha...Omaha Blue." I honestly do not know what the reference to Omaha means at this moment, but it was important that what I was witnessing was understood to be "Omaha." I was still in a light meditation, so I called my soul back to my body to write down the experience.

After journaling, I closed my eyes to begin meditating again. I was immediately taken to a location in the heavens. I found myself standing on a street with my daughter, Georgia. I looked up into the sky to see the height of the building before me. It was extremely large – maybe thirty stories or so and made of a white alabaster. I looked back at the door in front of me. I knew Georgia and I were supposed to go in.

Georgia was happy and unaware we were in heaven. I did not want to tell her because I wanted to see how she acted in the experience. She kept wandering around the building in front of me. On Earth, she will never lead or make a person follow her. Instead, she is always a step behind when we are

Rebirth III

walking together. But this time was different. She was exploring and happy to be there. I followed her through several paths and corridors inside of the building. Eventually, she found the end of the path we were on. It was a path that went to the left and at the very end met a stairwell that went up but was perpendicular to the end of the path.

As we reached the stairs, we passed an angel that I suppose was the "gatekeeper" to the area we entered. I knew it was okay that we were in this particular location, so I was not afraid that we would not be allowed to go in. When Georgia passed her, the angel looked at me and smiled. She let us pass, and we began to head up the steps. We were heading into a garden with tall trees and lush foliage. As I recognized where we were going, I began to lose harmony and returned to my body to journal the experience.

After journaling the experience, I again returned to the heavens. I was again standing with Georgia, and she was looking at everything around us. She said, "One of these things is inside of one of these twenty-six hundred things." I was puzzled what it meant, but I wanted to make sure I remembered her words so I kept repeating it in my head. We walked through the foliage and walked into what I can only describe metaphorically as standing on the bottom of the deep end of a pool, but it was sandy and the waters had receded. It was as if we were standing where the ocean once was very deep, but was being held from filling the place we were in. Around us, I could see the ocean covering the beaches. We were very clearly in a deeper section below sea level, but the ocean was not

The Written (cont'd)

filling the space. I decided to return to my body to journal the experience.

One last experience remained after I closed my eyes to meditate again. I was back in my condo, and my earthly mother was there (at least I think it was my earthly mother. For some reason, my earthly mother turns into my spiritual mother mid-experience). She was walking around my place seeing all that God had provided for me. I was excited to show her the guest bed and mattress. She tested it out, stood back up and walked around the other parts of my condo. This was the first time she had seen the place and was very intrigued with everything. This is when the experience began to become more abstract.

My mother faded away, and I noticed a black pipe running along the ceiling of my condo. This does not exist on Earth, so I was puzzled at what I was observing. I became aware of another presence in the room. It was my spiritual mother. Suddenly, through the silence, I heard a voice cry out, "What is it, Jonathan? Mom says you have something." The voice was different than any I had ever heard before. It sounded almost robotic, or synthesized.

It was definitely a female voice, but I immediately had the impression that the synthesized sound of the voice was because it was an effort of communication that transcended spiritual planes. The voice emphasized the word "it" in the first sentence. The second sentence would best be understood as, "Mom says you have something [important/special]." I knew that the concept of "something special/important" was being

Rebirth III

communicated, but the words did not quite align with the archetypal thought being relayed to me. I focused on the words and the voice. I wondered if the voice was the voice of my spiritual mother. When the voice first broke the silence, I thought it was my earthly mother speaking since that was who I had been interacting with, but it became quickly apparent that the voice was not hers. The only real possibility was it being the voice of my spiritual mother or the presence in the room with me.

As I thought about the voice and the words, I looked at the long black pipe above me. I began to realize it represented a conduit for the spirit. The idea of the spirit flowing through the pipe began to resonate with me, and there was a very difficult-to-describe idea of "something" at the open end of the conduit that was not blocking the flow of the spirit, but rather just floating there. If the pipe could be seen as opening up to a three-inch diameter from a half-inch pipe, the "something" floating in the middle of the pipe at the open end was about the size of a dime with the primordial substance flowing around it. But, the "something" appeared more like a glowing human form. I focused on everything being communicated to me, but lost harmony and returned to my body where I immediately journaled the experience.

The Written (cont'd)

July 16, 2014

During meditation today I found myself sitting on a park bench with an angel on either side of me. They were male angels. One was short, round, and older. The other one was older with gray scraggily hair, a gray beard, mustache, and wore horn-rimmed glasses. Across from us (and across a white stone walkway that was about twenty to thirty feet wide) there was another bench with a beautiful female surrounded on either side by two female angels.

The angels were telling me about some things to expect on my journey. It was my impression that the girl in front of me was receiving the same type of information from the female angels around her. For some reason, there was an emphasis on "the person who arrives invited will be provided a nice vehicle." As we talked, my mind thought of myself and the girl sitting across from me driving nice cars. I was shown the vehicle that the girl in front of me had been given. It was very nice and more expensive than anything I would ever expect to purchase in my lifetime. As I thought about it, I did not understand why I would be provided a nice vehicle when the one I had was already one that I was happy with. I pondered the circumstances and then decided to embrace the gifts that are to come my way. The angels emphasized to me that others I bring into Fort Lauderdale with me will not necessarily be provided the same niceties. Instead, they emphasized that "the person who arrives invited" would be the benefactor of the

Rebirth III

niceties to come, but that the others could enjoy the benefits of the niceties through "the person who arrived invited."

I understood that I was a person "who arrived invited" and so was the girl before me. Family, friends, and acquaintances that I invite into my life will not receive the same things in the way that I will be provided while I am here. I looked at the angels, and they let me know the experience was coming to an end and then sent my soul back to my body, where I arrived abruptly.

As I became immediately aware of my return, I thought about the experiences and tried to make sure I would be able to journal them. As I thought about the phrasing of the advice of the "vehicle," I am now unsure if it represented tangible objects or if it was geared more toward the vessel of my body. The concept was illustrated with cars, but as is the case in my experiences with the angels, concepts hold greater meaning than the object illustrated. I could even go insofar as to think that the word "vehicle" represents everything around me that enables me to live the life that God wills for me to live for Him and through Him.

July 17, 2014

A false awakening caused me not to be able to recall the journey from the night once I did return to my body. Again, it was as if I journaled the experience, but it was in the heavens rather than on Earth.

The Written (cont'd)

July 18, 2014

This morning's experience was quite possibly one of the most profound experiences I have had to date. While I would never claim to be a John the Baptist, Dante, or anyone else along those lines, maybe this is actually God's intention for me. For this morning, I awoke from one of the most detailed experiences I have ever had in the heavens – an experience that only after journaling it all and then researching what I was allowed to see – that I discovered the similarities in my experience and John's Book of Revelation, The Book of Daniel, Dante's Inferno, and numerous other ancient texts and stories from the ages.

This experience began with myself and two other male angels. The landscape was barren, rocky, and had a reddish hue. Darkness covered most of the landscape. As I came into harmony with the location, I knew I was in a place where I was able to see into the future. From here, it gets complicated, so I will do my best to explain.

While my soul was in this place, I was aware I had left my body behind on Earth. My soul was able to experience flash-forwards and commune with God. The visions of the future encompassed my mind and would eventually come true though the details were not always completely accurate at the time of my visions. And even though I knew that God communicated with me through these visions, I always had a hard

Rebirth III

time explaining to those around me what was to come…and an even harder time getting them to believe.

So, as I came into my surroundings, I knew this "was the last day" – "the last fight." The two other angels and I were tasked with ridding the heavens of the demons. We were spiritual warriors, an elite group of people selected to go in and save mankind. We were not big and muscular herculean warriors, but rather three that God showed favor through our dedication to Him. As we wandered through the barren land and darkness, the smallest of my two "spiritual brothers" ended up running into the darkness to fight a demon.

It was part of the large beast we were fighting. The demon/beast had seven heads and wore six gold rings. And while there were times we would see the beast as its whole, it would frequently disappear into the darkness and divide into smaller, but equally large and frightening beasts. One of the beasts had three heads, but I will get to that in a minute. For now, my spiritual brother was fighting one of the seven demons.

As he ran into the darkness, I realized this was part of the flash-forward visions I had experienced previously. I knew he would be okay and win, but that it would be a tough fight. I began to explain to my spiritual brothers that I had seen this part in the vision, sharing with them the ways that we had to fight in order to survive. As one of the brothers fought, I saw flashes of a field where the other brother went to fight a demon. The field was muted in color and on the crest of a hill. There was a dirt road that crossed in front of our path to the

The Written (cont'd)

field. The field had a fence – a two-plank style fence painted black. There were seven cows on the outside of the fence. Each of the cows were black and white spotted and faced left (which I assume would be west). I saw my brother fight and win. As these images filled my head, I began to see other flashes. I could not explain them to everyone, nor did I have time since my smaller brother was already engaged in a battle. Eventually all three of us became engaged in the fight with the demon where we managed to slay it enough to run and escape.

As we ran, we crested a hill where we came to be in the same location as the vision. I began telling everyone frantically that, "This was it. This was the big fight." My mind flashed forward to a battle with the three-headed part of the beast – a battle that, if victorious, would cause the whole seven-headed beast to fall. Again, I had little time to explain. The demon chasing us grabbed the taller of the two angels with me and took him into the field. All we could do was watch. My spiritual brother ended up winning in short order. Our battle was victorious again. As the demon vanished into the distance, I knew that the seven-headed beast was permanently wounded.

From the silence a voice rang out. It was female. I heard the words, "Good! Good!" The voice was initially confusing to me and caused me to lose my bearings. It sounded synthesized and had a strange echo with it. It was as if I was hearing a feedback loop with her communication to me. The only way I could describe the voice was as if it was being broadcast directly into my head. I looked around hoping that we could just

Rebirth III

talk in person since however she was communicating to me was not ideal. But, I never saw her.

Eventually, one of my spiritual brothers saw her and pointed her out to me. She was in a glass room at the edge of the "property" that we were battling upon. When we saw her, she began talking more to us. I put my right finger in my right ear to try to minimize the echo of the voice. I tried to focus on what she was saying, to hear her more clearly, but it was not helping. With my finger to my ear, I wandered to the left edge of the property to see if that would help with my reception of her voice. To my surprise, it did help clear up the echo.

As her voice came into focus, I turned to look at her from afar to let her know that I could hear her now. It was the first time I could really get a good look at this female angel. She was an elder, strong in stature. She was wearing a white robe that contrasted with her wavy dark brown hair that was pulled back into a bun. She had piercing brown eyes. When I saw her, I would have almost identified her as Persian, but with less pronounced facial features. As I focused on her words, I lost the ability to hear the voice of the spiritual brothers with me. And though I could not hear their voices, I knew that the taller of the two brothers was excited about what she was saying.

Now that I could hear her, I asked her to repeat her words. She said, "I've been trying to tell you that this would happen." As her voice touched my soul, I watched as three more angels walked across my path and into the darkness where we had first found the demon. This landscape was still

The Written (cont'd)

the rocky wasteland from when I first appeared. As I saw the three angels wearing white robes, I felt almost relieved at first – as if I could rest while they fought in our place. I knew we were engaged in a great battle and thought this was our chance to catch our breath from the fervor of the battle with the seven-headed beast. But as I watched them cross my path, I noticed they appeared naive and unprepared for all they were about to experience. I then had a sense of shame rush through me fearing that my trio of spiritual brothers had failed God, so that he had to send in the backups. The female angel sensed my concern.

Without me asking the question, she said, "No. This is what I was telling you. This happens every time there are three. I just chose those three. They have no idea what is about to happen to them. You can't let them get killed. They don't know how to survive." I immediately knew there was a greater process in place that kept feeding in groups of three angels after a specified amount of time. I knew that my two spiritual brethren and I had managed to defy all of the odds and had demonstrated favor in God's eyes. We had somehow managed to not just survive, but reach the final battle with the seven-headed beast. I ran back to the others feeling the weight of the heavens on my shoulders. We knew we had to finish this once and for all.

I was now aware that our triune represented the seventh ring that the demon was trying to get. While it was not immediately clear, it seemed that we had managed to take one of the rings from the beast along the way. We ran into an inlet in

Rebirth III

the mountainside. I began explaining to my brothers that my vision had not yet ended – that other things happened at the very end. As I frantically tried to relay everything that had been shown to me, I saw the ground before me rise up. Directly in front of us was the three-headed portion of the seven-headed monster. It let out Godzilla-like roars. It was caged, with a thick, rectangular piece of metal resting across the beast's heads. Great chains held the metal to the ground. It would be similar to someone lifting up a drainage grate from the ground below, but having it chained so as not to let it out.

This was a demon that we had already beaten. Its finger widths were the heights of each of us. It scratched and clawed its way trying to free itself from its cage. The beast's heads looked like a cross between ferocious dragons and vicious dogs. It had a tail that would appear with its claws. Its roars were screeching, booming and obnoxiously loud. I could see on one of its claws that it still contained a ring. All I could ever see was the top of the beast's head and its claws. It dwarfed us.

We walked over to it where it was fighting to get free. It was clearly beaten, enslaved to the cage holding it. I knew that we had beaten it once, but that it was still involved in the "final battle." As my brethren looked at it, Lucifer appeared. He was the seven-headed monster, but appeared to us in person. He was wearing a suit, skinny, and had slicked back hair. His facial features were pointed – the same man I have seen before in many of my other visions. It was clear he wanted to try to talk us into giving him the ring. He attempted to be sly with his words, but we would not have it. I looked over at the three-

The Written (cont'd)

headed beast. I could see it was the last part of the whole seven-headed beast that we would battle. I became aware that we had to procure the ring from the monster to be victorious…and that it would all boil down to this. This final battle was in my last vision.

Lucifer walked over to the large metal slab and forced it closed back onto the surface of the Earth. He wanted to demonstrate his dominion over the beast. He said some unintelligible comments to us and then indicated that "it was time." He disappeared into the darkness, and the three of us were left standing before the slab. I looked over at my brethren and said, "This is how it ends. This is the last battle I saw. I didn't see anything else, or how it would end – only that it would end right here in this scenario. It has all come to pass as I have seen, but I cannot see the end." One of the angels walked fearlessly into the darkness toward a small, dark opening into the cage that held the door that held the three-headed beast within the Earth. The metal slab had been raised just enough for us to enter.

I watched him go in, vanishing into the darkness. As the gravity of this final battle weighed on my shoulders, I knew that I did not know the outcome…but that the outcome was to be determined by our battle, and our battle alone. The two angels with me and I were chosen to make this come to pass. As I processed everything, my soul lost harmony and I returned to my body. It was as if a giant "To Be Continued…" message flashed before me in the greatest cliffhanger of all time, just before I returned to my body.

Rebirth III

I knew immediately upon opening my eyes that the seven-headed beast only had six of the rings and was trying to procure the seventh. And while it had six of the rings, I knew that the final battle would help return one more of the rings back to the heavens. I could not help but wonder if I was left in a cliffhanger and supposed to return back to the heavens immediately, or if it was intentionally left as a cliffhanger as a message for me on Earth to note what will come to be. All I know is that the overwhelming feeling I had as I lay there, having just experienced all that I had seen with the seven-headed beast, is that "this is my judgment day." I do not know how literal the words were to be taken. I do not know how much applies to mankind compared to my personal journey. But, I do know that I had an overwhelming sense that this battle marked the "final battle" of something greater that shall come to pass…something greater than just me and my personal experiences in the heavens alone.

The following morning, I read up on the "seven-headed beast" and learned about the seven seals in Daniel and the seven-headed beast in Revelation. I also read about the three-headed beast in Dante's inferno. As I type this I am overwhelmed with the sense that I not only saw the three-headed beast written about in Dante's inferno (Cerberus, the great three-headed dog that guards the gates of Hell), but somehow am serving as the bridge to explain how they are all part of the whole – the whole being the seven-headed beast, Lucifer. But most importantly, I think it was to see that six of the seven seals have been broken, and that the final seal is the final battle for all to come to pass. This is our judgment day.

July 20, 2014

This morning's experience was long, but I can hardly recall many of the details – rather, just a couple of the main takeaways. I was standing in a gorgeous setting – blue skies, manicured landscaping, with a large building before me. The building had three steps leading up to the doorway. An angel was with me as well as a child. At first I thought the child was my daughter since that would be the easiest earthly interpretation for my mind to make. But, the longer the experience unfolded, the more my mind understood the child to be another angelic form with me.

Eventually we walked into the building. As it turned out, the building opened up into some type of retail establishment. It was not overly big, and the interior seemed to be made of a darker purple-gray. The lighting was dim, but not dark. When I walked in, the child took me through the store. She led me over to something that was similar to a bedding section. We passed through racks of clothes and shelves of items on the way to this section. It was located in the back left corner, or north-northwest from where we walked in.

The child pointed to a pillowcase on the wall with a pillow in it. She wanted me to pull it down, so I did. The pillow was wrapped in an expensive silk-chenille case that was a beautiful

Rebirth III

purple. At that moment I did not think much about the significance of the color purple, but rather that the pillow was not a color I would ever buy for myself. The child said, "You should get the purple one. You already have the rest of it. You just need to add the pillow." I thought about it and smiled at her. I could see the gesture was not of want for herself, but instead it was to make me happy. She wanted me to be fulfilled with anything she perceived as missing in my life.

I told her, "I should get it. Let me walk around and think about it." I was not sure if I would actually get the pillowcase since it was purple, but I felt it was what I "should" do. I walked over to a shelf that was near the entrance. With my back to the door through which we entered, I looked at the boxes on the kiosk. The stand was about three and a half feet to four feet high with two shelves on either side stretching about five feet wide. The ends were capped with narrow bookcases probably about three feet in width, the same height as the stand, and had three shelves filled with books and miscellaneous items. On the stand, I saw a cardboard box that contained a musical instrument. I pulled it off the shelf and opened it up.

I pulled out something that resembled the neck of a guitar, but it was unlike anything I have ever seen on Earth. I heard the voice of the other angel I was with say something about how I should try playing it and see how I liked it. I gave it a try and was able to make some remarkable music even though I had never played the instrument before. I did not spend long with it before I put it back in the cardboard box

The Written (cont'd)

hoping I had not attracted attention to myself. On the box I read the words "*STEEL GUITAR.*" The words were in a narrow, bold black print and all capitalized. I repeated the words in recognition of reading them though I knew the instrument was not the "steel guitar" we have on Earth.

When I placed the box back on the bottom shelf (which was shaped sort of like a guitar), it leaned against the left hand side. It was the only one remaining. I noticed the packaging would not return to its normal shape. Where I had opened the guitar around the neck, the box now flapped about without form. It looked like the item inside of the box would have to be broken if judging by the box alone. I was intrigued by it but felt guilty for making something appear broken. As I observed the box, the child came back over to me and asked if I was going to get the purple pillowcase. I decided I would, and we walked back over to the bedding section where I took the pillow down from the wall again.

The child smiled at me, happy I was getting the item. I knew she was not happy for herself, but instead happy that I was getting it to "complete" whatever it was that I already had the rest of. In the literal case, I would have to assume it was the rest of the bedding set. But, in the spiritual sense, there is much more to be explored in this child's desire for me to complete my purple set.

Rebirth III

July 21, 2014

I was really exhausted tonight from work, so I was unable to maintain a great harmonic balance with my meditation. However, in the beginning of my travels, I arrived in the heavens in a bustling place. I am sure I must have looked disoriented as I was trying to gather my bearings. But as I was coming to grips with the landscape, a male angel approached me and said, "Are you Barry's son?" If there was something that was going to cause me to "pop-into" this spiritual reality, those words were it.

My mind reeled with possibilities. My first thought was, "Who would know my earthly father here?" My second thought was, "When have I ever been asked about my father in the last fifteen years?" I do not think I have heard my father's name mentioned directly since before I moved to Nashville, which predated me moving to Fort Lauderdale. I looked at the man slightly confused. I nodded in acknowledgement of his question. The angel's face became overjoyed. This particular angelic form was tan in complexion with darker hair. The man then blurted out, "Great! I can't believe it! I'm from Hawaii." I looked at him and struggled to hang on to the moment before returning to my body.

The man looked familiar, but I could not identify why I would have recognized him. And while words were not spoken in this particular capacity, my impression in that brief moment was that he knew my earthly father's spirit and identified me

The Written (cont'd)

as his offspring. There was some direct importance on my lineage with respect to what it must mean to others about me. Finally, there was a genuine surprise and admiration of this man being able to interact with me – as if my presence was a legend or myth or something along those lines. By no means am I trying to place myself on a pedestal or add some type of acclaim to my presence, but this is just what the unsaid words communicated to me in the interaction.

After returning to my body and taking notes, I returned to the heavens where the remainder of my experience seemed to involve me learning to swim with a child in a large pool. Perhaps this had to do with the "swimmy" feeling I had in not being able to find complete balance with the heavens.

July 22, 2014

I cannot recall much of what I experienced during my sleep or meditations. I did have a long, drawn out experience that began with me arriving in the heavens in a setting similar to when I met the man from Hawaii. The setting made me feel I was in a large outdoor setting, but inside of a great tent – like the kind you would find at a PGA golf tournament for workers and staff. The tent was busy with numerous souls mingling and walking about. That is all I can recall before I met with a couple of angels and taken from the tent for some type of training.

Rebirth III

July 23, 2014

A false awakening caused me not to be able to recall everything. I decided to stop using Minoxidil, and I feel I am a lot more focused than I was in previous nights. For many reasons I am glad I no longer use it. The first of which is that it was a decision based on vanity and was unnecessary. The second is that the application of chemicals to the scalp negatively affected my ability to find harmony within. This was a micro lesson on the macro: any chemicals applied to the body will cause the vessel to lose its highest harmonic capacity.

July 24, 2014

I was jolted into the heavens by a teenage boy's voice cutting through the silence. The boy said, "Maybe she came in to help you find the potential." The potential he was referring to was a potential energy within. My mind raced at the thoughts of the meaning causing me to lose harmony. I wrote down his words and returned to the heavens.

In returning, this time I heard his voice slice through the void again. "Perhaps you can find it better together. You just have to see how to harness the energy together." Once again, I returned to write down his words. I immediately was able to find harmony and return.

This time, the boy's voice said, "If you were at sixteen percent before, now you are at thirty-five percent of untapped potential." He continued on. "Your body is like this untapped conduit for potential. It is trying to be used and get out of you." My mind raced at the possibilities. I had always assumed that potential was the remainder of the untapped "whole" from whatever the source is. But the boy's words shared with me that untapped potential is relative to growth. If I was spiritually weak before, I only had a small amount of spiritual potential. As my spiritual strength has increased, so too would my capacity to reach into the whole. Perhaps the whole increases relative to my spiritual strength. This could very well explain why the elder angels always appear larger than life when I stand before them in the heavens. The thoughts caused me to lose harmony and return to my body.

I once again was able to find harmony to return to the heavens one final time this morning. In this experience, I was talking with my daughter. We walked around until our energy united. This buildup of energy would be akin to static electricity between two objects. When our energy united, an angel appeared before us. The angel explained, "This was a lesson in using each other to see something more."

July 25, 2014

This morning's experience began with me standing before three angels. At first we were in a subway. I helped a girl in the subway who seemed in need. I would not say she was homeless, or even spiritually weak. I just recognized she needed help

Rebirth III

from my vessel. It turned out that she needed to have "a prescription filled at a pharmacy on Old Hickory." Whether or not the reference to Old Hickory is important, I do not know. It is a major road in the Nashville area...one that I generally try to avoid. Regardless, I decided to help this girl.

She seemed very thankful. On the way, I crossed paths with my friend, Jason. I told him, "I'm going to your old stomping grounds." When he first moved to Nashville, he lived just off the exit of Old Hickory Blvd. and I-40. When I said those words to Jason, he immediately seemed offended. He did not like being identified with that particular location. It was enough to give me pause and try to understand whether I was actually interacting with my friend Jason, or whether it was an angel that my mind was associating with Jason. Either way, it did not matter at that particular moment. It was something to ponder.

I drove the girl to the pharmacy to help her get her prescription filled. As it turned out, it was going to cost $600 to have it filled. This was apparently why she did not fill it a day prior and seemed in need of help. There were two places to check out once it was filled. An older lady recognized me. She smiled and said she would help me take care of the prescription for the girl. She took her over to a kiosk that held the required forms and then helped her sign up for something that would offset the costs. There was going to be a delay in a response, so the girl and I went to a restaurant outside of the pharmacy to wait.

The Written (cont'd)

The restaurant was similar to a sports bar and grill. I had seen this particular restaurant several times in my experiences. The waitresses were generally very attractive and was partly why people enjoyed going to this place. I took notice of four waitresses inside. Two waitresses were extremely obese and nearly naked. The other two waitresses were extremely beautiful and dressed conservatively. While everyone else seemed to drink beer (or some type of alcoholic beverage), I ordered tea. Our waitress remembered that I usually ordered tea. It is something that intrigues her about me. I did not know that until she mentioned it to me in that moment though.

We ended up only ordering those initial drinks and left without hearing anything back on the prescription. We went to a house and met my sister. This did not seem like my earthly sister, but rather a spiritual sister. My sister became friends with the girl I was helping. Whether her name was "Joy" or not, I cannot be sure. But, that is the name I thought was hers as the conversation persisted. As it turned out, the two girls had dated the same guy in their past. After some time passed, we all went to a house for another meal.

My parents showed up. Again, these "parents" seemed like spiritual parents rather than earthly parents. I introduced everyone and gave them all time to get to know each other. My parents were concerned that Joy was using the prescription she needed filled to "cook meth." And while they all seemed concerned over that possibility, the evening ended with all of them becoming high on something indescribable. Maybe it was the moment. Maybe they actually ingested

Rebirth III

something. Either way, I watched as they all fell into a state of bliss, Love, and happiness with one another. I wondered how they found this "high."

I returned to my body, took notes on the experience and returned to the heavens. This time I found myself again with Joy. We were walking down a street and had some type of drink we were carrying in a gas canister. When I recognized that it may contain something we did not need to have, I poured it out. We hopped into a vehicle and set off to some unknown destination. As we were driving, a black vehicle that looked similar to a Land Rover signaled for us to pull over. I was nervous because I was unsure what I could have done to cause us to be pulled over.

In front of us, there was a three-lane road. When the patrol officer reached my window, I watched as one of the blonde angels I often see appeared from the distance. She smiled and was excited to see me. She decided to help us out of whatever situation we were in. The angel distracted the patrol officer and showed us the way to go. She hopped on a pink motorcycle and sped off. I watched as she fell off of the motorcycle once, but managed to get back up on it and carry on her way unharmed.

When we arrived back at the house, my parents seemed upset. In the moment, Joy dropped what appeared to be a bong which broke on the floor. I sensed that my parents were right about Joy, and I had been disillusioned in thinking that she was not a negative influence on me. I was tasked with

The Written (cont'd)

cleaning up the broken pieces of glass from the object Joy dropped as well as the rest of the house.

July 26, 2014

The experience this morning was extremely vivid. I found myself standing on a street in a location that looked similar to the North Beach shopping center in Fort Lauderdale. The important point is that the setting was a series of one-story businesses all with adjoining walls which spanned over several blocks. Between each block, there was a lane for parking.

As I walked through the plaza, someone wearing a medical mask ran out of a building. I watched as another person leapt through the large glass window in a storefront and began running down the street. They both wore blue surgeon's gowns. I knew at this particular moment that we were in the middle of a crisis. I walked around declaring for someone to "seal all of the buildings." This place had been in my experiences several times before, all prior to arriving in Fort Lauderdale. There are no other earthly places I have visited that seem similar. As it turns out, many of the locations I had seen prior to moving to Fort Lauderdale closely resemble or are identical to places here. It has definitely caused me to take notice of the uncanny similarities. The chaos of the moment lasted longer than I have words to describe, but I eventually lost harmony while I tried to help find calm and safety for others in that particular situation.

Rebirth III

July 27, 2014

While I did not have any experiences, I do think that it had a lot to do with being tired and not taking my vitamins. This was the first day I forgot to take my vitamin since I restarted them upon moving to Florida.

July 28, 2014

This morning I had a really long experience in the heavens, but I was unable to bring any of the experience back with me. At the time, I recognized the lucidity, but my body was overwhelmed with both a high sugar intake from the previous meal and was extremely groggy from not being able to fall asleep until late. I am not sure whether I have ever mentioned it in my journal or not, but I have been closely watching how sugar intake affects my ability to maintain harmony in the heavens. As of today, I am fairly certain that sugar affects spiritual balance as much as alcohol or any other substance introduced into the body. If for no other reason, it definitely makes me feel more sluggish throughout the evening hours, which results in a reduced ability to maintain harmony.

The Written (cont'd)

July 29, 2014

This morning contained another "false awakening" type of moment. I distinctly realized I had returned to my body from the heavens with a great amount of detail. But, because my mind wanted to return to the heavens more quickly than it would take for me to take notes, I recited the details over and over until I felt confident I would not forget any of the details when I returned from my next trip. However, if experience has taught me anything, it would be to never rely on "remembering" because each experience consumes every bit of brainpower possible, but I suppose my mind tries to become stronger in recollection each time. The victim in the matter ends up being me, for I end up with an inability to recall all of the details of the communication that God is having with me.

With that said, I can recall one extremely overpowering moment, though the details surrounding it are foggy at best. I recall talking to a female angel. She was wise and strong – a brunette it seemed. She continued to talk to me about "Joshua." My earthly mind wrestled with the context of her words during the duration of our conversation. At one point, she led me over to a mirror where she stood on my right side and mentioned the name "Joshua" one more time. As I puzzled over my own reflection in the mirror, as well as hers to my right, I tried to justify "who" this Joshua fellow was. For some reason, my mind continued to think it was the child of the woman I was speaking with. And, perhaps that is actually what

Rebirth III

was going on. But I was confused enough to ask the angel directly, "So, Joshua is your son – right?"

Her response baffled me even more. She seemed almost taken aback by my question, and every mannerism told me that I did not understand the context of the conversation even though at the time, I fully understood the details of everything she was telling me. My challenge was in understanding who she was telling me the story about. I felt it was about Joshua, but I could not understand why she would be telling me something about this person. It basically left me with a divine message wherein I was missing the key to understanding everything about it – the application of the message for my journey.

But as irony would have it, when I returned to my body from my second journey to the heavens, I could only recall the key, but not the message. So, here I am writing this knowing full well that I was imparted wisdom about Joshua – of which I can see it was the Joshua in the Bible, and the Book of Joshua specifically. However, I do not know what I am supposed to do with a key and no vessel for the key to unlock. So, that is where I will leave this. Hopefully, The Lord will share with me the context of Joshua this evening.

July 30, 2014

The events of this trip began somewhere around the 2:00 a.m. hour and ended abruptly at 5:00 a.m. It is important for

The Written (cont'd)

me to take note of this now because almost every experience I have had while in Fort Lauderdale has caused me to awaken at almost precisely 5:00 a.m. – every time. Events leading up to the grand denouement of each experience cause me to awaken between 2:00 a.m. and 3:00 a.m., but those are mostly the "almost" launches to the heavens. It is also important to note the 5:00 a.m. time because Bryan also awoke this morning at 5:00 a.m. from his vision... which was part of a shared experience between him and me.

My experience began with a frantic scene. I was aware of an angelic presence around me, but it was not visible. Instead, I found myself in the midst of a chase where I was trying to "stay alive." In retrospect, this is not the first time I have had this experience, but it is the first time I have been able to discuss it with clarity. Consider this a repeat experience from one of the nights in Fort Lauderdale that I was unable to recall the details of the experience.

As I was being chased, I realized that "we" were going to have to get "caught" and perform something I can only liken to an escape-heist to survive. The group I was with was being pursued by a negative force that wanted to annihilate our kind. Our impending capture was unpreventable. However, for us to be prepared in how we were to handle the situation and how we were to escape seemed to be the message in the experience. The group I was with was comprised of either five or seven souls. I was not quite sure which one it was, but I continued to think of "five or seven" every time I thought about the number of those with me. In this scenario, I felt like the

Rebirth III

leader of the group, but not a commander. It was more of a recognition of direction that the group seemed to respond to in kind.

Our plan of action was to "strategically get caught" but not by those chasing us. We met in a large music hall that was set in a scenic park. Night had fallen, but the inside of this grand Romanesque building was lighted and filled with the hustling and bustling of a large group of people. Even though the plan was to look inconspicuous and for each of us to go our separate ways, we knew this was the destination where we would be caught.

It was at this point we all split up. Bryan was one of those in the group. We all attempted to evade the negative force that was trying to annihilate us, but at the same time, the plan was to somehow get caught by the other legal forces looking for us. I was the last to get caught. As I began to be pursued by the "Feds," I made a break for the outside. I ran a great distance across grassy fields before climbing a mountain covered in green grass. This mountain was tall – not quite Mt Everest tall, but along those lines.

As I reached the top, there was nowhere else to go and I allowed myself to be arrested by the Feds. For some reason, it was important that the Feds capture me instead of whoever was actually chasing me. I was arrested for trespassing on the mountain, rather than for anything greater in scope. On the way to be booked, I saw each of my friends from our group being led to booking as well. Each had his hands bound behind his back, being ushered from behind by the person who

The Written (cont'd)

apprehended them. Not all of them were apprehended by the Feds (which seemed to be an important part of the plan). Those who were arrested by other "local" authorities had not been caught by the negative force, but rather by a lesser legal authority that was going to add minor bumps in the plan.

So, as each of the group passed by me, I would pull them aside where they took my lead and did something to one of the Federal officers with me – which caused them to be put under Federal arrest. The plan was working. We were all led to a holding cell. The cell was twice as wide as it was long and was made of steel or iron bars, reminiscent of old western jails. On either side of the width of the holding cell were large doors made of the same steel or iron that the cell was made, but each had a single diagonal bar across it.

In the holding cell, I could tell that not only were we building a strategic force, but we were drawing others previously inside of the cell into our circle. It was as if we were assembling an army without anyone – even those joining us – knowing what was happening. It was slick and covert. It was very important that no one knew anything about each of us. We each had to hide our identities and even act out of character to blend in so as not to draw attention to our intentions.

I watched as some of the group talked in accents and about subject matter that would be frowned upon by God. But this seemed necessary so the negative force would not know who we were, or even where we were. The Feds were not the negative force. For some reason, they seemed like a protective force even though we were "caught" and arrested by them.

Rebirth III

One of the guys in our group started acting very gay suddenly. This was extremely out of character for him because I knew him to be more of a ladies' man – a man that women swooned after, steaming after his masculinity. I was taken aback. Then, out of nowhere, he attempted to kiss me on the lips. I knew it was an act and did not resist, but nor did I kiss back. I would describe it as a fake kiss where friends joke about kissing someone but the act just appears that way from a distance. He did not try to kiss me, but rather just pressed his face close to mine. I was frustrated, but I did not want to blow his cover. I took notice of a few people walking by which made me realize there was a reason for his actions in front of that particular group. When they left I looked at him in a way that must have said, "Never again." He told me that he did not want to be approached by those guys who were gay, and that this was the only way he knew how to keep them away. Needless to say, I was uncomfortable with the circumstance, but I knew that it was all an act.

As the jail filled up, I knew that we would have to have everyone's help to escape and overturn the corruption that got us here. We began forming groups within the jail. As our group materialized, the cell door on each end opened by themselves and the song "Staying Alive" started playing. It burst through in vivid sound. It was an audible queue to help ensure that I did not return to my body without remembering the experience. It was sort of like an angelic shock-and-awe moment to help me remember. In that moment, I recognized

The Written (cont'd)

the song's purpose. Suddenly there was a loud "click," and I returned to my body where I journaled this experience.

Later this evening I spoke with Bryan who told me about some of the loose details he had recalled from his experience. His side was the missing portion when we went our separate ways. He remembered the outdoors, being chased, the smell of wet wood. As we talked about all of the details, and I shared with him the brief incident of the Joshua vision from the day prior, Bryan was able to start tying much of our experiences together. I would Love to share our hour long conversation here, but I think that much of that was intended for him and me to understand the following points. In the end, the important takeaways that I will only mention in brevity were Amos, Chapter 5, verses 1 – 7. Verse 7 specifically talks about Joshua and the ties to wormwood mentioned in Revelation.

July 31, 2014

This morning I was taken to the heavens to speak with a female angel. She was one of the angels I see regularly – an elder among the angels. But, as I have said before, the word elder is only meant to indicate seniority and not physical radiance. She is definitely a beautiful angel. While we were together, she was trying very hard to get me to remember a word – a name possibly. Bryan and I have shared with each other how these types of experiences are almost impossible to explain, but for the reader, it is important to understand that

Rebirth III

understanding the language of the angels is unlike anything on Earth. It is as if my soul is learning to speak their language, but simultaneously attempting to translate it into English, archetypes, symbols...anything that can help decipher the words. But all of that complex translation happens seamlessly without recognition of what is actually taking place. Instead, for me, it manifests as watching myself seemingly unable to recite back words in English to the angels.

In this particular experience, she spoke a word that was unfamiliar to my ears. I struggled to repeat it even though I could hear the word echoing in my head. It was like trying to sing a note but every time my voice rang out, the note was wrong. The word she attempted to tell me was something along the lines of "Acacia." And, it very well might have been the word acacia even though I know the word in English and should not have had trouble reciting it back to her. However, when I tried to repeat the word back to her, I understood the first two letters to be "A" and "C." I understood that part very well. The angel would repeat those two letters back to me and the sound that they made. She spoke the word "Ace" but I repeated it as "Asa." I understood that she was trying to communicate a name to me and seemed content that I was repeating the word "Asa" to her. She would repeat the full word back to me in its entirety to try to get me to say it, but I never could get it.

In the midst of the lesson, I heard another word that I believe must have been "battlefield" but my mind seemed forced to understand it as "butterfield." I began saying the two words

The Written (cont'd)

together: "Asa Butterfield." I became excited that I had come to a conclusion of what she was trying to tell me, but I knew it was not correct. I knew the word "butterfield" was not correct, but my mind forced it to follow the word "Asa." I became so frustrated at myself for not being able to repeat her words that it caused me to lose harmony and return to my body. Immediately upon journaling the experience I was aware that the words were likely "acacia" and "battlefield," but I looked up "Asa Butterfield" to see why my mind was set on forming those words together.

As it turns out, Asa Butterfield is the actor from Ender's Game – a movie about a child saving the world even though he thinks it is a training exercise. The parallels to Asa's role in that movie and my own life bring chills to my body. Is it possible that everything I am learning is not training anymore? Is it possible that the angel was trying to illustrate to me that I am not in a game with my travels, but rather in the real battle? Could it be that I am one of the children chosen that will help save mankind, perhaps being forced to make impossible decisions along the way? It is very possible that all of that is true, but of course this is not where the understanding of the experience ended.

This evening Bryan called me to share with me an occurrence from his day. It just so happened that he called in the midst of me talking to a "lost" person for about an hour on the street corner in front of my residence. The timing was impeccable. While I will not go into the details of my conversation in

Rebirth III

this book, the gist was that I was experiencing a role reversal – seeing others through God's eyes.

When Bryan and I connected on the phone, he shared with me about him saving the life of a woman while he was completing his respiratory training in Gadsden, Alabama. He began the story by telling me about four nurses that found him while he was eating a meal and led him into a "Code R" that was happening. Bryan came to find out that a "Code R" was the same as a "Code Blue" at the hospital he normally works at. It essentially means someone is no longer breathing and is about to die.

Listening to Bryan tell the story, I could only think that his experience was as if he was experiencing a trip to the heavens with the four arch angels. The situations he was put in, the way he was able to respond, the end result of the four other nurses placing him in a real-world situation of an event that he had only practiced on a test-dummy and having him save this person's life – it all seemed just like the way the angels train him in the heavens. When I pointed this out and helped him see that he was experiencing "heaven on Earth" with the four angels, he was overcome with emotion. I knew he understood it when it was happening like that, but he was hesitant to place words in describing the situation as I have described it.

His experience – coupled with my earlier conversation with the lost man on the corner of the street – led our conversation in directions neither of us expected. I felt compelled to tell him about the Asa Butterfield vision, but I wanted to share it with him more under the context of Acacia Battlefield. I did

The Written (cont'd)

not shape the story any differently than I wrote it above, I just wanted to explore the idea of the words being "Acacia" and "Battlefield" rather than "Asa Butterfield." Bryan felt compelled to share with me his thoughts.

In the conversation, there came a point where I wanted to tell Bryan a pressing thought I had about the words, but every time I attempted to tell him, my phone fuzzed out on a specific set of words. I said, "Bryan – you know what was made of Acacia wood right? If the word really was acacia, then it could be talking about [....fuzz....]." I said the word but he did not hear it. So, thinking it was just a connection issue with my phone, I repeated those same sentences over again. I am not kidding when I say that the phone fuzzed out in the exact same place. Bryan asked me again to repeat it. I asked him if the conversation had any other reception problems before, and he told me it had been perfectly clear. I was sitting on a bench outside my apartment building during the duration of the call with a full signal, so I noted the two signal interference issues as likely a divine signal. This type of occurrence happens frequently with Bryan and me. Certain words and certain phrases are fuzzed out to help us know we are either saying the right things or are not supposed to say those things aloud, even though they are the right things. It is a divine interference in our communication.

Knowing that what I was about to repeat a third time was going to be significant, I asked Bryan to repeat what he heard exactly. Each time, the very last phrase I had said – the answer to the question "You do know what is made out of acacia

Rebirth III

wood, right?" – was lost in a signal interference. With more excitement than I had when I began the sentence before, I blurted it out one more time. "The Ark of the Covenant. The Ark was made of acacia word." Each time I said those words, the phone fuzzed out. I continued on. "It has to be. And it supports the seven years. And if the Ark is made of acacia wood and the second word was battlefield, then it could be possible that all of the chaos taking place in the other hemisphere right now is related to..." I didn't have to finish my sentence. Bryan chimed in. "the discovery or the use of the Ark of the Covenant." We both knew this was most definitely one of the messages being communicated to me. Sometimes, though, it takes both of us to work out the details.

But if understanding the significance of the word "Acacia Battlefield" was not enough, an even greater seven-and-seven moment was about to occur. Bryan began by telling me some of what he recalled about the Ark of the Covenant and the destruction it could unleash. He mentioned how four angels were on the outside of the Ark and it was covered with a blue cloth. I stopped him mid-sentence. At that moment he had no idea what he had said. I said, "You mean like the four angels that were with you today during the code blue?" He was speechless. There before us was the divine architecture of the day's events unfolding in a glorious manner. To someone without sight, without ears, the day's events would have been a smattering of weird but justifiable experiences. But if one was to step back and see it from God's eyes (no irreverence intended), it could be understood in a way like this:

The Written (cont'd)

"Jonathan has been communing with my angels pretty regularly. Even though he doesn't always remember everything, let's give him what he needs to see that everything taking place on Earth right now, and the roles I have planned for him and Bryan, are not to be seen as games or training. Training is now over and this is real. The Ark is on the verge of being [used or discovered] on the battlefield as I foretold would come to pass – just as I shared with John, Daniel, Amos and many others in previous generations. But that is probably too much to try to communicate to him and have him return with from the heavens. So, instead of taking the chance that the message is missed, let's make sure he can connect the dots. As for Bryan, he already understands how the end of days is unraveling. He sees the world's events for what they are, and he is acutely aware of the details of every story in the Bible. But, he needs to see that his role is no longer in training either. He needs to see it as real. The challenge with Bryan is that he has not been communing with my angels in heaven as much recently for [whatever biological or astrological reason]. But he has been noticing my works around him on Earth. So, let's let him see it in the real world. Let's role-play his life in a way that echoes similarities to his most lucid experiences in the heavens. In fact, let's sign the events of his day in every way we can. Let's begin by having him surrounded by four medical elders who will pull him from his place of rest, escort him to a room, and rely on him to save a person's life. Let's put him in scenarios he has never been in and let him react on faith as he does in the heavens. When he has questions, let's have the

Rebirth III

nurses answer as the angels would. And, when all of this comes to pass, he will walk away understanding the spiritual parallels, but not fully understand the story, just as Jonathan won't quite understand the full story of the words I shared with him. But after each of their days unfold in the ways I intend, their souls will seek each other out and commune upon the events and understand the great message they need to understand today....it cannot wait a day longer."

And so it was, this is how God began to share with Bryan and I what our roles would be and what events would soon come to pass.

August 1, 2014

I awoke to a great swirling feeling – as if I had just returned from a great travel to the heavens – but was unable to recall any of the information. I went to bed late and fell asleep while meditating. I think my body's demand for sleep prevented me from finding harmony.

August 2, 2014

My experience this morning echoed similarities to the great revelation of the seven-headed beast several nights ago. In the moment, my mind did not quite understand everything going on in detail, but my soul seemed to understand the situation fluently. The scenario was a run down school. Destruction

The Written (cont'd)

had plagued the landscape around us. All of the buildings were broken or damaged some way. Colors were muted and it seemed to be night above... at least that was my impression since the sky was dark. But, now that I write this, I realize I have never described day or night in this particular way. So, it stands to reason that the sky was dark though it was day, but that is only a best guess. Darkness was a fact.

I saw orange streaks in the sky as if fire was destroying whatever was above. I was with two others. Among the three of us, we comprised a fighting unit. As I can only describe the events that led us to this school in rudimentary earthly words and concepts, the best I can explain is that we were being pursued across the galaxy by some evil threat. My awareness of being in the surroundings came clearly into focus as we arrived in front of the school. It seemed as if we had been running across "the galaxy" trying to lure the force behind us to this very setting.

While that explanation may seem like something from a science fiction movie, the scenario was hardly like that. The term galaxy should be more observed as "all eternity" and the term "evil threat" should be understood as "the opposition to the holy." Our unit of three souls was one of the last remaining units fighting this great battle. We were clearly outnumbered in quantity, but much stronger on an individual basis. It was possible for the three of us to defeat entire armies of evil's forces, and quite possibly Lucifer himself. And though we had strength on our side, I knew there was no margin for error. It

Rebirth III

seemed there was an immense weight on our shoulders that if we didn't succeed, evil would overcome the holy.

As I surveyed the landscape around us, I saw death and carcasses everywhere. There was no life at all. No plants. No vegetation. No animals, insects, birds, or reptiles. The stench was enough to make my stomach turn. In all of my experiences in the heavens, the sense of smell is the least frequently utilized. During heightened sensory moments, it generally affects sight, hearing, and touch. But this is the first time that I was so clearly aware of the sense of smell – and not only that, but the sense of something so rotten and stomach-churning. There were several times I nearly threw up from the smell. It was the most disturbing feeling I have had in any type of astral travel.

The school before us was white, and its doors were chained shut. I turned and saw one of the negative forces off in the distance. I understood the force to be a "creature." It was flying toward us in the distant sky at an extremely fast rate of speed, but it was without form, so I could not describe the appearance of the creature. We turned and ran into the school knowing that we would have to split up in three separate directions so that we could lure the creature to a place we had chosen for battle. I ran in one direction and continually had to catch my breath, but not due to being winded. Instead, it was more like I was not as strong due to the increasing distance between the two other souls in my unit.

The lack of strength caused the stench of death and the carcasses to make my stomach turn even more than I thought

The Written (cont'd)

was possible. So each time I had to "catch my breath" was more akin to stopping to "gag and nearly heave up my insides." Each time, though, I could only stop for a brief moment before I would continue running. We were each being closely pursued, though I cannot really describe how we were all being pursued in three directions by one creature. My thought process stumbled through understanding, but I knew that having no rationale was better than bogging down my mind in trying to rationalize the chase.

The three of us eventually found our way into a large science laboratory. When we arrived, I knew we had successfully lured the creature to the place we had planned. We all stood together with a large black table top behind us. It was the same kind of table found in school science labs, but larger. As the creature approached, I was aware of its great size. I looked upward to where its face would be when it stepped into view. The only thing that separated us and the creature was a great wall that divided the science lab from the hallway outside. The door did not shut, for it was already destroyed. My senses became overwhelmed at this moment, and I began to lose harmony with the heavens. My periphery began to fill with a bright white light, and then there was a brilliant flash, and I was returned to my body.

Rebirth III

August 3, 2014

I had several experiences today during different meditative times. Each one was brief, lasting about two minutes on Earth and occurring almost immediately upon shutting my eyes. During the first experience, I recognized my heavenly surroundings. I began to wonder about my past and how it was viewed to the elders. I immediately heard a voice cry out from the heavenly void. It was a male voice, gentle and kind. The voice said, "Thirty? A young lamb, bricks [I didn't understand the next word, but I was shown a concept of a pile of bricks that looked like rubble, though it was going to be used to build something]." As I focused on his answer, I lost harmony. I understood the definition of a young lamb to be biblical in nature. But, having the word bricks immediately follow the concept of a lamb will require further exploring.

I journaled the experience and closed my eyes again. I immediately was taken back to a heavenly void. It was swirly at first, but I eventually found balance in the feeling. My field of view was obscured, and my only area of focus was directly before my eyes. In front of me, I was handed a bag. It was black and open, held by two angelic hands. Inside was the fish symbol used in Christian culture. I had been debating on signing up for Christian Mingle in the hours earlier, so my mind interpreted the symbol to mean something about that action. I spoke into the void, "There is no one out there on that site that will want to date me." This time, a more stern voice

The Written (cont'd)

boomed and resonated in the chamber. I could tell we were no longer in a void, for a void would have no echoes. The voice said, "There is one that exists." I interpreted it as literally only one person.

On that note, I returned to my body to write down the experience. I quickly attempted to return one more time. This time I arrived in the exact same scenario as before. Again, I was handed an open black bag by the same angel. It had an orange life jacket in it, folded in half and something that represented a paddle board. I recently decided I would start paddle boarding and purchased one the other day. I have only practiced one day on it, but I know I am going to enjoy the sport. Regardless, seeing the bag open before me only gave rise to two questions. The first – "Does the paddle board symbol show me what I am supposed to do with the girl that was in the previous vision?" And while that would make sense if one was to interpret the series of visions only in earthly dialogue, I believe it to also contains a second meaning.

Last week I prayed about my desire to learn to paddle board. I heard God's voice and listened to his signs. He provided me the answers I needed and the confidence to understand that He is providing for my heart's desires in this Promised Land in so far as I do not take advantage of His generosity nor allow my intention to shift to the right or left from where it should be.

Later in the afternoon, I had one more brief experience. It, too, only had a duration of a couple of minutes. In fact, I was not sure how long I would meditate, but I set a timer to

Rebirth III

beep after 11 minutes since I had an errand to run. But, as soon as I had my experience, I was jolted back to my body to find that only two minutes had passed.

When the experience began, a male angel was standing with me. I was handed a scroll that contained a questionnaire that was answered by "the girl planned for me to one day be with." I understood the scroll to contain the written word of her thoughts and actions to a series of compatibility-like questions. These questions seemed important for a spiritual union to take place. I scrolled through her responses quicker than my mind could comprehend. Somehow though, my spirit knew what was on the page without having to process the meaning. I struggled with this concept as I scrolled through hundreds or maybe even thousands of questions in a matter of a couple of seconds. Finally, my mind convinced my spirit to stop on one question so I could try to read it.

As I tried to read it, the words remained blurry. I could not decipher a question, much less an answer. When the angel noticed I was trying to understand it well enough to bring it back with me to Earth, he swatted at the scroll and made it continue scrolling faster than I could understand, then he took it away. As I was reading the questionnaire, I knew that the girl was twenty-six years old and that her answers were somewhat misguided and naive to what she really meant. I was not disappointed, but rather concerned that the angels would not accept her as a spiritual counterpart for me. I hoped that the angels would approve of the girl's answers.

The Written (cont'd)

I tried to ask them if they could help her change the answers to what they should be (as if she was not going to pass a literal written test for the angels). But they did not seem to acknowledge my plea. There seemed to be importance placed on me being aware of how a younger mind can warp understanding of spiritual concepts, for even my thirty-three-year-old mind is naive to another that has more experience than I. As I pleaded with the angel in unspoken words, another male angel walked through a door on my right and into the room. As soon as he saw me standing with the angel, his voice cut through the silence, "Mack (which I understood to be the beginning to Michael with a longer ah sound for the second letter)! What are you doing?! I've got this." The angel seemed frustrated at the other and walked briskly to us. He grabbed the scroll that was in my hand which suddenly caused black and white snow (like on an analog television channel with no signal) to fill my periphery and white noise was all I could hear. I suddenly felt a thump to my chest and I opened my eyes on Earth.

August 4, 2014
Afternoon

While each of my experiences was brief during mediation, I decided that it would be best to try to return with as much information as I could each time. Often, just remembering a couple of words is a difficult task at hand. The experiences that

Rebirth III

occurred during my mediation could easily have continued to unfold into much longer experiences, but the details in the beginning seemed so important, so I returned to my body to journal each experience.

During the first experience of my mediation, a swirly feeling was felt by the right side of my face. The word "Hiroshima" was said as it passed over my face as it swirled and created a bigger arc to my left. It felt like it was swirling along a Fibonacci spiral vector. I immediately was overcome with confusion. I had no idea why the word "Hiroshima" was just imparted to me, so I returned and wrote it down.

When I returned, I again found myself in a void without form. The darkness turned to a fiery red, and a demon made of iron emerged. He was holding an iron helmet in his left hand and had no face in the iron opening of the armor around his head and neck. The void was filled with a horrible metallic and burning sound. The demon was more like what I suppose a Sentinel would look like. The demon's voice cut through the air. It was bold, and deep. "Years ago the mud-yellow waves fell down upon you. Years ago [something about a parachute]." I wrestled to understand the line about the parachute. I recited the demon's words over and over and decided it was better to write down what I understood than to try to understand that which I could not and risk losing the rest of the message. I returned and wrote it down.

Almost immediately I returned. This time, the void was filled with screams and destruction. It was all audible with no visual queues. Everything was, again, without form. A higher

The Written (cont'd)

pitched, almost squeaky, male voice cut through the screams. The voice was directed to my ears. It said, "I warn you. We all die. Even you do." I tried to force my eyes to open in the void, or seek out just a little light to bring the void into focus, but to no avail. The screams were tortured souls. This I knew. I returned to my body and wrote down the words I heard spoken.

Again, I returned. This time there were visual queues. A royal blue orb flew over my head. It changed shape into a teardrop with a very sharp point. As it reached a formless and smoky representation of evil, the orb inverted itself…or perhaps I was upside down. Either way, the blue orb-teardrop seemed to ward off the evil spirit. An angelic voice cut through the void. It was the voice of whomever was controlling the orb (or maybe was represented by the orb). The voice said, "No. We will kill all of you." I tried to focus on the visuals, but they lost form. I quickly returned to journal the experience.

I closed my eyes and this time was led to a basement. It was dark, damp, and had a wooden-plank stairwell leading down into it. The walls were made of cinderblock. I watched as an evil spirit was brought down into the basement. The spirit was placed in a chair under restraint. From the silence a robot-like voice began to cut through. It was saying a prayer or specific incantation. It was very formal, and I was caught off guard by just how formal and ritualistic it appeared. It began with the words, "Thou shalt…" but I cannot recall the words immediately following. There were a couple of lines spoken, and then I heard, "For thou shall not harken before me." Knowing I already could not repeat back the missing lines af-

Rebirth III

ter the first "Thou shalt" I decided to return and write back the words I was able to take away from the experience.

Still not done with my travels, I once again returned. This time, the void became engulfed in red and filled with flames. A blocky, almost Lego-like form appeared before me. It was the representation of Lucifer. I have never seen him appear in this form – only in the form of a man in rose-colored glasses. He looked at me and erupted in a dreadful voice, "Stop! This marriage thing shall not come to be. It is a waste." And just as quickly as he appeared in the heavens, he was gone, and I returned to my body. I am not quite sure what "marriage" he was speaking of, but I have to think it is pertaining to my spiritual walk. I also took it as potential that I would meet a girl to be with and that Satan was unhappy about this union…but that may just be my own wishful thinking.

I wrote down my notes and returned once again. This would be the final brief-experience during my meditations. As soon as I appeared in the heavens, I heard the voices of three angels. They were peaceful, calming, and presented an overwhelming feeling of warmth and Love. The first angel said, "Nicely done." The second angel said, "He has done well." The third angel said, "He is ready to enter." Each of those comments were spoken without pause between the lines. With this, my form was turned so that a tunnel appeared before me. Perhaps it was a tunnel leading down, such as into a pit. Perhaps it was directed up and I was on my back. I did not have any way to gain my bearings, but I thought that the direction was "down" from whatever direction I was orientated.

The Written (cont'd)

My periphery began to have flashes of white light. It was as if an engine was revving up. My mind began to swirl as the ascent was starting to occur. I knew I would forget the words I heard if I did not return, so I broke harmony with the moment to journal the words I heard. This was my last experience; I was unable to find harmony with the heavens again during mediation. And, I suppose that makes sense because my soul was sent on a journey in the moments prior. It only makes sense that I broke the attachment between my mind and soul and would not be able to "reattach" it during the conditions of this mediation.

August 4, 2014
Late Afternoon

Another quick experience during meditation took me to a beautiful garden. It was beautifully manicured, but in a natural way. I was walking along a winding dirt path that flowed like a river, or like the body of a serpent. The trees contained bright red apples. The bushes had red berries budding on them. To my right was an angel dressed in white. He was an elder with a long white beard and white hair. He wore a dark band around his head. I could not look at him directly so my description of him is only my impression. He was much taller than me and took me by my right hand (he was on my right side) and began leading me through the garden. I knew instinctively that this was the Garden of Eden even though I was

Rebirth III

not told the name of the location. I have been in a couple of gardens before – quite possibly this same one – but never did I hold onto harmony long enough to understand anything about the surroundings. This time was different though. While it was extremely brief, it was also extremely vivid. The angel was talking to me as we walked, but I was not able to focus on his voice as I was focusing on the surroundings initially. Almost as quickly as I arrived in the garden, I lost harmony and returned to Earth.

August 7, 2014

My experience this morning was extremely vivid. I can only explain this one as similar to the parables Jesus shared with his disciples as documented in the New Testament. While I have obviously had a wide variety of experiences – many deep with symbolism that I may or may not have understood at the time, this message was delivered to me in a way far greater than could have been communicated by a simple story alone.

It began with me witnessing two girls fighting over religion. One girl had an olive complexion. The other was black. They both carried a tremendous amount of sass when it came to the way they delivered communication to each other. The vision began with the black female holding a large planter's pot. It was made of clay and was the size a person would use to grow a small tree. While I am just guessing, I would say it

The Written (cont'd)

would hold somewhere between three and five gallons of liquid. But, this pot held only dirt and soil. There were no plants growing from it, and it seemed that the lack of plant growth was symbolically what started their communication.

They were fighting over religion, though neither ever said any words that would communicate religion was the source of their argument. It was only the impression I had as I witnessed their argument. They were arguing in a childish way wherein the more words they said, the louder they became, and the greater amount of sass in their delivery took hold. It was as if the louder and more words were said, it would help them win the argument. Eventually, the black girl holding the pot with soil in it lifted it up and dumped it on the olive-complected girl's head. Soil fell all over her and made her angrier than before. The girl with olive skin said, "Oh, no, you didn't..." But as those words rang out, something unexpected happened. The pot that appeared to hold only dirt revealed rooted plants hidden within. They were just hidden beneath the dirt. There were two blue hyacinths that had bloomed and blossomed beneath the soil.

The two girls looked at it briefly, but resumed their argument. The olive-skinned girl ran around the room in search of a pot to dump on the black girl's head. She wanted to return the gesture – an eye for an eye, if you will. It was important for me to witness these antics. As she ran around the room in search of a pot with no plant growing in it, she realized that she was not going to find what she was looking for. She walked over to a plant that had a large, bulbous root base. The base

Rebirth III

was much, much larger than the plant itself and resembled the shape of a teardrop on its size, though the bulb was about the size of a basketball. It was not sitting in a pot, but instead was wrapped with a silver ribbon-like tape that served the role of a pot. The silver ribbon helped the roots grow. The plant was a chrysanthemum, though at this moment I was not sure if the plant I was seeing was actually a chrysanthemum, for I have no idea what a chrysanthemum looks like (I had only heard the name).

She picked up the plant and began unwrapping the ribbon around its roots. She said, "Oh. Oh! You aren't going to find reason to use the Chrysanthemum? It has meaning too!" Without words and only in construct, she began to reveal to the black girl how the word Chrysanthemum holds two parts. She emphasized the "Chrys" at the beginning and held it in the same religious context as "Christ." As she did so, she began speaking about Christ. I was not able to understand all of the words in their fast-quipped conversation but the gist was that the plant represented Christ in some capacity. The black girl replied, "Oh, yes, I am!" She grabbed the plant from her hands. But, instead of using the plant as a weapon in the context of their fight, she wanted to keep the plant and nurture it. They seemed resolved in their fighting, and this portion of the experience faded.

The next day, the two girls appeared to be friends again. They began to journey out into the waters that were near where they had their spat the day before to "find what else was hidden from view." The waters were turbulent, but not overly

The Written (cont'd)

deep. The two girls made their way through the waters and turned right into a hidden inlet. This portion of the stream was cleverly tucked away and was a place where the waters found calm. The surface of the water appeared like glass, though the rushing stream behind them divided the two locales. The olive-skinned girl suddenly proclaimed, "Oh. Oh! What have we here?"

They walked through the waters and over to one single plant floating in the water. It was a "blue lotus flower" though the flowered portion was closer to a purple/pink color. The roots of the plant were hanging deep beneath the flower. They were both overcome with excitement. The olive-skinned girl asked the black girl if she would "use it" to which she replied, "Oh, absolutely."

They both seemed unsure whether they should tell others of this special place for fear that it would be destroyed. There was an emphasis on needing to keep the location clean and spiritual, but without those words. It was only an impression given to me. They puzzled over what they should do and decided they would return to continue exploring the place, but would hide it from others to keep it safe. They turned through the calm of the waters and waded back from where they came. They were the only disturbances in the water, which was important for me to observe. These two beings were the only reason ripples in the water existed in this otherwise calm and serene place.

As I processed the moments, I understood the significance on a spiritual level, but knew I needed to understand the sym-

Rebirth III

bolism in/of the flowers once I returned to my earthly body. It was at this point that my soul left the heavens. When I awoke, I was on the shores of Thailand. It appeared I had washed up on a beach there. I was in a safe place and felt protected. Immediately, my mind spun as I began rationalizing where my earthly family was as I asked myself the question, "Would I be emotionally okay to be this far away from everyone I knew – my daughter included?" I felt saddened in that moment thinking about my daughter being "a world away." But, almost as instantly as the sadness crept in, God's warmth and Love filled my spirit. I knew in that moment that, no matter where the journey may lead, God was protecting my family as well. And just like that, I felt peace. I stared at the sun in the sky as I continued to lie on my back on whatever shore I had washed upon. I felt resolve and calm in all that I was doing, for I knew The Lord was watching over me. It was at this point I returned to my earthly body.

Immediately after journaling the experience, I looked up the meanings of the flowers involved in the experience. I was fascinated to find that the blue hyacinth is native to Israel and Northern Turkey. With all of the emphasis on Israel in the End-of-Days, it suddenly made sense that the flower (representing life, the spirit, God's truth) was hidden beneath the soil, though it was revealed when the two began to squabble. The hyacinth is said to have received its name from Apollo – the sun God. It was the flower that grew from Hyakinthos blood when he was accidentally struck by a discus while Apollo was teaching Hyakinthos to throw.

The Written (cont'd)

The Chrysanthemum's meaning is actually derived from splitting the first portion of the word from the second. The same first portion that was divided in my experience was divided to help in understanding the meaning of the flower. "Chrys" means golden. The second portion of the word means "flower." Unsurprisingly, the appearance of the flower in my experience was identical to how it appears on Earth, though I would never have been able to describe the appearance of the flower before today. It is also important to know that the Japanese hold a "Festival of Happiness" every year to celebrate this flower. Also, Confucius once suggested that the Chrysanthemum be used as an object of meditation. It is thought that a petal of a Chrysanthemum placed in the bottom of a wine glass will encourage a long and healthy life.

Before even delving into the meaning of the lotus, it is important to note that both of the first two flowers hold extremely significant spiritual meanings and represent locations as well. Both meanings center around the sun. Knowing this heading into my brief research on the blue lotus, the symbolic meaning was already beginning to be unveiled. The blue lotus is regarded as one of the most sacred plants known on Earth. It grows from the mud and blossoms under a full moon. Every ancient culture has held it in high regard to its meaning. It, too, can be used in a tea or wine to encourage spiritual enlightenment.

From Buddhists to Egyptians, this flower appears as a focal point in their spiritual teachings. The blue lotus (purple in color as I saw in my experience) represents the victory over the

Rebirth III

senses, of intelligence and wisdom, and of knowledge. Its center is unseen and is the embodiment of "perfection of wisdom." In Egyptian culture, the plant was associated with the sun god, Ra – the bringer of light. In Hindi culture, it represents resurrection and purity. The leaves and flowers are born high above the water. In all cultures, the flower is compared to an enlightened being who emerges undefiled from the chaos and confusion of the world.

So in the brevity of the message shared with me in the heavens, a story about religion was told. Locations were given through the flowers. Colors were given to communicate a specific message. The actions of the two women and the way the story was told communicated the religious turmoil that exists in Israel – why it exists, and what will come of it, where the story will unfold, how the spiritual message is to be seen. I will not expand further, for the beauty in the message is in the numerous meanings the message holds. But I wanted to share this portion of the message to help trigger thoughts to those who may be trying to understand how God works and how Divine messages are made.

August 8, 2014

This morning was filled with three distinct experiences. The first experience began with the sounds of splashing water. I had no visual queues – only audible. An angelic female voice spoke in the silence. She said, "The dharma initiative began

The Written (cont'd)

with [what sounded like Jowahsheea, but not quite]." I immediately understood the word to be an archetypal representation of "who." And while that may sound like a strange way to explain what I heard, the spirit tends to speak in an archetypal fashion, rather than a literal fashion. I also understood the term "dharma initiative" to mean "how the concept of dharma began." As I attempted to repeat the phrase for my memory, I struggled to pronounce the last word she said. I tried very hard to say the word, but it was as if I did not understand the word well enough to know how to pronounce it. The angelic voice repeated the word several times to help me try to say it. On the third attempt, I lost harmony and returned to my body. I took brief notes about the experience and attempted to return to my meditative state.

This time, I found myself with no understanding of the context of events that I was about to witness. The only way I can describe the event was that "I witnessed the passing of crystal while I was with another." Everything else – all details of this moment – are impossible to put into words. Perhaps I was not supposed to be able to relay the moment with any more understanding than the words I am able to write down, but after I returned to journal the words, I returned to the heavens for one last experience. This experience was much more detailed than the previous two – however, I believe the first experience of the morning held the most meaning (as I will discuss in just a bit).

This experience began in a Latin restaurant. There were two Latino women sitting on my right. The restaurant was

Rebirth III

plain. The table we sat at was a well-worn wooden table. I knew as I was eating my food that money was in short supply for most of the people around me. The lady directly next to me on my right was a regular of the establishment. I listened as she asked the waitress for a special dish that had a fruit that appeared to be similar to a plantain, but was not anywhere related to bananas or plantains. The waitress told the lady they only had one of these fruits remaining and that it was not in the best condition. She was worried that if the lady placed the order that the chef would replace the fruit that she wanted with mangos instead.

As I listened to them talk, I was overcome with a craving for this mystery food. I began to ask the waitress about the dish they were talking about when she replied that I could only try it on a Wednesday. I was a bit puzzled by the response and sat back to listen to the couple and the waitress continue to discuss the dish next to me. The couple seemed to be hesitant to buy more than one dish. It was as if they would not have enough money for other purposes if they chose to order this food. This caused me to be even more perplexed since the waitress had already said they only had one of those fruits remaining. I interjected in the conversation and asked if "the price of the fruit was similar to that of how a single plantain is more expensive than a bundle of bananas," but they did not understand my question. At that point I lost harmony and returned to my body.

After journaling this last experience, I began combing the internet for any understanding of the word that I could not

The Written (cont'd)

pronounce from my first experience of the morning. I tried phonetic spellings. I read up about dharma, searching for any name or word that could have been similar. I began looking up Hebrew letters to see if the word had any relation to my minimal knowledge of Hebrew, though that seemed like a reach. Nothing.

I finally had the realization that I have been given Sanskrit words in previous travels to the heavens and that perhaps this could be Sanskrit. Unfortunately, not much is to be found on Sanskrit in English translations. I continued attempting phonetic spellings of this strange word that I could not pronounce. And, since I could not pronounce it, it left me even more confused as to how it may be spelled. I eventually ran across the word Joshi (which I knew was not right) and discovered it was rooted to the word "Jyotishi." Finally it was all beginning to make sense.

The spelling that the word was rooted in did not appear in any English document I could find, but I again found another word that was similar. It led met to learn that the word I sought was "Jyotisha." It is essentially the ancient Hebrew understanding of astronomy with the root of the word meaning "radiance of the moonlight." Now it all made sense. The simple sentence that took so much effort for me to unravel in meaning essentially said, "The travels to the heavens, the girl that appears in the visions under the moonlight, and the ancient study of celestial bodies is what gave way to the understanding of Dharma." The word Dharma has no western equivalent, nor a definitive translation. The closest that

Rebirth III

can be made is the phrase "the path to righteousness." So, essentially, I was told in the purest words that could deliver the intent of the message, a confirmation in continuing the path that I am following.

August 9, 2014

This morning I journeyed across the stars and arrived in the heavens. When I first arrived, I was escorted by an angel on my right side. This has been increasingly common for me recently. Perhaps my awareness of the angel is just becoming stronger. Maybe the angel is just letting me see him. Maybe he has been there all along, but it is a detail I miss because of the marvelous nature of the experience itself.

As we were walking, I stopped in my tracks. This was the moment my consciousness fully kicked in, and I understood my surroundings in full. I looked at the angel with me. He was bright, and I had a hard time discerning memorable features. I guess there is a moment that the mind says, "It is now or never," when it comes to decisions. So, as I stood there absorbing the gravity of the moment, I decided to just ask what was on my mind. I said, "I feel terrible for even asking this because I know I must ask it all of the time. But, what is your name? That is the one thing I can never seem to bring back with me, and I know I must know it. I'm really sorry, and I hope you know I mean it respectfully."

The Written (cont'd)

The angel was glowing in the brightest white light, his presence already overpowering in strength. I suppose it was a rather bold effort to ask the name of such a divine presence, but it has been a question plaguing my curiosity since these experiences began several years ago. Names arise. Faces arise. But, tying names and faces has proven to be one of the most difficult tasks for me. I am uncertain why. Perhaps names should best be viewed as "unimportant" where the actions speak louder than the identity a person converses with in the heavens. Perhaps I have been told the name many times, but I just have not been strong enough or allowed to return with such a grand piece of information. Whatever the case may be, I have feared even more greatly calling an angel by the wrong name. I imagine that could be perceived as a greater misstep than asking the name again. At least by asking, I knew I was being honest and true, and my intentions were just.

The angel looked at me as I awaited an answer. It was just the briefest of moments, but the angel's face became more defined in the white light. His features were sharp, but small in definition. I would use the word "svelte" but that would best be served in the description of a feminine presence. This angel was clearly masculine and radiating the essence of strength. So the features seemed a little counterintuitive in verbal description, but fit perfectly for everything I was witnessing. The angel's eyes cut to my core. His look was stern and intimidating, yet I did not feel intimidated as much as partially ashamed for having to ask the question. But somehow, I knew that he understood all of those same feelings I was describing. It was

Rebirth III

as if he shared in my consciousness through his gaze. Without words, he gave me his name. His lips did not move. His eyes did not blink. "Michael."

This was the first time I had ever heard the name Michael in my experiences, though he is perhaps the most documented of all angels. I have assumed I have interacted with him on occasion, but have never fully expected to feel the gravity of the moment in such a way. I realized that my "guide" on so many occasions in the heavens has been this same angel. It is not always him, but this was one of numerous encounters with him. Imagine realizing suddenly that a "blank name" that has recurred so frequently in this written history of my travels to the heavens was just unveiled as the great archangel, Michael. That is what I realized in this moment. It was not just the name. It was the realization of the divinity to all that I have been experiencing.

For a few moments, I could not process anything outside of this one fact. I did not lose harmony. Instead, it possibly helped me find greater focus. After a few stunning moments of sheer white light in my periphery, Michael walked me over to a group I was meant to join. The setting was hard to explain since it was represented archetypally, so I will save an attempt at a description. The highlights are that the group, including their leader, was all sitting around a table when I arrived. As I joined the group, I knew I was supposed to be there, supposed to be led by the leader. In an instant I recognized the leader as Noah, though every description in earthly terms would only do this man a disservice. In fact, I am not sure how to relay his

The Written (cont'd)

appearance in any words. It was more like I saw a man that represented history, God's favor, leadership, notoriety, a noble nature, humility, yet proud stature. Somehow that is the only description I can give of Noah, save for a beard.

The group I was with all seemed to be at various levels along their spiritual journey. I could not tell if they were mortals in spirit, or spiritual beings. I paid attention to the conversation, though words from Noah were few. He spoke in actions. There were remarks in the group about us following a path that he was leading us to take. Within the group, there was a girl that seemed so familiar. In the beginning my mind tried to rationalize her as someone I knew on Earth, but was unsuccessful at finding resolve in her identity. Finally, I realized she was one of the other angels that appears in disguise around me regularly. It is as if she is there to watch over me without letting me know she is there. In the past, this would be the angel that I have called out and said things along the lines of "I know who you are," which would cause her to change shape into her more familiar angelic presence.

There is always a strong sense of Love and admiration from her. In simplest terms, I would say "she liked me" but in earthly terms, this would be misinterpreted. And even while I can describe the feeling like this in words while in mortal form, I also long for her when we are near in the heavens. There is an undeniable potential for a perfect Love, something that all earthly Love I have ever known pales in comparison to obtaining.

Rebirth III

While we followed Noah on this path, I could see that she was curious of me – of my actions. Eventually she walked past me to catch my eye. She was heading to an elevator. I am not quite sure where we were or how we got to this place along the journey, but the shading was of an emerald green. As she walked toward the elevator, I felt confidence in her identity and wanted to let her know. I headed toward the elevator after her. When I caught up to her, she turned around quickly with her back against the wall. She was brunette and beautiful. The light was still green in hue, but dim.

On Earth, this would have been a passionate moment – like something out of a movie. But in heaven, this experience would prove to play out differently. She looked at me with the most beautiful eyes. I said, "I know you aren't who you think I think you are." She looked startled, realizing she had been "caught" while I was excited to talk to her up close. As soon as her eyes glazed over in recognition of my recognition, there was an explosive sound and she disappeared right before me.

I found myself standing beside a pool. The scenario had changed, no doubt from my attempt at calling out the angel-in-disguise. I had already been given Michael's name, so I guess I was really hoping to find resolve in other angels' names. I was not upset at the scenario changing. Instead, it seemed fluid and intended. In the pool, there was a black mother and two of her children. I would guess her children were around the ages of four and six. The two children climbed out of the pool ahead of their mother. The youngest one was wearing a striped pink and white bathing suit. She ran

The Written (cont'd)

a few yards from the edge of the pool and then squatted to use the bathroom. I assumed she was still wearing a diaper, so I was not concerned about it, but I wanted to let her mom know. I had overheard their conversation of the mother telling her children where the bathroom was, so I pointed to the bathroom and helped the little girl find where she needed to go. I walked over to the edge of the pool. The mother was a little more heavy-set than most people I interact with in the heavens. She seemed to be moving more slowly to the edge of the pool. She was wearing a black one-piece bathing suit and large black sunglasses. I let her know what had happened with her child, and she seemed very thankful.

As I was speaking with the mother in the pool, the brunette angel appeared behind me. It was as if she just popped into existence to find me. She walked over to me. I looked around and noticed that everyone at the pool was now gone. Her words were simple. "How did you know?"

We were now standing with a small, round table between us. It was white. The sun glistened off of the surface. We began speaking about how I figured it out. The conversation proved to be more valuable to me than to her because I was able to better understand through spiritual words how I knew. I knew I struggled in some of my explanation. She asked me multiple times throughout the conversation, "So that is how you knew?" But, each time seemed like more of an effect than the cause she was looking for. I eventually pulled out a gold ring from my right pocket. I set it on the table before her with my right hand. It was like a man's wedding band, pure in its shape

Rebirth III

with no blemishes. She looked down upon it; the sun was glistening off of its sheen.

I could not say how I knew to pull the ring out, or even where the ring came from, but it seemed like showing her the ring was my attempt at communicating to her the answer she was seeking. The ring held a significance of why I was in the heavens – how I was able to visit. It seemed to communicate that I had been chosen, or shown favor, or perhaps something like a divine relic of recognition that I understood enough to be allowed access to the heavens. She looked up at me in surprised awe, but apparent understanding. The sun was above, and all that I can recall in those moments was the circular table with the ring glistening in the sun light, her eyes and a moment of "understanding" that occurred between us. It was then that I returned to my body from the heavens.

August 10, 2014

However brief, and though it is without context, I found my spirit standing in a shower struggling to find harmony. I felt a loud thump and realized I had been hit on the back of the head – knocked unconscious. I returned to my body.

August 11, 2014

I met three girls over the weekend while out paddle boarding. They were visiting for the weekend and we did not

The Written (cont'd)

share too much conversation – just the occasional hellos and goodbyes. But I mention them for two reasons. The first is that I have most definitely seen the blending of heaven on Earth in my time here in Ft. Lauderdale. Much of my experience here has caused me to question whether I have left Earth behind all together. The significance of there being three girls should be obvious in the context of all of my projections lately. So, there is a part of me that questions the existential nature of our interactions. The other reason I mention them is because even if one were to bring undeniable verification to this existence being of-the-clay-fact, these three girls still were used to represent something special in my heavenly experience this morning.

It began with me walking into a dimly lighted amphitheater. And, while it was my understanding that I was standing in an "amphitheater," the locale more closely resembled an indoor theater with a stage. There were long rows of seats that were constructed of plush, red fabric cushions with steel frames – the type that is used in typical movie theaters and concert halls these days.

I walked in. I began to move down an aisle to a seat that had been saved for me. There did not seem to be anyone in this theater except for the three girls I had met this past weekend on Earth and me. Of the three, there was one girl that I felt a pull to instantly when I first met her. It was that rare moment that takes your breath away and everything in your periphery fades into the distance. There was only her. She was the center of my view and radiated a light from within that my soul found in song. As great of a moment as it was, I dismissed

Rebirth III

any thought of trying to be anything more than social because of how different our stages in life were comparatively speaking.

It was even enough of a recognizable divide on Earth to bring me pause and cause me to pray for philosophical understanding before I went to sleep. As I prayed, I began thinking about what "Love" meant for each person involved. These thoughts were echoed in my prayers. For me, I have always had this Disney-ideal view of it. Ironically, these three girls all worked at Disney World a few hours away and were just enjoying a weekend at the beach. But, I had never stopped to see it from the other side.

I began to realize that Love from a female side should be much different than the Love from a male's side. I had never thought about it before – mostly because women in the United States try to always be equal to men. But they are not. One is not superior to the other. They are just different. The differences collide to create a perfect bond. The attempts at equality-in-all-ways is really a distraction from allowing the self to fall madly in Love with the other in the way that God intends.

I began to think about the differences in ages and how the places of each other's journeys change the way each other would be viewed. The concept of an equal Love was turned upside down. For every effort I knew I would one day make in Love for another, I recognized the differences in how that would be perceived by a woman at different stages of her life. To make a long story short, I began to realize that for a perfect Love to exist, there has to be a maternal/paternal aspect to the

The Written (cont'd)

relationship for nurturing and growth to occur. If each person is dead-set on a single feeling as the anchor, then the room for growth no longer exists. But, with Love as one of the strings to an anchor, the other ties must have some aspect of maternal/paternal bond to it. I have always viewed the Love I have to give in a nurturing way, but this was the first time I understood the aspect of how it actually has elements of paternal traits within it. Of course this caused me to think about how I have actually longed for a woman who demonstrates maternal Love as well as the passion of Love raging ferociously in every aspect of the relationship.

I never quite understood this is what I needed, nor did I understand that is actually what I have to give. Do not misunderstand this for anything incestuous or anything along the lines of mother/father issues for myself or the other. This is understanding the grand design of how every action we take falls into the category of teacher/student, student/teacher and transcending that into all other aspects of our lives. If two people Love each other madly, would they learn from each other and teach each other? But perhaps those words are too strong, because it would seem that the effort to teach would indicate master, and the effort to learn as a student would indicate a subservient role – and that is not what is intended. Instead it is the very effort to be paternal to a female spouse and for her to return a maternal nature to her husband. Without the actions understood as such, the effort to "care for another" is lost in hollow action rather than maternal/paternal intention. Anyway, I could write about this topic for quite a while and still

Rebirth III

feel these words leave a high potential for the reader to think I was expressing mother-father issues – which is most distinctly not the case.

So, I say all of that to set the stage for how that moment shared with one of the three in the group caused me to seek understanding in the greater meaning of Love and life. This brings us back full circle to the moment I walked into the amphitheater. Of the three girls, the one that I felt a pull toward was sitting in the row in front of me. The row I was summoned to come down had her two friends sitting there. While they were all bunched up in a group, I was supposed to sit to the left of one of her friends, with her diagonal right in front of me. All three girls were extremely happy to see me, demonstrating a lot of enthusiasm toward my presence. But of the three, the brunette girl was truly the happiest, which warmed my heart.

The girl to my right was eating something as the lights dimmed and the presentation began. I am not sure what the presentation was about for it seemed to end abruptly. I assume that it was more for me to understand the idea of what was happening versus any specific details to come from it. When the presentation was over, the lights faded out. When they faded back up, we were all standing in their house...which was somehow connected to the amphitheater. It seemed to sit in the same place, but it was like tuning to a different channel to bring the house into focus.

It was late and each of the girls was ready to head to their bedrooms to get some sleep. I was still sitting in an amphithea-

The Written (cont'd)

ter chair when they began to get up and go to their rooms. I pretended to fall asleep to prevent any awkward "where do I sleep" questions from arising. I wasn't tired, so I pretended until they all turned out their lights. The brunette girl's room was to my right. She left the door open, which I understood to be a hopeful gesture from her to me. I just pretended to stay asleep. After they left I just sat in the chair, wide-awake. One of the girls came back in and noticed I was awake. She asked me to throw away her trash (from the food she had been eating previously) since I was still awake.

I got up and walked to the bathroom tripping over something along the way, which made a loud noise. I was sure it was enough to wake everyone up. When I was walking back to my chair, the brunette girl called me into her room as I neared her door. I stepped in the doorway to see what she wanted. As it turned out, she was sleep-talking. She asked me a couple of questions to which I gave answers, but I was more entertained that she would not recall any of the conversation.

The other two girls became aware of the conversation and in a protective way, asked me to walk their dog. They knew I had no ill intentions. They were just overly protective. So, I obliged to walk their dog. When I walked into the hallway, there were two dogs there to greet me. One was larger and well trained. The other was a small, white, bratty dog that seemed to only answer to its own desires. It looked like a Maltese/Chihuahua/Corgi mix. As I walked to the door, the bigger dog sat down while the other dog darted out the crack as I began to open the door. I had a moment of panic and saw

Rebirth III

myself having to chase down a deranged puppy in the middle of the night. But, to my relief, it only darted out ten yards into the grass to relieve itself. While I was outside, a male angel told me how to handle the dog. He showed me how to hold it and make sure it listened to me. It was brief advice, but worked very well. After it used the bathroom, we came back in.

The entire scenario was repeated start-to-finish two more times. They were almost identical except for a few small details. In the second experience, I sat one seat further to the left of the two girls in the amphitheater. I knew this was a second-pass at the experience and since I already knew they were eager to see me from the first experience, I felt at peace not demonstrating too much affection toward them. Even though I knew exactly where they were in the amphitheater when I walked in, I pretended not to see them until I sat down. It was strange because I think I was nervous, though I tried to demonstrate confidence and apathy.

The third time went just as the second except when the time came for me to walk the dog, it ran outside much more quickly than the previous two times. It came back quickly as well, but in its haste, it trudged back through the river of urine it left behind causing its paws to become very wet. It was as if the dog understood the drill was recurring just as I understood everything was repeating. The dog was trying to be more efficient and quicker at relieving itself for me to see. This simple action helped me understand that the scenario was not always exactly as it was before and that everyone participating had the potential to change the outcome each time. The other dif-

The Written (cont'd)

ference is that the angel was not outside the third time to give me instructions on how to handle the dog.

When I walked back in with the dog I was called into the brunette's room again. This time she was wide awake. As I stepped in the room, I saw that she was now in the form a small child that was sitting between the edge of the bed and a cream colored nightstand with three drawers. She looked like she had fallen between her bed and the nightstand and was stuck. She was sitting on her butt with her right leg extending out between the bed and the nightstand. The other leg appeared bent which was causing her to be stuck. While her voice sounded older when I entered (like in her early twenties), the voice did not match her form.

I walked over to her and picked her up and placed her back in bed. This was a moment that I felt such a great difference in size between each of us. I felt like a giant picking up a tiny doll. I recognized the size must represent spiritual growth like how I see elder angels. The elders would be similar in size to me as I was to her. I could not tell while I was looking at her if she was really a child, a fairy (yes, this actually popped into my mind), or the adult brunette I met in a form but represented in form by her spiritual growth.

As she was lying in bed, I covered her up and tucked her in as a father would do for his child. She was so happy to see me. It was the kind of happiness one would hope to see in those they Love. I felt such a great amount of Love for her, but in a fatherly way. It was as if I was a caretaker, or someone she looked up to rather than someone of passionate Love. As I

Rebirth III

looked at her tucked in the bed, she kept saying words I did not understand. I originally thought she was trying to tell me her last name so that we could stay in touch, but then I realized that the first name I knew on Earth was not the name that was being given to me. I immediately recognized that the three girls were used to help me understand a lesson in my life in a way that I would only fully understand after the experience completed.

I wrestled with the two words I was given. This felt like a flashback to the other day when I was given a Sanskrit word I knew nothing about. The first "name" I was given sounded like "scaenici." The last "name" was shared to me in syllables, much like the names of the great angels have been shared with me before. This time was much harder for me though. The word broke apart into a first easy syllable. It was either "Meg," "Mega," or "Meta." But, by all accounts, this part was easy for me to understand, and we moved on to the other part of the word, which was much harder. After several attempts of trying to repeat the word, my best effort put the word as something like "le galania." Still, that did not seem quite right. It was at this point the vision faded and I was jolted into my body.

After journaling the voyage, I immediately googled the words and tried to figure out (at first) if I had been genuinely given the brunette girl's last name. I scoured all of the resources I could find, ultimately not arriving at anything. I then decided that the experience most definitely was allegorical and not representative of an earthly truth. I scoured the internet for words that phonetically sounded like the syllables I had

The Written (cont'd)

been given. Finally, I arrived on the same webpage that I had seen once before (over a year ago). It was a webpage that I had been unable to find since a great vision from Bryan.

In that vision, Bryan was given a name that he found almost impossible to understand. It was given in syllables but he still could not put together the words well enough to find anything. Eventually we discovered information on Megalensia/Megalesia. It is a festival held in honor of an Ancient Greek goddess of the same name. Almost nothing is known of her, but the Greek's called her Magna Mater – the great mother. Bryan and I eventually uncovered other ancient texts with variations of spelling to the Greek goddess's name, and we eventually found references to her being the great female angel that controls all.

I suddenly realized that the name I had been given was this same angel's name. It came from the representation of a brunette child in a motherly/fatherly kind of way. I think the word must be hard to understand because there are no characters to adequately represent the sounds of each syllable. I have not yet discussed it with Bryan, but I imagine we will likely find similarities in our confusion. Further research on the first "name" showed that "Ludi scaenici" was the drama performance held during the Megalesia festival in Ancient Rome. The festival placed a lot of emphasis on this drama portion and must be why each of my three repeat experiences all began in an "amphitheater" that was portrayed like a modern theater with a stage.

Rebirth III

This also brings significance to the earlier vision about the how "Jyotisha was the reason behind the Dharma initiative." This would indicate that Magna Mater (The great mother) is the same as Jyotisha (the radiance of the moon...the girl we see in our dreams and during meditation under the moonlight). This is just my first pass at interpreting the experience, but I am confident that I have now been shared the name of Megazalea from this angel directly.

August 12, 2014

Though this morning's experience was brief, it was very direct. It began with me being shown how I have been "shipped stuff." While that term is vague, the important takeaway is that my King, my Creator, has been providing me resources that will help me on my journey. In particular, the paddle board that I purchased was at the forefront of the deliveries. The reality is that I purchased the paddle board across the street from my apartment and carried it back with me – so it was never "shipped" as my experience presented. But, I understood the meaning nonetheless. It was explained to me that the paddle board would be my "vessel." I knew at the time that the word "vessel" implied much more than a buoyant board floating in the water – it was analogous to any other "vessel" in life. I soon saw myself in the water with a group of people listening to me speak. They were around me in a semi-circle. After being asked, I took the paddle board that was

The Written (cont'd)

floating horizontally before me and split it — breaking it into two paddle boards for two others to use. The paddle board that was before me appeared to have never been broken as I bore witness to having three paddle boards in front of me. One was the source, the other two were the original halves I broke. After seeing myself perform these tasks in my experience, a voice asked me if I "wanted to remain over the domain."

At that point I awoke and journaled the experience. At the time it seemed more abstract than I have just journaled — but that is how these types of experience tend to occur. First, something abstract is presented. Then, after meditating upon the experience or in days to come, the meaning is revealed. For me, breaking the paddle board in two was representative of Jesus breaking bread among his followers and sharing wine. While I am not trying to place myself in any kind of comparison to Jesus, it is important to understand the actions that he took were left in writings so that one day we may each strive to find Christ within ourselves. I began to understand that in all I have been provided, that I need to take steps beyond the metaphorical to share Christ.

In the days following that experience (as the meaning was becoming more apparent), I found myself in the waters outside of my apartment where people would seek me in the water to speak and carry on conversation. I know they were not seeking my identity as much as they recognized my King's beacon shining through this mortal vessel encumbering my soul. The first few days my paddle board became a conversation starter

Rebirth III

among others. But several days into it, something special happened. The topics of the questions became more apparent in how the people around me sought more than just answers; they wanted to understand the spiritual side that their mind could not quite put into words. It was in these days that I began to learn to speak to people about Christ and all that He has done for me.

August 13, 2014

This morning's experience placed me in a post-apocalyptic setting. There is nothing specific to help me describe the setting. Rather, I just knew it to be the aftermath of an imminent ending to the Earth. I took my paddle board and journeyed across the ocean for what seemed like an eternity. There was no end in sight to this journey. Eventually I arrived upon a beach. I took a backpack that was broken and heavy and placed it over my shoulders. This location was green and mountainous. It seemed as if the Earth was moist with water, as if the oceans had either just receded or heavy rains had subsided. I journeyed for what seemed like hundreds of miles. Every bit of the experience seemed to last every bit as long as my understanding of time and distance allows.

I eventually arrived at a farm. I recognized the farm as the home of one of my relatives. Perhaps it was my spiritual grandfather's home. In the front yard, there was a broken tractor. It had the appearance of a well maintained tractor from

The Written (cont'd)

the early 1900s. It had two round headlights offset from the front of its rust-colored front end. The grass in this particular area had been scorched from the sun and was not as green as it once was. If I understood the journey across the ocean and to a wet shoreline as being a remnant of an apocalyptic flooding, then this part of the world was remnant of an apocalyptic scorched Earth – as if both flooding and scorching coexisted in different parts of the world.

    I headed into the house and saw my grandparents and father there. I could not decipher if they were my spiritual parents and relatives or earthly parents and relatives projected into a spiritual world around me. When I walked inside, I noticed sixteen candles placed before me. It is important to understand that the sum total of candles was sixteen. An angel that resembled my Aunt Cindy made a purple candle, separate from the rest, for my father. My grandfather seemed to think a pink candle represented something about me. This would not be the first time that the color pink has been presented to me in the heavens. There was the pink motorcycle that arrived with an angel, pink azaleas, other pink flowers, and now a pink candle. And even though these candles were made separate from the sixteen I initially saw, the sum total of the initial candles and the purple and pink candles remained sixteen.

    I returned from the heavens to write about the experience and was able to return once again. This time I arrived at a location somewhere between the beach and the house from before. And though I was along a shoreline, the mountains were what helped me understand my location. An angel

Rebirth III

walked with me across the beach. There were graves everywhere, but unmarked. Upon each of the graves was a small white piece made of linen inserted into the ground with a stick. On each piece of linen was the word, "Official." The angel led me up a mountain to a chapel on my right. To the chapel's left was a cemetery with more graves. The sun was setting as we faced west. We stood on the green mountaintop overlooking the ocean as the sun sank lower in the sky.

August 15, 2014

The experience this morning was broken in detail. It began with me among a group of islands. I saw boats and a cruise ship that was much bigger than the islands themselves. The cruise boat had a large pool on the roof. I witnessed as men jumped into the pool and somehow were able to climb through to the ceiling of the room below. When this happened, I was taken to the ceiling to see them arrive at the top of the room below the pool. But somehow, it seemed the pool was in this room as well. The imagery transitioned to me standing on a street and witnessing a car wreck. In that moment, I had to save a child. The girl who must have only been seven or eight, turned out to be okay. There was another boy child in the wreck. He was in one of the vehicles that was more severely damaged. The boy had a tag around his wrist as if he had been marked for dead. The girl I helped rescue knew him.

The Written (cont'd)

August 17, 2014

I arrived in the heavens to find myself in a flower store. It was more of a boutique plant store than a typical greenhouse. It was less ornate than a florist though. The only comparison I would have is something like a small pet store that held plants instead of animals. I walked over to a plant that was in a glass vase. It contained two stalks joined at the root. I split the plant in two to take one of the plants home with me. After I left the store, I realized that the plant was much more complicated than I needed to serve my purposes. After I arrived home, I tended to the plant in the glass vase. The vase was square – a more modern appearance than round vases.

After some trial and error, I discovered how to make the plant exist by placing it in the L shaped corner of the glass vase. For some reason, it seemed the plant needed to be placed in the corner for its survival. That part of my lesson was important. Perhaps it needed two sides to support it as it formed the third side. I could not be certain. I just knew that where the plant found its strength was important in the moment. The plant took quite a while to grow, but once it began to flourish, it grew at an unwieldy rate. The plant seemed unmanageable at times, but I continued to try and better understand the plant. As challenging as it was, I eventually caught up to the plant's rate of growth in my understanding of its needs. It took a little time, but I eventually arrived where I needed to be.

Rebirth III

I returned to the flower store with the plant. There was another person in the store looking for the same plant as I had just spent so long understanding. This person wanted one larger and one that appeared unkempt because (as the person indicated) it would be easier to "get what was needed." I took the opportunity to set my vase and plant down on the counter and give it a name. I looked at the other person and said, "Or you can take this one which has already been mended." I had the impression that I understood great intricacies and how to uncomplicate them for others. Somehow this was the most important theme of the experience. The person in the store needed something simple even though I knew how complicated it could get for them from underestimating the challenges forthcoming. It was a lesson of my actions in helping others and a spiritual lesson for anyone who reads these words.

August 18, 2014

Upon arriving in the heavens, an angel continued to ask me if I was ready for eight-thirty. At first I first said, "Yes." The angel reminded me of a friend I have named Kip, though I knew it was not him. I thought the angel's question about "eight-thirty" was in regard to a time for the two of us to commune for some special occasion. After we parted ways, I continued walking around and exploring the heavens. After some period of time had passed, I received a text and was asked again, "Are you ready?" When I first saw the text mes-

The Written (cont'd)

sage, I thought I must have missed it, and that was the reason for him sending me the message. When I looked at the time, I saw it was 11:30. I immediately apologized to the group of people I was with at that time and rushed off to meet the angel.

When we met up, I still had no idea what his intention was. I did not know if I was dressed appropriately, or if there were any other preparations I needed to make. When I arrived, I realized I needed something different to wear. Just as suddenly as I realized I was not appropriately dressed, I appeared in a sporting goods store and began choosing a blue/white reversible tank. It was basically a reversible basketball jersey with no insignia. This particular jersey was rare. It was even more surprising to me that they were only $24 each. Though the price did not reflect it, most people did not buy this item because they did not know about it. It was somewhat of a hidden treasure among a sea of other shirts. After I picked up the jersey, I had to get one other item that cost $50 (though I could not identify what item I was picking out in earthly terms). At the register, the two items rang up to $82.75. I realized I had not spent enough money and grabbed a couple more tanks. I knew the total needed to be over $100, but I was okay with that. It felt required of me and right.

I returned to the angel where he accepted my apology and we ventured off to whatever it was that we were going to do. At this point I realized the clothes I purchased were unnecessary, but they were metaphorical for something else he was trying to tell me. As we journeyed off into the distance, my

Rebirth III

sight was limited, and I could not see what was going to occur, nor did I understand the intentions of our actions. I just knew I was being led to do something of importance...blind.

I had a false awakening but was aware it was false. As I concentrated to get back to the heavens, a wireframe cube formed around my head. It was subdivided into nine cubes per face but only the edges were visible. It continued to swell and shrink proportionately to my breath. I observed that the cube was demonstrating a spiritual strength through my breath. Though I tried to continue to travel back from where I once came, I was unable to learn more about "eight-thirty." When I awoke, I began to understand that "eight-thirty" was not a time, but rather a date...as was "eleven-thirty." I could recall in hindsight that each time I heard the numbers spoken, I always looked at a watch to see what time it was. This was the reason that I understood the numbers as times versus dates. However, nothing was ever defined.

Upon returning to my body, I googled the numbers (initially as a time). The first result that appeared was "Luke 8:30." Numbers shared with me in my heavenly experiences have almost always managed to reference Bible verses, but it is as if my mind blanks out that possibility each time. When I saw that Luke 8:30 was the first result, I smiled. Luke is the book that I am directed to on most any occasion from the angels. I read the verse. The verse was in regard to Jesus asking, "What is your name?" I could not help but become excited.

Before I went to sleep, I prayed for God to help me understand my next steps. I specifically said, "Do I have Christ in

The Written (cont'd)

me in the same way that Jesus demonstrated Christ within him? And, if so, how can I demonstrate this to others?" The reference to the verse shows that God had cleansed my soul, cast out the demons, and that I was being tested with understanding my spiritual name. Knowing that God spoke to me through Luke, I understood to read Luke 11:30. "For as Jonah was a sign to the Ninevites, so also will the Son of Man be to this generation." Both verses were in reference to helping me understand my similarities, my differences, what the future holds, and my purpose in comparison to how Jesus served God. In this moment I knew that the Angel I had spoken with was none other than Luke. This is why this same angel continues to reference Luke.

August 19, 2014
Early Morning

I was taken to the heavens and found myself in a room. A letter was handed to me with a name I did not recognize scrawled across the bottom of the page. I was supposed to read the letter written upon the scroll, but I struggled to understand any of it. After struggling for a few moments, a pair of angels imparted knowledge to me that "their daughter Hilary will be passing through on their way to [an unmentioned location, but I thought it was Chicago]."

At first I thought maybe the letter pertained to Hilary. It was an interesting mix of emotions. I could not understand if I

Rebirth III

was being shared this information supplementary to the letter, or if they were one in the same. I also could not discern why I was being shared information about Hilary. Was I supposed to meet her? Did she need help? I tried to reread the letter. This time I understood the words. In summary, it was a Love letter, or rather a declaration of Love. However, the Love spoken about upon the scroll was describing Godly Love rather than romantic Love. As I read the letter I continued to hear the word "AY-NUC" repeated over and over. The pair of angels seemed passionate that I understand how much Love was in the letter and how important it was for me to understand not just the words, but the words "AY-NUC" and "Hilary" in relation to the scroll as well.

I returned to my body and wrote down the words. Once again I journeyed back to the heavens. This time I found myself standing before a mirror. I was smiling. I gazed at my smile and realized that I needed to clean my mouth. There was a film across my teeth which made them look weird. It was as if I was seeing in another spectrum which revealed very unflattering nuances about my mouth.

The following day I would speak to Bryan about the visions. He immediately felt inclined to point me in the direction of the song "Battle for Britain (the Letter)" by David Bowie. I had never heard the song, so I obliged. It was easy to see why Bryan wanted me to read the lyrics to the song, for it would seem that the song was an ode to the same spiritual concept. Also, when I shared the word "AY-NUC" to Bryan, he immediately told me I heard the true pronunciation of the Biblical

The Written (cont'd)

figure we know as Enoch (pronounced EE-NOK). Bryan also began to see ties to the experience I had days prior where an Elder angel with long gray hair spoke with me, but then left me when I began asking questions.

Everything now made sense. The angel I saw a few days prior was indeed Enoch, but it would seem he had to seek further permission or council before he continued communication with me. It appears that, by the Grace of God, I have been allowed to take the next steps forward and receive lessons directly from Enoch. It was important for me to understand that the words I was reading were indeed the words of Enoch – one of two humans we know who were taken from the Earth in bodily form and up into the heavens. For the record books, Enoch is pronounced with a long A sound and a shortened U sound. The CH at the end has a garbled KUH sound rather than a short K sound.

August 19, 2014
Late Afternoon

While this experience happened on Earth, I still wanted to take note of it today. Earlier, I prayed to God asking Him to help me find strength to answer questions correctly to those around me. One typical question I get asked frequently is, "What do you do?" (as in for a career). It is a normal question to field, but I have been tasked with living my life as if I am entertaining angels at all times. To answer with an earthly ca-

Rebirth III

reer is most certainly not the answer I should give. I asked for forgiveness in my short-sighted answers I have given to that question thus far during my first days in Fort Lauderdale. As I prayed, I voiced that I would task myself with answering more along the lines of "My current vehicle is….but I am here to do whatever God calls me to do." I felt resolved in my prayer, but hoped that God would grant me the opportunity to strengthen my iron.

Just moments after finishing the prayer, I went to a Thai restaurant to pick up dinner. As I waited for my order to be cooked, two strangers came in and sat down beside me. One seemed to have some sort of a physical disability or handicap, so I offered to help get the door for him. Almost immediately upon my gesture I was asked, "What do you do?" There was not a lead in. There was not an introduction or "thank you." There was only the question. I was overwhelmed in almost complete disbelief that God was speaking so boldly to me in response to my prayer. I knew this was my chance to respond the way I had just expressed to God I would in this situation. And it was not just a time to practice. This was a test. This was Divine intervention – a divine test. I answered the man with confidence in the way I shared with God how I thought I should respond. The man smiled and seemed pleased with my answer, then he went on his way.

The Written (cont'd)

August 20, 2014
Early Morning

This morning I had many vivid experiences, but false awakenings and overconfidence in my ability to remember would cause me to not be able to bring any of the experiences back with me.

August 20, 2014
Late Afternoon

While this is not pertaining to anything in the heavens, this was a great experience on Earth I wanted to make sure I journaled. Today, I came back in from the beach. As I walked by the pool, I ran into Kelly and her daughter, Ava. Kelly's family is from England, and they visit Fort Lauderdale several times a year. We shared in a great conversation wherein Kelly began to tell me about a book she ran across in her apartment today as she was cleaning. She tried to recall the title and could only remember "Toll." I immediately recognized it as "A New Earth" by Eckhart Tolle. She was excited I knew about it. I spoke highly of the book and told her she should definitely re-read it when she finds time. I explained that it was a very inspiring book.

Kelly brought up the book to me because we have had spiritual conversations from time to time, and she saw a similarity in my point of view and the way the material is

Rebirth III

presented in the book. Kelly then asked me what I thought about Fort Lauderdale. This was a loaded question from a prayer I had just prayed the day prior. I was very quick to pick up on God's action through Kelly's question. I did not hesitate to compare my experience in Fort Lauderdale to how a person walks through doors in a house to enter into another room. I explained that, to me, Fort Lauderdale is a special place that God prepared for me and that when I leave this area for any particular reason, that it is like entering into a different reality. I stopped short of explaining how I saw everyone as angels, or at the very least, messengers of God. Kelly was moved and warmed by my words. We eventually parted ways, but it was a moment that I wanted to remember in writing.

August 21, 2014
Early Morning

This morning I traveled to the heavens. What I witnessed was full of symbolism in a context that would probably make more sense to me than others reading. It began by my witnessing an angel breaking up a fight between two technology executives. The angel told them that he wanted to see how they fought outside of the subject area. In context, the two fighting executives seemed to work for Microsoft. The angel represented Apple. By no means is this placing bias into the scenario though. This is just how it was presented to me.

The Written (cont'd)

After the angel broke the fight up, he took me with him through the heavens. He let me get a drink at a restaurant since I was thirsty. I took notice that they "did not hand out cups except only to the good." They handed me a cup to drink. While in the restaurant, I witnessed a crazy person come in and complain about the cups (or lack there of). Another person began complaining that drinks were located in another building, not in this restaurant.

August 21, 2014
Daily Experiences

Over the last few days I have had the pleasure of getting to know a young couple from Canada visiting for the week. Their names are Chris and Maria. We shared in a lot of great conversation in the days prior, but never did I expound upon anything spiritual. Today, though, Maria asked me questions that begged for me to share a small portion of my personal journey. I did not have to say much – maybe just a few sentences before Maria exclaimed, "I knew there was something about you. I didn't quite know what it was, but I knew. I knew it." Maria's face was shining with light, though others probably did not see what I saw in that moment. She had a spiritual recognition in me but did not quite know how to put it into words until this moment. She continued on, "So you want to be a healer?" I could tell she was trying to add logic to her spiritual understanding.

Rebirth III

I replied with, "Aren't we all already? You just have to know how to use it." Maria smiled in recognition. She continued asking me other questions that were applicable to her life, and I obliged in sharing a spiritual perspective. Maria eventually mentioned the book, "A New Earth." This was the second time in as many days that this book has bubbled up to the surface of a conversation. To me, it was flattering to hear the comparisons – not for my ego, but rather because the truth in the message I was sharing with the world around me echoed the truths Eckhart Tolle has shared through his books.

Maria then went on to ask me about a Japanese scientist that demonstrated how intention affected the growth of plants. What she did not know is that this particular scientist was at the heart of my scientific research before I paid undivided attention to God's voice again in my life. I told her I knew exactly who she was speaking about and then asked her if she had read about him, or saw him in the movie, "What the Bleep?" Maria seemed shocked I had seen the movie. Honestly, the only reason I knew about the movie is I had a random knock on my door in Nashville from the sister of a friend of mine that dated a guy that lived down the hall from me.

Aside from a casual hello, I had never really spoken to her. But, for some reason she felt led to come over to my apartment, sit down on my couch, and then tell me that I needed to watch a specific movie. To others on the outside, they may hear "girl randomly comes over to a guys house she doesn't really know to *watch a movie* and (…ahem…) hook up." But, the truth is just as I explained it. Inexplicably, this

The Written (cont'd)

girl came over and asked to watch a documentary that talked about spirituality through Eastern science.

I fired up Netflix and as the movie started, she wanted to tell me about all of the people in the movie she knew and how it pertained to her life. She explained that before I got to know her or how she practices Chiropractic, that it was necessary that I watch this movie first. After the movie was over, she walked back to meet her sister and the group of friends over at my neighbor's apartment and left to go home.

So, the fact that this movie had resurfaced in conversation was not too surprising I suppose. But, it did not stop there. As Maria and I were talking, another woman and her child walked over to us. She had not been involved in the conversation at all and had just walked up. She said, "It is called 'What the Bleep Do We Know?" This is person number three that not only had seen this movie, but also became involved in a deep spiritual conversation with us. There are truly angels among us each and every day.

August 22, 2014
Early Morning

This morning I traveled to the heavens several times. Upon arrival in the heavens my first time, I was standing beside a black angel adorned in a white gown. I was listening to his conversation. He seemed unaware of my presence, or perhaps it would be more accurate to say "of my awareness" in my

Rebirth III

presence. He was making jokes with another angel and having a good conversation. I turned and saw a female angel to my left. I began to lose harmony and told her, "Hang on. I am trying to balance my spirit." But, unfortunately, I lost harmony and returned to my body.

I traveled back and found myself standing upon a beach. There was a female that was wearing pink. She had been stung by a "man of war" (jellyfish) because she wanted to touch it with her chin. As I stared at her I took notice of an angel beside me. It was as if he was showing me her actions for a reason. Overhead, a flying vehicle scorched by. It looked like an older cream-colored Volkswagen van with chrome bumpers without wheels or wings. It swung into view from the top right of my periphery and curled up and around to the right before all of the airbags inside inflated and the vehicle crashed into the water. As soon as it landed, it drove through the water and wrecked into the beach. Undeterred by the crash and the wreck, the vehicle kept going. As it passed us by, I saw a driver on the right side of the vehicle (in America, the drivers sit on the left side of the vehicle). She had blonde hair and was beautiful. In this moment, she looked headstrong and serious, intent on finding control of the vehicle.

The angel and I sat down on the beach. He gave me jelly beans as we stared upon the ocean. He told me he wanted me to swim out with him because there was a full moon. He went on to tell me that early in the morning hours with a full moon overhead, it was perfect for sea life. It seemed the fish would be safest under a full moon. We chatted about other things.

The Written (cont'd)

He seemed unsurprised by the flying car. We laughed at how cartoon-like the whole experience seemed.

August 22, 2014
Daily Experiences

One of the people I first met here in Fort Lauderdale is a man named Paul. I could immediately recognize Paul's spiritual strength, though neither he nor I mentioned it to each other. Today was the first day that we spoke more than a few passing words. Paul approached me while we were each in the ocean and asked me why I moved to Florida. I knew this was one of God's tests. I responded, "Because this is where I am supposed to be." That answer is usually enough to make people smile and understand I am following a greater plan in my life. But this time was different. This time Paul pushed onward. "How did you know you know?" he asked. He did not just ask how I knew. He asked how I knew that I knew I was being led. I responded, "Because this is where I was told to go." He continued on. "Who told you?" he asked. "God did. He told me to. It is part of my journey. I moved here sight unseen." I responded quickly and without pause. It was obvious that God had surrounded me with angels, and these angels wanted to help mold me and shape me as best as could happen. Maybe there was even a little curiosity in their questions as well, for I am half the age of everyone around me.

Rebirth III

Paul continued his line of questions. He seemed unfazed by my responses and more intrigued in my confidence than anything else. After I responded that "God did," Paul quickly interjected. "You mean IT did" to which I responded, "Yes. IT is a better way to say it." He smiled and seemed satisfied that we were one of the same faith and that I understood his words of how God was greater than a name that could be said. Paul's insistence on "It" to describe God was a modern way of saying "the Name of the Ineffable God."

Feeling resolved, we continued chatting about other things and parted ways. A short while later I saw Paul on the beach in the company of some of the other residents in the building. Through my eyes, I saw a group of angels all sharing lunch together. He motioned for me to come over. When I approached, I could tell that Paul wanted to invite me into his world. He wanted to introduce me to the two women that he was sitting with. They were having lunch and seemed curious at my arrival. Paul said, "Ladies, this is Jonathan. He was sent here by God." Literally, that is how I was introduced. The introduction was overwhelming. In an earthly sense, one's spirituality is a personal aspect almost always left unto themselves. It is not usually something that is projected upon other people, especially in introductions. No one really says, "This is Jonathan the [insert your choice of religion here]." But Paul's words managed to shift my perspective from modern times to the origin of mankind. He introduced me at the most intimate level he could with the other angels on the beach with him. It was important that he let them know that I was a child of God.

The Written (cont'd)

The three angels represented a divine trinity of truth in that moment. All three had spouses but were just enjoying the company of other angels.

All three represented the angels I see in my travels to the heavens. There was a brunette female, a blonde female, and an overly masculine male. To some, they would have feared an introduction of such grandeur – fearing that they were becoming a mockery unto others. But to me, I saw truth. I saw light. I saw everything that I thought God had been showing me in one demonstration of angelic grandeur. The two ladies offered me lunch, and I dined in the company of angels. After lunch was finished, we each went our separate ways to enjoy our day on the beach.

When I walked away from Paul's group of friends, Maria motioned for me to join her and Chris. I walked over to them. Maria subtly held up "A New Earth" – the book we had discussed a day prior. She then shared with me how my discussion with her helped Chris become motivated to go to yoga with her that morning. She was so excited that in only a few days, she and Chris (her boyfriend) were able to find a closer connection through the words I shared with them.

The day wore on, and I eventually went in to prepare for a fundraiser I was invited to by another lady in my building. Part of me was excited. Part of me was dreading it because I knew it would involve socializing over wine. I enjoy the taste of wine, but I loathe the way I feel after consuming any alcohol. I always feel as if it causes me to derail from my spiritual alignment that allows me to commune intimately with God. It is

Rebirth III

not that I believe alcohol is bad. But I do believe it inhibits a person from communing with God in the manner I have become accustomed. And while the fundraiser turned into a wonderful event for me where I met many Lovely people and shared inspiration and hope to others, God's plan for me attending the fundraiser was built upon what would occur in the cab ride to the benefit.

    Since arriving in Fort Lauderdale I had only been out for a night on the town on one occasion. And while I took a cab ride that night in July to the restaurant I was led to go, the story that night was not about the destination, but the journey in the cab as well. On that particular night in July, I knew I had been led to go out (against my personal desires). When the cab driver picked me up, I asked him how he was doing. The cab driver was overcome with emotion and began telling me of his strength in the midst of one of the darkest times of his life. Without ever saying it, I could tell he did not have an apartment, house, or home. He was doing all he could and admitted he had thought about taking his own life but recognized it was not something he could do because of his faith. And while I have written about this encounter in my other writings, the important take away was that he recognized Christ within me as we spoke. The cab driver sobbed, and I could tell that this conversation was truth. As he dropped me off, I asked him to take my by the ATM. I recognized God's financial blessings in my life, and I wanted to do the same for him. I tipped him $100 on the cab ride and prayed for blessings to enter into his life. The rest of the evening was just the

The Written (cont'd)

charade of God's plan – the reason I thought I was led to go out that evening, when in reality it was about the journey getting me there.

So fast forwarding to tonight's plan for me to go to the fundraiser, I again (just as in July) had my eyes on the destination, oblivious to the spiritual story that would unfold on my journey there. When the cab driver arrived, he looked familiar. We never made eye contact. It was just a moment of me stepping into the backseat of a cab. As he took me to my destination, I asked him how his night was going. The cab driver began by telling me that this particular night was better than the others, and then went on to say how every day was getting better than the day before. We passed a homeless man on the street which prompted the cab driver to begin saying how sorry he felt for that particular man. He went on to explain how he always tries to make sure he helps the homeless – especially the ones that most people do not realize are homeless because they hide it well. I just listened as the man began sharing with me a story of how he was once in the darkest time of his life – only a month or two prior – and had found himself homeless. He explained that he hid that fact from others and even alluded to having suicidal thoughts, but refrained from those words. I immediately knew the cab driver was one in the same as the one that drove me the only other time I had taken a cab in Fort Lauderdale. I did not let on I recognized him though. I just listened.

The man went on to share with me a story about a homeless man that he was allowing to stay at his house that evening

Rebirth III

and how he also made sure to buy the man a six pack of beer and whatever else he wanted to feel Loved. The cab driver continued telling me that while he did not have much money, he always makes sure he gives everything he can give to help others because he was once in their same shoes. He went on to tell me how, when he was struggling, he was helped in ways that even he cannot explain today and alluded to the night I gave him $100 in July as he shared how God worked in his life. He went on to say that now he was able to make his $1000 rent payment, and while he does not have furniture, that was the first step in moving forward.

This man got it. He understood. And, for me, I saw how $100 turned into $1000 for this man. I know he may have been helped by others along the way. But, without us even exchanging eye contact, the man shared with me the story of the night he received help from one of his riders and how he was better for it today.

On my return ride home, I somehow managed to have the same cab driver that returned me home the first time I went out in Fort Lauderdale. He was a different driver than the first, but over four total cab rides over a month apart, I had managed to get the exact same drivers. On my way back home I asked the driver about his day. He was nice, jovial, and his spirit shined brightly. When we reached my destination, I tipped him the remainder of the money that I had won in a raffle a week or two prior. It was not much money, but more than he expected. He was so thankful and continued to look at me like he did not know what to say. When he found his

The Written (cont'd)

words, he continued repeating, "Thank you. Thank you. Thank you for choosing me tonight." As I stepped out of the car, he said, "You don't know what this means. God will return this to you." And he went on his way.

Before I returned to my apartment, I walked out upon the beach. I spent time in prayer reiterating that I felt blind and really did not know what I was doing. As I said, "Father, I don't know what I am doing, but I am doing what I think you are telling me to do," one of the stars in the sky overhead flared brighter than the light of the moon. It grew in size several times over. I immediately recognized it as a sign of acknowledgement from God. As supernatural as it may have seemed, this was clearly a message intended for me in that moment. I went on to also pray about not being able to recognize which angel was Rafael or Gabriel when I travel to the heavens. I explained that I thought I had met Gabriel, but I felt ashamed for not being able to identify angels of their stature and greatness.

And while that wraps up most of the spiritual encounters today, I also want to take note that over the last month, I have now met a one Vicki, two children named Victoria, and after tonight, two other women named Victoria. It may not be important on the surface level, but everything is not as it seems. Until Fort Lauderdale, I had never met another Victoria save for my very first girlfriend in college.

Rebirth III

August 23, 2014
Early Morning

This morning I experienced many visions, but could not manage to bring them back with me. I could only recall small flashes of the visions even though each of the experiences was extremely strong at the time. I felt like from the time I shut my eyes, I was traveling among the heavens for the entire duration of the night.

August 23, 2014
Late Afternoon

Today I was invited to dinner with a group of people I had met on the beach. We have spent the last several days getting to know each other, and they were very curious to learn more about my story and my religious foundation. When they invited me, I picked up that they had been planning a dinner for me for a few days. The restaurant we went to was one of the nicest in the area. As we sat down, I overheard the waitress say, "So he is the guest of honor?" while she looked at me. It was a curious moment and very unexpected.

At the restaurant, they insisted on me having everything I wanted and asked for my opinion on group appetizers. It was as if they wanted the dinner to be a celebration for me. I was uncomfortable with the focus on me and continually let them know that the group appetizers should be what everyone else wanted. The conversation was very spiritual all night long. There was a point in the conversation where I was asked my age. They seemed fascinated in my perspective relative to my age. "Thirty-three," I responded. Immediately I heard, "The age of Jesus." This was not the first time I had heard reference of my age to "the age of Jesus." It was not as if I thought I was equal to Jesus, but rather that God was letting me know of the divine symbolism in my age and my purpose. On this evening, I shared in a wonderful dinner in the company of beautiful souls…and for that words cannot express my gratitude.

August 24, 2014

This morning's experiences were very poignant, but lacked in detail. The experiences began with me being pulled across the sand. It was sort of like being hog-tied and dragged to a place not of my choosing. When we arrived, I was given a golden ring. It was a solid band, like a wedding band. The room filled with brilliant flashes of white light. The next thing I knew I saw a black man in a white robe paddling on a paddle board across the water to meet me. He spoke with me about "my company" though I cannot recall any more details.

August 25, 2014

I was taken to the heavens where I walked around blissfully. I was learning how to properly wield the spirit as my

Rebirth III

protection: to use it not as a cry out for spiritual defense, but rather as an instrument of practical application. I cannot explain exactly how this method of application works, for it involves complete surrender of the senses. I was anxious to try it out but knew I was I entrusted with something that required great respect.

Eventually, an angel led me to a group of people that were all fighting over the land. I knew the land was purposed for a specific reason from God, and that He was very upset that mankind would act so disrespectfully toward His gifts. This was a place in the mountains that needed protected. As the arguments continued, lightning and thunder started swirling above. I knew it was God's voice expressing His anger. This made me that much more upset. I wanted to prove to everyone else that God's voice was real. I stepped into the crowd and began making pillars with each hand to cause the storm to unleash its fury. I knew God did not need me to do this, but I wanted to demonstrate to others His strength.

They watched. It was clear that I was riling up the storm. They became fearful. The angel with me told me to stop, but I could not. I was not strong enough to continue with my intention or strong enough to stop. At this point a giant blow of destruction exploded in our area causing me to be blown away and into the company of the angel. God destroyed the land around us. I came to find myself being cared for in a cave by the angel. I felt ashamed that I would have attempted to demonstrate God's wrath without being strong enough to

The Written (cont'd)

handle it myself. The angel did not think I was wrong, but also thought I could have made a different decision.

When we came out of the cave, I learned that God had destroyed all of the lands that we had been discussing. Each of the destroyed lands were all in a mountain area that reminded me of Chattanooga, Tennessee. The angel then took me on a tour of the future of those places. The place where I intervened was now a beautiful garden – just as God intended it to be. It was named after me, though. When we appeared, there was a city council argument on taking care of the land. Our presence immediately made them straighten up and provide the resources needed to help keep the land a protected park and sacred. They seemed fearful of me, but respectful.

August 27, 2014

Though it was bright and not easy to see due to its greatness, I navigated the Rainbow Road last night. I was fascinated by all of the colors passing by. It was not a road that cars drive upon. Instead, it was more like a tunnel of rainbow light, with a more defined path of rainbow light beneath my feet. When I arrived at the first stop I was greeted by an angel that asked how I had arrived there. I said I took the Rainbow Road – that it was my first time being able to do it on my own. The angel seemed dumbfounded that I had navigated the Rainbow Road to this destination. There were no words, but it was as if the angel, while impressed and confused by my ac-

Rebirth III

tion, seemed to tell me that I should not do it alone. I felt he wanted me to move on from this particular stopping place, so I took the Rainbow Road to the next destination. It was another beautiful heavenly landscape – mostly white. After looking around I began to lose harmony and returned to my body via the Rainbow Road. It is important to say that the Rainbow Road felt like it always curved to the right.

August 28, 2014

To date, the experience I had in the heavens this morning was so impactful that it must surely rank in the top portion of the list of experiences I have had in the heavens. In fact, it may sound counterintuitive to understand what I am about to say in the way I intend, but the situation was so profound that I did not even realize I had a portion of the experience when I first arrived back in my body. The portion that was blurred from my immediate memory was so real it was like a real-life experience that seemed like it must have happened to me on Earth in the previous days. My senses clung to the moment just as my earthly senses cling to the experiences I am blessed to have during my waking days here on Earth.

The experience brought me face-to-face with Enoch...the very Enoch written about in the Bible. This is one of two men that is said to have never experienced death on Earth, but was raised to the heavens in honor of Divine servitude. In speaking of my previous experiences, with Bryan, there is one specifical-

The Written (cont'd)

ly where Bryan thought an "unnamed" angel must have been Enoch in my travels. I did not know what to think at the time, but I was open to the possibility. In the following days I was allowed to read a book in the heavens that most surely had been written by Enoch. His voice was what I heard through the words as it told a story of Divine Love. I was also continually told the name "AE-NUK." At the time of reading the book and hearing the voice, I did not think it was the same as "Enoch" that we know about in the Bible. But once I returned to my body I realized that Enoch had communicated to me through written words. When sharing the story with Bryan, he thought that it was possible that Enoch was not allowed to show himself to me, or possibly that I was not able to see him yet. Regardless, it was an interesting experience.

However, this time, I found myself standing face-to-face with Enoch. The heavens were filled with the whitest of light around us. There was another angel to my left who was my guide. It was a familiar angel – a true elder, wise with the spirit. As I stood before Enoch I soaked in the moment. He was extremely large indicating his spiritual strength. He wore a white robe and had pepper-gray hair. He had a long, straight mustache and beard in the front. His hair was long and straight. He had it pulled back in a loose-fitting ponytail. I did not see his ponytail until the end of the vision.

As I stood before him, I listened to his words. He was bold, proud, and clearly strong in divinity. The only question I could seem to muster flowed right from my lips. I asked him, "How were you able to ascend in mortal form?" He looked at

Rebirth III

me with eyes large in wisdom and wonder. He said, "I never sinned one single time." He said this with an air of pride in his purity – and rightfully so as anyone who lived sinless deserves to hold some amount of pride. I replied to his answer, "Really? Not once?"

I was extremely baffled at my own inadequacies in his presence. It seemed like there was a rush of confusion in my mind. I wanted so desperately to follow in his path and ascend before a mortal death, but I thought that it must surely be unlikely since I had certainly sinned in my life before I found His Grace. However, in the same context, I thought I was having this very conversation to give me an ideal to strive toward. It was as if his circumstances were unique to him, but that I could live a sinless life moving forward and be in the same graces. These concepts were floating through my mind as I waited for his reply.

His response was simple, if not a little understandably arrogant. He simply nodded and said, "Not once. That is why I was allowed to ascend." He then turned and walked away into the light. I watched as his flowing white robe was consumed by the light. The ponytail of his long hair that reached all of the way down his back was the last to vanish into the light. As I stood there processing all that I had just witnessed, the angel on my left must have seen me rationalizing if it was possible to live sinless for an entire existence because he went ahead and chimed in, "It is true. He has never sinned." With that, my periphery filled with a white light.

The Written (cont'd)

The next thing I knew, I was lying down with my head in the lap of "the girl" – the beautiful angel mother that has a warmth and Love indescribable by any earthly understanding. I was staring up at the sky while she rubbed her fingers through my hair and touched the side of my face. It is the most warming Love I have ever felt. As I "came to" in the moment, I heard her voice talking to me in a way that a parent would talk to child in their arms. There was music in the background. All of my senses kicked into a hypersensitivity-mode when I realized how clear the music was. I recognized the song, but not from anything here on Earth. However, it seemed to be of an earthly recording.

The song had a higher-pitched male voice singing a chorus. After the words ended, the song went into a brilliant jazz-like musical bridge where a saxophone played a beautiful, slow, melodic solo. I wanted the chorus to return because I felt like I could sing along to it. I was repeating the words over and over in my head. But, as I repeated the words, the music fell into the background. I found myself standing in the rain being told to run toward something in the distance.

In the moment, I understood what I was running toward, but there were no earthly words to describe the destination. As I ran, I began to lose my balance and, in stride, went to step onto a curb and sidewalk with my right foot. As soon as my foot made contact with the curb, I lost my balance and toppled over. It was the result of my soul starting to lose harmony with the heavens and the spinning sensation beginning to take

Rebirth III

over. I was helped up by "the girl" and continued running ahead. Before reaching the destination, I awoke in my body.

I immediately jotted down the words to the song that I heard playing in the background. And, while these words are going to sound like the Richard Marx song "I'll Be Right Here Waiting For You," the song was not the Richard Marx song. The words that I was able to bring back were, "Wherever you are...[something]...Whatever you do...[something]...waiting for you." I knew that the words were eerily similar to the Richard Marx song, and I fear that my earthly mind tried to relate the song in the heavens to a song I knew on Earth, so it is possible the lyrics are not entirely correct.

I ended up googling the lyrics to see if there was another song that may show up. The only other song that came up was a song I had never heard. It was called "I'll Always Be Right There" by Bryan Adams. After listening to the song, I can say the song is extremely close, if not the exact song. However, there was no saxophone solo in the recording I found, so that does give me doubt I found the right song.

But, if there is a shining beacon of light within the message — if you are to listen to the song, "I'll Always Be Right There" in the context of the great angelic mother-figure singing it to you, the message could not have been more precisely akin to the song I heard in the heavens. Hearing the words to that song in the voice of "the girl" brought me to tears of happiness. Whether the song was the song I heard or not, it led me to this song that could be understood in the same context

The Written (cont'd)

of the song I heard in the heavens. And, for that, I am humbly thankful.

August 29, 2014

While the experience this morning was brief, it contained a very interesting element within it. This is the first experience where I recognized archetypal messages in real-time with the context of the heavenly presentation. This experience began with me strolling around a building. I was seeking "food" and in search of a "food stand." I knew that my desire for food had nothing to do for sustenance for my stomach, but rather for my soul. In this, I recognized that food was archetypal for knowledge. And while I recognized the symbolism in real-time, the entire context was presented without me veering from staying "in character."

As I strolled around, I eventually found a food stand. There were others there in line. Others were standing around eating. I walked right up to the stand and ordered some food and ate it very quickly. I was not fulfilled in that moment, so I continued walking around in search of another source for food. Eventually I had to return to the stand I had just left in order to ask for directions to another stand. I was told that I should go visit a particular stand quite some way off. Without hesitation, I headed in that direction.

When I reached the stand, it was closed. It appeared that the angel running the stand had just closed up. He was exiting the stand to leave for the day when we saw each other. I asked the angel if there was something "lighter" I could eat. I told him I had been sent his way. He asked me what I meant by "lighter" to which I responded, "Hummus." I repeated "hummus" twice before I said, "or something along the lines of grilled chicken."

I honestly have no idea why I said hummus. It is not anything I eat on Earth. I actually cannot be completely sure I have ever had it. My curiosity has never led me to ordering it. But regardless, the angel smiled and said that he did have some grilled chicken. I asked him, "How much?" He said, "How about when I return you just help me out with a small project at work." I agreed and he walked off. I did not receive any food at that moment. And, while he walked away, I digested the entire archetypal meaning, though still mildly curious as to why the situation revolved around food. I eventually returned to my body where I tried to rationalize whether earthly cravings interfered; however, I had no desire for food or drink at this particular time.

August 30, 2014

There were just two brief experiences that happened to me this morning. The first was a voice that shouted out at me as my spirit began to leave my body. It was not mean or negative. It just startled me – which caused me to return to my body. Later in the morning, I found myself standing on a

The Written (cont'd)

shoreline of an ocean or a bay, watching a large tanker ship head straight toward shore. It managed to traverse the shallow body of water at a high rate of speed. As it neared a very shallow depth and less than a hundred yards from the shoreline, it made a hard left turn (my right). It veered off comic-book style and journeyed south.

September 1, 2014

This morning's travels were numerous but each one was brief. As my body found its right state for travel, I heard static popping all around. It was enough to cause me to lose my balance and take notes. Upon traveling again, I arrived on a beach. The sky was illuminated by the glow of moonlight. The water glistened under its glow. I stared at the ocean and saw someone in a suit wash up on the beach. As I ran down to see how I could help, I could see in the distance an entire boat had capsized and many of the people had drowned. I stared in disbelief unable to move.

I returned once again and arrived in the heavens. Though the details are inexplicable in earthly terms, this experience involved something about fish-like creatures without heads. It was important that I understood I was without a head. I returned to my body.

As my body settled into a meditative state once again, I saw a hand reach down and touch its palm against my naval.

Rebirth III

My body seized as if I had just received a burst of electricity applied directly to my stomach. I awoke.

My next attempt brought me before an angel. The angel said, "It is not a construction by hand, but a construction that man already did." The angel spoke these words as he pointed out at an unwanted/undesirable artifact shape in my condo. The experience was in the heavens, but the unwanted shape is not an object that exists in my condo in an earthly sense.

After journaling the last experience, I returned to the void. A voice spoke to me: "Sea of abolition. A sea of tears." Though I did not have any context or understanding of why I was being shared the words, I returned to my body to write down the quote.

Once more I traveled back. This time an angel spoke the words, "In the further sweet molasses that is below." I looked below us and saw a white and chocolate swirl that represented knowledge. I lost harmony and returned to my body.

My next attempt was met by the words of an angel only while my soul was formless in the void. The angels spoke, "The fervor of a joyous maora major." I am not sure what the word maora is, but the word was pronounced "MAY-OR-UH."

Once again I returned. This time, my angel was represented by three pillars. He was talking to another about how difficult the communication has been with me tonight. The conversation was being spoken because of the importance of "a potential ending" upcoming. My understanding is that it had more to do with the end of times (aka Revelation) rather

The Written (cont'd)

than the specific moment I was in. After this experience in the heavens, I travelled back and forth several more times, but could not bring the messages back with me. In the process I "gained a head."

September 4, 2014

My experiences this morning consisted of more sporadic, contemplative thoughts in the void. There was a stream of thought where the idea of "being naked" came up. The angel that was near me supported my decisions on "when to be naked" because "I took care of my body." Another angel seemed pressed to say that he thought "I was indecent to others at times." As the two angels conferred, they both agreed that I knew exactly "when to clothe." When I returned from the heavens, I understood the significance was greater than the physical explanation alone. The angels were speaking about my spiritual exposure to others. This is a time when I am learning what to say, when to say, and how to say the correct spiritual words around others. Their words put into context the efforts of my actions to date, and granted me perspective in my approach for the future.

September 9, 2014

The travels to the heavens began underwater near a glass panel. There were three of us – myself and two angels. I no-

Rebirth III

ticed an explosive device located on the panel of glass. It seemed the "only way to win" was to allow it to go off, which would take our lives. As I stared at the explosive charge, time literally stood still.

The next experience took me to a "dark gray version of Atlanta." I went to a football stadium that I thought was the Atlanta Falcons' stadium. When I arrived, I realized it was not. When I looked above, the sky was gloomy. I had a sense that the setting portrayed a post-apocalyptic future. As I stood in the stadium, I recognized I was in the presence of "my father." I cannot say that this was my earthly father, but rather my father in heaven. As we stood there together, I remembered him taking me to a football game as a child. I thought that this setting could be representative of that particular time.

The inside of the stadium had a wall that was made of dark concrete and dark tinted glass. It looked similar to the outside of the BMI building in Nashville. The wall also contained two giant spires on either side of it. I could see another stadium in front of me and another park/stadium to my right. The three stadiums formed a triad. I asked my father if this stadium was being torn down to make way for the new one. The other angels around me seemed puzzled by my question. I was instructed to look at the field.

In the midst of a baseball game being played I saw a young Dale Murphy. I asked if it was really Dale Murphy, but the angels did not entertain my question. I was told his son was "the second." At this point I realized it was not really Dale Murphy (the famous Atlanta Braves player whose career pre-

The Written (cont'd)

dated my life), but rather a metaphorical representation of a Christ-like figure among the sport of baseball in Atlanta. In fact, I would come to discover that even Dale Murphy's personal life was lived as Christ-like as possible. So, the metaphor of seeing Dale Murphy on the baseball field was fitting. The number he was wearing was 16. His jersey was a dark, midnight blue. I tried to recall whether he played first base or second base during the first game my heavenly father took me to. It is important to note that I never saw Dale Murphy play a game in my earthly life. My father saw me struggle with this thought and said, "He played second." As I watched him on the field, I knew I was not watching a baseball game, nor a football game, nor was the player Dale Murphy. In that precise moment, I puzzled over what my father was trying to tell me.

Eventually I left the stadium to find myself seeing the spot where the new stadium would be built. It was along a river. It was divided in two parts on the west side of the nice stadium that was brightly lighted. When I arrived, I wanted to make sure I was in the right spot. I walked across a platform and made a comment about "half of it already being purchased for the construction." My father immediately corrected me. He said, "You mean the whole, not the half."

As I continued east across the platform, I turned right. There was a female angel in front of me waiting for me to accompany her to the next destination. We were standing along a one-way street that headed west. I wanted to wait and go East, but was told that "it was far too expensive now." The

Rebirth III

angel said, "It could only be done the long way by starting west and making a u-turn." She imparted a vision to me of how I should travel west and make the u-turn. The vision made me feel like the attempt to go east would take forever. But, as we waited for our ride to come, we each decided to walk forward and take matters into our own hands to speed up the process. It was in these moments that I lost harmony and returned to my body.

The experience of seeing a Christ-like figure in a sport and being told that he had a "second son" was, without a doubt, telling me about the second coming of Christ. The number he wore was 16 – a number that has recurred in my travels to the heavens. In sum total, $1 + 6 = 7$. Seven is a divine number. Man is represented by the number 6. So, it could be seen that the number 16 is representative of Christ on Earth...or better said, the Son of Man. It should also be mentioned that Ed Leedskalnin always talked about his "Sweet Sixteen." Though popular culture makes out his writing to speak of a girl that he once Loved, Ed's true meaning should make more sense to those reading these words.

When I returned to the heavens, I heard the voice of God. He said, "Michael will turn five in May." I returned to my body to write down His words.

Upon returning again, I saw a series of Fibonacci spirals hopping around like an ocean wave moving together in a race to help save everyone. But, I saw there would be no one worth saving. The wave was no longer connected to the whole. The

The Written (cont'd)

ones in the front were pushing against the boundary of the wave. I wanted to pull it all together to help save everyone.

Returning again, I heard a voice in the void. "Did he contact Ginger?" At that moment I was given the vision of a ninja. I returned to my body.

I returned to the heavens once again. When I arrived, I heard a voice say, "Maybe it will work on humans like it did on the angels." As the words echoed through my mind I walked into a garage. I was extremely excited that I had just been told the solution to a great problem. I began running to the door. Music filled the air. The song was old, in the style of a Kenny Rogers song, but noticeably older. I heard the words, "I'll be waiting…" The song was in a folk country style and so loud in the moment that I had to stop and take notice. I lost harmony in the moment and returned to my body.

Once again I arrived in the heavens. I was surrounded by a group of angels who were talking about my physical form. They talked about my hair looking good and "where it should be." It is important to note that I have been letting it grow out and it has been many months since I last had it trimmed at all.

I returned to the heavens again. I found myself in the middle of a lesson. The angels were explaining to me how the "government" used to employ 1% of the population, but now it does not. There was no longer 1% of the population doing what is needed to uphold spiritual peace. As the lesson was spoken, I was impressed the number "fifteen thousand" instead of the "thirty thousand" that I understood to represent the 1%. Numbers raced through my head. I knew that the

Rebirth III

population of the United States was around 300 million, so at first I thought the numbers I was given were in relation to the United States alone, but I realized 1% would be three million, not thirty thousand. But, in the context of the numbers given to me, I understood the number to be three hundred thousand, which would mean less than one hundred and fifty thousand were "spiritually sound." After I returned to my body and began to write down the numbers I received in the heavens, the Lord spoke to me and told me that these numbers were in relation to the one hundred and forty-four thousand that are mentioned in the book of Revelation as being taken up into heaven.

Once again I returned to the heavens. I was lying underneath sheets on a bed. A female angel walked over to me and pulled the sheets off of the bed saying they were dirty. I was confused because I had just washed them two days prior. I looked at a spot that she was trying to draw my attention toward. There on the sheets there was a stain that looked like a slime green color. I tasted it (unsure why) to discover it was just a "light stain." I decided to take the advice from the angel and wash my sheets anyway.

One last travel to the heavens this morning placed me on a beach gazing out upon the ocean. I saw a large dorsal fin of a shark rise out of the water. The image rattled me inside causing me to lose harmony and return to my body.

Third Revelation

It would take almost three months to the day from my travels to the heavens on September 10, 2014, to be baptized in the light of understanding. Today, as I write this on December 12, 2014, the spiritual recognition of what I bore witness to hit me like the weight of the sun. It was on September 10th that I witnessed a wedding in the heavens. I stood next to an angel that was guiding me through the heavens. She was beautiful, but I was mostly soaking in the experience of the wedding we were attending.

I watched as a bride and groom took the stand and said their vows. After the wedding, the angel took me to a place where she was trying on white dresses. The dresses were most certainly wedding dresses, but in that moment I recognized that I had already attended a wedding. She tried on two separate dresses, as she looked to me for advice on which one she should wear. All I could do was stare. I never offered a suggestion. I was mesmerized by her beauty.

While this particular experience carried a certain weight with it when it occurred, it was not until the past couple of days that I started putting all of my journal entries into their final forms when the greater meaning of this experience was revealed. As I have been journaling, I have split the journals at

Rebirth III

places that seemed impactful for the books – where the last entry would carry the most weight. But, in my initial draft of Book VI – Rebirth III, I had continued to write even as the length grew twice as long as the other books before. So, as I sought a place to break the book into two during editing on December 12th, I randomly (through divine grace) selected this date as the last entry.

As I re-read the entry I had no expectation that it would be all that it turned out to be. Instead, I was just guessing the correct halfway point to split the book. At the time of the experience I would not quite have the context as I have now to understand the moment. But in the recent days as God has shown me the significance of the dates in Daniel and Revelation and revealed the upcoming arrival of the anti-Christ and of the Messiah, the meaning has become clearer.

For in this third revelation, it was revealed to me that the angel was the Bride of Christ – a concept that I had not yet wrapped my head around in the teachings of Jesus. The Bride of Christ is akin to how I witnessed a child dying nearly a year ago in the heavens. This was the moment that God showed me I was engaged. The wedding was to help me understand the idea of marriage. The angel wearing the white gown in the context of the wedding was to help me understand she is to be my bride.

And though I can only assume many things can derail a marriage and that many other factors could come into play, on December 9th, God shared with me a message that offered further clarity to the defining moments leading up to the day of

Third Revelation

my Wedding Banquet. Most certainly the days ahead will test a soul beyond the norm. But just in seeing the bride-to-be, I can only hope that I can be a worthy groom.

The definitions to such experiences have never been written. And to be honest, I was unable to put it all together until He revealed the next piece of the story. I cannot be sure what the Wedding Banquet will reveal, but all I know is He must have my complete and devoted attention. For even if everything God has shared with me is just the way I had to learn how to one day meet my Father, I will still sing Hallelujah for all time.

The number of experiences God has shared with me since the Day after Thanksgiving in November of 2011 has been an undeniably exhilarating ride. Rebirth III begins with the moments after He caught me and the moment I felt fear and questioning subside. The end of Rebirth III leads up to the moment of seeing my Bride. I pray that one day I am blessed to see her again – hopefully dressed in white, on a podium in front of heaven's angels, as they witness my words of forevermore and the promise of forever upholding my vows.

...

September 10, 2014

This morning I was taken to the heavens. A brunette angel greeted me with an over-abundance of Love and joy in her mannerisms – more so than is imaginable. It seemed she was

Rebirth III

smiling nearly the entire duration of my travels. The brunette angel was one that I have seen on several other occasions. She is so beautiful and is always delicate in her ways with me. It seemed this particular experience in the heavens held more gravity than usual, though that would be downplaying the significance of each and every moment in my other experiences in the heavens.

While the experience took a little while to gain clarity, the brunette angel led me to a celebration event. We were standing in the midst of a crowd of hundreds of other angels. We were located somewhere in the middle of the group. The brunette angel stood to my left. Before the crowd was an elevated stage and podium for the angel who seemed to be leading the ceremony. It did not take me long to realize we were attending a wedding.

I was not sure who the two souls were that I witnessed being wed, but I understood that the ceremony was extremely special for all those gathered. I watched intently, trying to discern any detail that could help me understand why it was important that I witness this wedding. Though I could see the bride, the groom, and the angel leading the ceremony, they were all too far away to discern anything recognizable. I assumed that just witnessing a wedding in the heavens must be the intended message.

While the wedding ceremony took place, the brunette angel to my left kept trying to get my attention regarding the dress she was wearing. Initially I did not notice the details of her dress, for every time she fell into my view I became lost in

Third Revelation

her beauty – the type of moment where all of the details fade away except for the romantic dance of two souls, spinning each other around in the moment. But as the ceremony was taking place, it became increasingly apparent there was something she needed for me to see.

Though in earthly terms it may seem like an impossible description in the moment, in this experience she was changing dresses seeming at will. At first she was wearing a white gown with a single strap over her right shoulder. The dress shimmered like satin and fell across her form in the most beautiful fashion. She then changed gowns into a strapless white gown with a longer, more flowing train. As she continued to change dresses, I understood that she wanted me to tell her which dress I liked best on her.

I must have seemed like no help at all because I was speechless in those moments as I was mesmerized by her beauty. While I was locked in a helpless gaze, she indicated that she liked both the single-strap dress and the strapless dress, but was unsure of which one to pick. She also showed me a couple of other white dresses with lace, but they were not as radiant and svelte as the other two. She seemed to lean toward the single strap dress, but wanted to see which one I liked best. While both dresses were stunning, I do not think I actually ever was able to compose myself to offer an opinion. If I could describe this moment in earthly terms, it would be like a girl wanting to make sure she looked as beautiful as possible in the eyes of her man, while her man was speechless in her mere presence. All I could do was stare, locked in her flawless es-

Rebirth III

sence, which was bound upon mine. These were the last thoughts I had as my soul lost harmony and returned to Earth.

At the time all of this was occurring, I was not seeing the entire experience for what it was. I saw myself standing with this words-cannot-describe-how-beautiful-and-loving brunette angel in the heavens, while witnessing a wedding in the heavens. I would not understand until after returning to my body on Earth and beginning to journal the experience that the dresses she was showing me were wedding dresses for her wedding day. Perhaps the wedding was an event that I needed to see in order to understand the context of the gowns she was showing me. Perhaps we really attended a wedding in the heavens, which she used to foreshadow events to come. Perhaps I should just trust with patience that the purpose of the entire presentation will one day be revealed. Whatever the case may be, all I know is that on this day, I stood before the most beautiful bride-to-be with an essence so ineffable that "perfection" falls short in describing her.

Requisition

At some point along the way, a blur between my original understanding of visions and being taken spiritually to Heaven began to occur. Throughout these words, it should now be clear that God has revealed Himself in all of His grand Glory. I journeyed to Fort Lauderdale, answering His call. The journey has been the greatest blessing in my life. But, just the action to follow His call to Fort Lauderdale was not enough. He still had much planned for me. In the beginning, I thought I was learning to follow His will. By the end of this book, I realized He had something greater planned. All that He intended for me to see would be revealed in the coming months.

Though many may see the journey I had experienced thus far as just an intriguing viewpoint on a person's spiritual walk, the greater importance will be revealed in Book VII – Glory. When I began writing, I thought that my journal entries might fill one book. Never would I guess four. The three books entitled Rebirth should be viewed as the days of spiritual rebirth leading to a marriage ahead, where all will be revealed in His Glory.

...

*From generations and generations to come,
this is the revelation of Our Father's daughter,
the Bride of Christ.*

...

www.ingramcontent.com/pod-product-compliance
Lightning Source LLC
Chambersburg PA
CBHW021139080526
44588CB00008B/120